transformat

transformations

the architecture of penoyre & prasad

black dog
publishing

Contents

Introduction

We have called this collection of works and essays "Transformations" for two reasons. First, because we enjoy seeing the beneficial changes that architecture brings to the people, the briefs, the sites and the neighbourhoods of our projects. Secondly, we take pleasure in the changes the projects make to ourselves. Just as every site demands its specific and fresh response, so we are challenged to review and refresh our architectural preoccupations.

This book is written with clients and users in mind. Architecture, like any specialism has its own language and we have tried to strike a balance between communicating to non-specialists and retaining the depth of the subject. In detailing the positions and influences that have informed our approach, the essays are intended to reveal and share our way of working and our exchanges with architectural culture. Interleaved with these are 25 key projects from the past 19 years of practice. All of them are the product of collaboration within our practice and with our co-consultants and constructors. Behind each are committed clients who have challenged and supported us in equal measure and who have shown faith in the power of architecture to transform everyone's life for the better.

The south-facing facade of the restaurant of the Snape Maltings Concert Hall shaded with horizontal timber louvres, 1999.

Place, Time and People

Thomas Muirhead

When they left Edward Cullinan's office in the mid-1980s, Greg Penoyre and Sunand Prasad were inspired by everything from Le Corbusier to traditional Japanese building, Californians Maybeck, Schindler, Green & Green, or the Australian architect Glen Murcutt. Inheriting Cullinan's "total commitment to making architecture with people and for people" Penoyre & Prasad have continued to strive for an architecture that uses signs and signifiers to make itself comprehensible to non-architects. As the practice has grown and new people joined their sources of inspiration have moved closer to classic modernism, and any investigation of their work will soon uncover the influence of Alvar Aalto, Louis Kahn or Mies van der Rohe. "How" asks Prasad "can we fulfil the need for architecture to communicate, whilst also keeping it authentic and rational?" Much of the success of their work derives from this internal dialectic between an intention to be serious about architecture, and an intention to make buildings to which non-architects can relate.

One of their earliest projects, a GP group practice in Walworth, 1986, consists of an intricate arrangement of quite small rooms slotted into a former builder's yard behind some south London Victorian terraces. Overlooks, daylight, and the need to retain rights of way across the site are exploited to create a "Chinese box" of indoor and outdoor spaces, with clerestoreys that bring daylight into the deepest parts. The result is a spatially complex, layered organism of small architectural events that adapt to the existing buildings and fit in with them. The sinusoidal metal roof rises to the same height as other nearby roofs; this finely tuned interaction between old and new begins to emerge as one of the enduring features of their work.

New Maltings in Suffolk, 1987, is another refurbishment: in a series of alterations to a house originally designed by Cullinan, their new roof gives the building a lunging, aggressive aspect of great power. The addition of new overhangs, which act as sun-shading, exemplify their interest in allowing environmental design to influence architectonic form. The introduction of oblique lines into what had been the house's orthogonal layout, and its newly upheaving roof profile, are now becoming characteristic of their work. Poised and tense in its landscaped grounds, this house seems to emerge out of the earth.

The Residential and Daycare Facilities in Essex, 1987, are a complex of vaguely agricultural buildings visible from a distance, their monopitch roofs nodding this way and that. The modesty of these buildings, and their tough rural quality, makes them communicative as a homely but robust neo-vernacular. This project further developed Penoyre & Prasad's experience of health and care-related projects, translated into a quasi-domestic, easy to recognise way of arranging spaces that mixes elements of modernist design with allusions to the Arts and Crafts and the traditional vernacular. This friendly group of buildings has a directness that belies the sophistication of its layout, internal planning, and handling of proportion.

In The Rushton Street GP group practice in Hoxton, London, 1991, four GP practices are accommodated in two arrays of rooms arranged along a double-loaded central circulation space. This basic layout is manipulated until the central space, with its niches and recesses, becomes a promenade where waiting to see the doctor becomes an opportunity for people-watching and conversation; out of such small and humane things, architecture can enhance civilised life. On the street, a recessed space in front of the entrance creates a small meeting place where people can wait for each other and perhaps converse. Such apparently insignificant minutiae of everyday life animate all of Penoyre & Prasad's "architecture for people".

Woodlands Nursing Home, Lambeth, London, a competition-winning design begun in 1993, builds on Penoyre & Prasad's increasing expertise in the design of buildings for the elderly. There are no locked doors nor any feeling of institutional confinement; even when not quite sure of their bearings, residents are free to wander about in complete safety. Dominated by the now-familiar monopitch roof and wrap-around high level corner window, with clerestoreys that bounce daylight down internal walls into the corridors, the home is divided into four "houses" for ten residents each, whose rooms are arranged as two approximately L-shaped blocks, pulled apart to create a semi-enclosed courtyard. By carefully setting floor and ground levels, it was possible to recycle the demolition rubble to create a raised garden. The glazed link block is a device that begins to reappear in many projects by Penoyre & Prasad.

Eastbrookend Country Park Visitors' Centre, Dagenham, Essex, begun in 1995 and used for the environmental education of school pupils, is a small building in a big landscape. In such a setting, the aluminium "roof with a kink" seems to echo the shape of birds in flight. The construction method makes extensive use of sustainable and recyclable materials. Thanks in part to the input of Max Fordham and Büro Happold, the whole building is a showcase of environmental design. It stands on steel screw foundations which without damaging the ground, can in future be removed at such time as the building may be demolished. Thick-wall construction gives high natural levels of thermal insulation, and large south-facing windows enable the building to benefit from natural solar gain. A ha-ha protects it from vandals without any need for walls or fences, and steel shutters can be brought down to cover the big windows. The cross-section facilitates transversal ventilation; natural airflow for cooling the classroom passes from outside through big transversal ducts passing between the two floors. These giant sculptural ducts offer an exciting overhead view in the ground floor corridor. The plan is an arrangement of poise and elegance: an interplay of orthogonal rooms softened by the curves of the bullnosed stairs

and the 'cubist' shape of the enquiries desk. Front and back, this building has a taut sense of controlled proportions and massing. An exceptionally successful composition of steel frame, glue-lam beams, and aluminium or timber cladding, it enthusiastically expresses how everything is put together in a kind of low-tech high-tech, evident (for instance) in the galvanised steel plate that bolts the timber roof joists to the glue-lam beams that support them. The dramatisation of the roof creates lofty spaces on the upper floor and a quite different feel at the lower floor — more intimate, with lower ceilings, a different acoustic, and offering a horizontal raking view across the landscape.

In its planning, the Sydenham Youth Centre, Bridgwater, Somerset, 1995, has affinities with New Maltings, the remodelled Cullinan house in Suffolk: single-loaded orthogonal rooms, counteracted by a curved wall that generates a change of direction of flow within the plan, from formal to informal, leading to a double-height social space. Characteristically in much of Penoyre & Prasad's architecture, the use of various colours and materials breaks down the composition into different parts.

In 1995 following an international competition win design work began on The Pulross Intermediate Care Centre in Brixton, south London. This hardly seems like a health care building, such is its informal character. The accommodation is subdivided into two blocks arranged for the best orientation, and a curvilinear entrance hall wraps around the front of them to create an unemphatic, but strong composition. This project unobtrusively resolves many practical and technical issues in a "building for people" in which what ultimately matters is not the background expertise (which nevertheless has to be outstanding) but the building as finally experienced by the users, who may indeed not notice the conceptual moves made in the design. Among the most important of these was to tie the new building into its context by using the same type of brick as the nearby terraced houses, and to carefully harmonise its massing with the domestic scale of the area. In a repetition of the landscaping strategy used at Woodlands, the demolition rubble was recycled on-site to create gardens on two different levels, the upper one accessed via a series of little bridges that create a delightful sunken walkway.

A limited competition in 1996 brought Penoyre & Prasad the commission to upgrade an important piece of 1930s architecture, Wolverhampton Civic Hall, designed by Lyons & Israel in 1938: a proto-modern stripped Neo-classical building composed of rectangular brick and stone volumes. Penoyre & Prasad adopted the same orthogonality, and added new volumes which were clearly separated from the older brick parts. A large number of other internal alterations, and some masterly restoration work, infused the old building with a bright contemporary feel, demonstrating how old buildings can be injected with new vitality without betraying their original identity. The new parts are added carefully and the old parts expertly restored, in a spirit of enjoyment of the architectural merits of the original. The glass boxes resolve a number of internal circulation problems and add another level to Lyons & Israel's compositional language; at night they can be illuminated to transform the building into an ephemeral architecture of coloured light.

The Maltings at Snape, acquired by Benjamin Britten and Peter Pears in 1965, is a grouping of agricultural buildings, full of character, set in the flat Suffolk landscape and dominated by big dramatic roofs. As they appeared in 1996 when Penoyre & Prasad began to work on them, the buildings had been adapted by Arup Associates and acoustics expert Derek Sugden to make the Maltings one of the UK's most important concert halls. Penoyre & Prasad were asked to resolve a number of technical and functional issues that had emerged out of using the building: improved auditorium lighting, a new restaurant, improvements to the entrance hall, and other modifications to improve back-of-house access and delivery. The jewel of this piece is the new restaurant, created by adding a new volume on top of a former malt store. As at Wolverhampton Civic Hall the separation between old and new is carefully expressed, in this case by a long clerestorey window that frames panoramic views. The structure of the new roof, elegantly expressed inside as steel portal frames that are allowed to stand proud of the

ceiling, deliberately echoes in simplified form the magnificent auditorium roof by Arup Associates; seen from outside, the two sit in counterpoint with each other.

In 1997, following a successful competitive interview, the practice started designing the upgrading of Vincent Harris' 1932 Sheffield City Hall, a major work of twentieth century British architecture that required detailed knowledge of every nook and cranny in its fabric. By exploiting the interstitial spaces in Harris' design, Penoyre & Prasad found places through which new ventilation systems and circulation routes could be run, in ways that would not disrupt Harris' grand auditoria and beautiful rooms. Movement into and through the building was reorganised to meet current building regulations and improve the flow of people. Whereas in Harris' day the lower orders were segregated by forcing them to use a separate route to reach the top balcony, this level is now directly accessible from inside the building. Penoyre & Prasad's elegant new additions (stairs, lifts, counters and other fixtures) are deliberately orthogonal to set off Harris' Neo-classicism and the interplay between these two languages, especially at night when the building comes into its own, is dramatised by new coloured lighting.

The Charter School in Dulwich, south London, 1999, required the refurbishment of a school designed in the 1950s by the Architects' Department of the London County Council. Penoyre & Prasad reorganised circulation between the isolated blocks of this building, whose multiple points of entry had been designed for an epoch without vandalism, violence, or intruders in schools. The new single controlled entrance was positioned in a modified corner block of the original layout; its internal courtyard was given a roof supported by a steel tree structure to become the new entrance hall for the whole school. From this point, new covered walkways were introduced to enable sheltered movement all round the school; vertical circulation was improved by adding enamelled steel clad lift towers to each block. The six-storey teaching block was re-clad using a variegated pattern of glazing, panels and ventilating louvres that united the irregular elevation into a single composition. A giant bright orange 'belvedere' marks out the new Sixth Form Centre. In this painstaking and subtle refurbishment, the architects took the trouble to understand the merits of the existing building; as much as they imposed their own thinking on it, they were also influenced by it.

In the same year they designed a masterplan for Gravesend in Kent, an "urban healing" operation to atone for the tragic demolition in the 1960s of several streets of what would now be considered valuable Victorian terraces. From the beginning, their approach was to design in three dimensions, widening the designated study area to allow for careful consideration of the surroundings, and organising the site edges to reconstitute a memory of the lost streets. Typological studies ensured that inside dwellings the most important rooms would enjoy good orientation for views and sunlight, and winter gardens would help reduce energy consumption whilst enhancing the quality of domestic life — so much more desirable than the pointless, unusable balconies thoughtlessly stuck on the front of too many new residential developments.

The Bradbury Centre in Belfast, 2001, occupies a prominent corner location at the end of a Victorian terrace, and projects slightly forward from the line of these houses to offer the oblique entrance found in so many Penoyre & Prasad projects. The interplay of a solid bullnosed block with a glass bullnosed block and between them, the entrance, subtly guides people into the building, past the reception desk into the internal atrium. Also in Belfast, The Arches Community Treatment Centre, 2001, is partly the refurbishment of an existing building and partly the addition of a new building set parallel to it. Between the two, an interior street rising through all floors offers a variety of upper level balconies, where people can stop and look down into a giant space day-lit from above. This division of a building into two parallel blocks with an informally designed circulation space between (and which plays a role in heating and cooling the building) was the basis for the design of the earlier Rushton Street GP practice and has been reiterated many times in other projects.

The Richard Desmond Children's Eye Centre, designed in 2002, is a vertical sequence of consulting and reception/play areas, with short stay residential at the top. The entrance hall incorporates a coffee bar, shop, and information point, but the main facilities are on the upper levels: an outpatient department, a day surgery unit, a research floor and the short stay hostel. The enormous south-facing glass facade has a projecting orange 'belvedere' that marks out an important reception floor and recalls the analogous belvedere at Charter School. This south-facing wall of glass is protected from solar gain by a flight of metal "seagulls" carefully placed (with assistance from artist Alison Turnbull) to achieve a cascading effect down the front of the building. Although seen from the front this is Penoyre & Prasad's most powerful urban building, aggressive in a London manner, various elements in its design also invite it to be perceived obliquely; as in many of their other projects its appearance is even more intriguing from along the street, in foreshortened views.

Nearby in Bethnal Green, The Rich Mix Arts Centre (design started in 2002) was a former garment factory refurbished as a place of interaction for the expression of London's culturally and ethnically 'rich mix'. Many internal finishes and fixtures have been designed by local artists; other parts of the interior are deliberately left 'raw' and will be fitted out later to suit changing community needs. The project was designed for 'loose fit', in which many things will change over time; the architects limited themselves to essential internal restructuring and upgrading, including the addition of an extra floor and three cinema spaces. The most visible feature is the new sunscreening, which creates a two-layered front facade. The vertical steel components of the existing inner facade are picked out in secondary colours and in front of them, adjustable banks of louvres, which can be moved ad-hoc by the users of the building, transform the whole frontage into a three-dimensional ever-changing work of abstract art.

Ashburton Learning Village in Croydon, 2003, was designed and built using PFI, which is intended to keep costs under tight control but tends to produce generic, thin-looking buildings in which the architects have little or no control over details, finishes, and fittings. Penoyre & Prasad made a policy decision to accept these conditions and to prove it is still possible to lay down the strategic architectural and urban ideas of such a project: how to locate the building on its site, the articulation of its parts, and the internal planning of its most important spaces. Its environmental design strategy can also be established at an early stage and Ashburton incorporates many sustainability features: photovoltaic cells, rainwater harvesting and natural ventilation. The main architectural effort was focused on setting out the essential urban and architectonic forms and spaces. Internally the building is configured around a full-height galleried concourse as the central feature of a large, complex building that houses a school for 1,200 students, a public library, and a music centre. Its irregular site enabled the three teaching wings to be skewed at different angles, with landscaped open spaces between, and the various blocks of the building are composed so that the higher teaching wings are set well back, with the lower parts arranged along the front so that the architectonic masses step up and away, eliminating any looming effect and bringing the scale down where people approach the building. To relate the building to its context its most important civic element, the new library, was located on the main road. Although the PFI process resulted in a flatness that is perhaps due to the lack of articulation between one part and another, the basic planning and volumes are successful and the sun-screened elevation of the library, well integrated with the entrance hall, is genuinely elegant.

In 2003 the practice's experience on schools led to a commission to prepare a schools exemplar, an advisory document for the government's future school building programme. Educational experts were brought in to develop research on how future schools should be organised, and technical sections analysed environmental performance, the reduction of carbon emissions, and how planning, construction methods, and technologies can create a low energy buildings. The design component of the report brings together some design principles investigated at Ashburton and elsewhere, and culminates in some 'exemplar' schools for different types of site. It exploits many design features already matured in Penoyre & Prasad's work: subdivision of the rooms into logically planned smaller blocks with service spaces between. Corridors thus never become too long and are social spaces rather than passageways; the blocks can be arranged in different ways by skewing them; clerestoreys that let light into otherwise inaccessible parts of the plan; and full-height central "streets" also serve as environmental control zones. Curvilinear spaces such as entrances and assembly halls are freely arranged round the foot of the buildings.

Collier's Gardens elderly care home in Bristol, 2003, is a faintly rustic, picturesque, playful grouping of 50 flats for elderly people, arranged across their site as two-storey, monopitch-roofed buildings, bending and twisting to create at one end an irregularly shaped communal hall, and at the other an informal garden that opens out towards the back gardens of the houses that surround the site. This extends the scale and feel of these residential surroundings, offering the possibility that the elderly inhabitants might chat over the fence with their neighbours. As in their other projects for the elderly, Penoyre & Prasad achieve quiet, humane effects that seem domestic and friendly but are based on energetic, bold architectural decisions.

The refurbishment of Prior Weston Primary School in Islington, London, required the modification of an existing 1950s school by adding three new teaching blocks with a new entrance hall and library between them. These additions and alterations created interior views without corridors, through open-plan configurations that lead from room to room, without doors. Despite some minor noise problems this has been so successful that the concept of the door-free, corridor-less school is being further examined by the practice. Construction was an impressively fast-track process: two weeks after winning the competition a planning application was submitted and the project was built during the school summer holiday using a proprietary engineered timber cassette system that accelerated construction. No foundations were dug; the building simply sits on the ground.

The Heart of Hounslow Health Centre in west London, 2004, houses health, social, and mental care services and outpatient spaces. As a Local Improvement Framework Trust (LIFT) scheme, it had to be designed for adaptation to a different use at some future time and this limited the degree to which its health care functions could be expressed. Penoyre & Prasad therefore identified those aspects of the project that would not need to change; the result is a layout that builds on the "generic architecture" elements worked out in their exemplar schools research. Breaking down the building into smaller parts, these are skewed this way and that so that there are never long straight corridors. This gives the building a picturesque character without sacrificing the logic of its orthogonal planning. The way in which the two undulating wings of cellular accommodation touch each other seems very relaxed but is in fact meticulously calibrated to simplify and dramatise the internal circulation.

The University of Portsmouth Library, originally designed 1977–1988 by the distinguished practice Ahrends, Burton and Koralek (ABK), was almost doubled in size in 2004 by Penoyre & Prasad, by adding two floors of book stacks and reading carrels, an IT area, cafe, seminar rooms and a new issues desk. Although unpredictable and imaginative, the new project is respectful of ABK's work. The new accommodation is arranged round a secret courtyard in a curving one-storey block set asymmetrically in front of the main three-storey part of the library. This dramatic move skewed the approach to the ABK building and once again expressed what is possibly the deepest drive in Penoyre & Prasad's approach to architecture: their desire to create an oblique entrance. The curving new wing links the library to a cross-campus system of pathways, and its interplay with ABK's building creates an exhilarating new internal space at the conjunction of the two.

Olney Campus near Milton Keynes, 2004, sits on top of a hill and almost seems to have been designed from the roof down, so important is its profile against the sky. Always appearing different from different viewpoints, the roof loops up, down and around. This roof, and the obliquely arranged entrance, contradict the strict, orthogonal layout of the building's plan and its complex, perfectly equilibrated elevations. In a new departure for Penoyre & Prasad, the use of a single material for the whole building gives it a formal coherence much more assertive than in previous work; it communicates a tautness and unity that promises interesting future developments.

Unlike more dogmatic British architects, Penoyre & Prasad's architecture does not rely on an abstract, pre-existing syntax but on a loose vocabulary of more or less fixed elements, many of which have been discussed above, such as the insistence on an oblique approach to the entrance, the fragmented roofscape, and so on. From one project to another, these recurring design elements are modified in different ways to suit the job in hand, and the reworking of these elements is determinant on the overall architectonic form of each building. In a way this seems a very English pragmatism, and may suggest analogies with Kenneth Frampton's concept of "critical regionalism"; but in other ways it is mainstream European and has distant affinities with the work of architects like Rafael Moneo or Renzo Piano, who like Penoyre & Prasad allow each project to emerge out of the conditions of the particular time and place. Designing each building becomes an unpredictable new experience that Prasad describes as a process of discovery. Penoyre & Prasad have been exploring an architectural idiom that is not part of any movement and for which no manifesto could be written; but they are not working in isolation. In 1973 Bruno Zevi analysed the most important buildings of the twentieth century and elaborated seven "invariables" by which all good modern architecture can be recognised: (1) reformulation of the relationship between form and function (2) the use of asymmetry (3) non-axial perception (4) decomposition of form (5) experimentalism in construction (6) perception of the building only possible by moving through it, and (7) re-integration of architecture and the city. Quite by coincidence, or perhaps not, Penoyre & Prasad find themselves exactly in tune with Zevi's invariables of authentic modern architecture.

PURPOSE

*Buildings have to satisfy the demands of their use by people for intended purposes; so it
might follow that their designs should be developed directly from considerations of use and
purpose, from function. But things are not so simple. This chapter explores our approach to
the complex relationship between form and function.*

Form

The search for form is a central preoccupation in architecture; form in the sense of the physical
and spatial presence and experience of the building. Although architecture is also about problem
solving, about processes, and about the re-use of previously proven design strategies, architects are
not remembered for the difficult problems they solved or the effective processes they used; not even
for how well their buildings worked for the intended purpose. They are remembered for the forms
they created and to the extent that these were compelling, engaging, ingenious, beautiful, logical,
instructive, exhilarating, inventive. Today the image of a building in the media, as much as or more
than the direct experience of the building itself, can over influence design. This may lead to such a
dominance of form as to drive out other values, like functionality; that lie at the heart of the architect's
duty to provide the best possible design to help the activities of her or his clients.

That an architect feels the need to say such a thing in the twenty-first century would have
surprised the pioneers of the Modern Movement in architecture: the architects of the Arts and Crafts and
related movements; the late nineteenth century engineer/architects; and the great Modernists from Adolf
Loos to Leslie Martin, who span 50 years of architectural momentum, from expensive private houses for
the Viennese bourgeoisie to post-war mass housing replacing London's slums. For the one thing that
unites them all is a belief that a building's function both in terms of its use by its occupants, its wider
social purpose, and the means of its making, must be at the heart of design. This core belief, together
with the associated demotion of applied decoration and rejection of other historical conventions, are
what sets apart the Modern era in architecture from all that went before.[1] It was later to become known
as Functionalism, a term used as often to criticise modern architecture as to illuminate its practice.[2] There
is much more to the celebrated works in the canon of modern architecture than can be summed up as
'functionalist', but a great mass of buildings built in the second half of the twentieth century in towns and
cities all over the world really are functionalist in the pejorative sense that the term is often used.[3]

Our practice's work is rooted in a close interest of people's use of buildings and urban space
and in the means of making them. To that extent we willingly embrace Functionalism. But rather than
directly leading to form, function enters into a dialogue with form, into a dialectical relationship. By
pushing against functional needs form is sharpened.

Working with pupils from
Archbishop Michael Ramsay
Technology College on the DfES
Design Exemplar Project, 2003.

Communication

When we started in practice in 1988 modernism appeared to be in a state of crisis. In the journals there was a three cornered fight: a revived classicism, so-called postmodernism and the continuing modernist tradition of which we saw ourselves as fierce adherents.[4] In hindsight this looks like a battle between the tragic, the comic and the optimistically pragmatic. The first two were shortly reduced to a rump in mainstream architectural culture, finding niches in business parks, beach resorts and private houses. However, they offered some very important lessons to a refreshed modernism. Lewis Mumford, Jane Jacobs, and others, by brilliantly laying bare the workings of the city as an organism had already criticised modern architecture and planning for its neglect of the space in between buildings in favour of the buildings as freestanding objects.[5] The classicist critique, articulated with particular force by Leon and Robert Krier compelled renewed attention to the urban public realm and the making of place. Robert Venturi and Denise Scott-Brown had pointed out the alienating effect of modernism's supposedly dogmatic insistence on the primacy of simplicity and consistency, which they argued was out of synch with a world whose essential condition was complexity and contradiction.[6] This led, for example, to the inability of modern architecture to use signs and symbols that had meaning for the general population. Inspired by Venturi, Scott-Brown and others, the postmodernists of the late 1970s and 80s made the communication of 'meaning' a central aim of architecture. In all but a few witty hands the results were clumsy, and the superficial meanings rapidly became stale. But the critical point remains valid and gives us a key principle for our architecture: conscious communication is a prime purpose of a work of architecture. What exactly to communicate is a challenging question, explored later here in the essay "Art".

The most interesting early critiques of modern architecture were the ones 'from within' and amongst the most effective were from Team 10.[7] This group of European architects, who were in their youth in the 1950s, clearly articulated a growing conviction: that modern architecture had abandoned its ethical and rational core and become just a style — the so-called International Style, whose grand gestures and dogmas they rejected. What really mattered was close observation of the ordinary and everyday aspects of human social behaviour; the subtle details of the relationship between form and

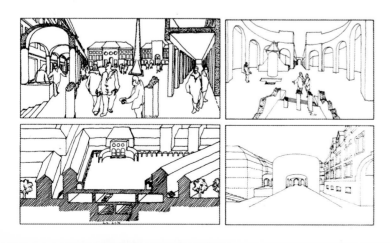

use; a close reading of the landscape and urban context of the project; and an ability to synthesise these into understated new forms. Almost 30 years after their first manifestos, Team 10 still exerted a big influence on us starting out in practice in 1988, not so much through the forms they created, but through their way of thinking about architecture and its relationship with people.

Use

In one of the practice's first projects, The Walworth Road Surgery, there was a lengthy exploration with the doctors and nurses of how they saw themselves working and serving their patients in the future. Dr Roger Higgs said of us "they take a good history", using the terms he would use to describe what a consultant needs to do to gain a whole understanding of a patient's condition. Working closely with our user clients we worked through many potential layouts to solve what was a particularly difficult combination of brief and site, in the process developing an intuitive understanding of the fundamental issues of the project.[8]

A few years later we won the competition to design Woodlands Nursing Home for elderly people with various forms of dementia. None of us ever having designed a nursing home, I arranged to work some shifts at the hospital ward where the future patients and staff were based, covering the 24 hour life of the facility. Anthropologists call this "participant observation" and though it is only one of many tools for understanding a 'problem' it is very effective in revealing certain underlying factors that are likely to improve the design. On the Woodlands project these were both environmental and operational. Our

Opposite left: Robert Krier's sketches of his Charlottenplatz-Schlossplatz scheme.

Opposite right: Recommendation for a Monument by Robert Venturi from *Learning from Las Vegas*, 1972.

Top: Team 10 at work, Spolento, 1976.

Bottom: Cartoon of our consultation process for Walworth Surgery, Louis Hellman, 1993.

discoveries included registering how zimmer frames pushed along by large men made a tremendous noise scudding on lino and terrifying fragile elderly women; learning what a height of achievement was felt by a carer who after patiently coaxing an old man for several weeks persuaded him one day to go as far as the front door of the ward and open it to reveal the world outside; noticing that there was no provision for handily storing the huge quantities of paper towels required in bathrooms.

In 2004 during early design stages of the Treehouse School for autistic children all three of the architectural team carried out participant observation in the existing temporary school. In the detailed discussions that followed we were far better able to understand what the staff were striving towards and gained design insights that would not otherwise have been possible.

In these projects the client wanted a design that would respond to their ambitions for innovative practice, whether in caring for dementia or in the education of children in the autistic spectrum. In most of our projects clients have such ambitions and while it is possible for them to set these out in a written brief, it is impossible for architect or client to fully understand their practical implications without the contact suggested above. We call this early part of the design process "immersion". By this we mean getting absorbed in the world of the client and users of the buildings in order to gain a deep understanding of how they work and what it is that they are after, even if they have not (yet) articulated it. Equally, with the more straightforward projects, immersion in the clients' and users' worlds will help us ask questions and probe their tacit assumptions in such a way that the operational brief and the design grow together and become explicit and shared. The purpose of deeply assimilating the brief is to enable the designer to think outside its apparent limits to open the way to unexpected design solutions that go beyond what the clients could have dreamt of.

Immersion is impossible without effective consultation with users, which has been a fundamental part of our approach. But good design cannot arise from simply following what anyone with a stake in the building wants, which is anyway often impossible because of conflicting opinions. The users of buildings have vital operational knowledge, but their views of possible futures are generally limited by their past experience. It is our job as specialists, with a deep engagement with architecture, to communicate ideas and explain the rationale for designs while also exercising judgement and giving clear advice. To do this we have to be committed to listening and that means ensuring that there is a shared language in place for discussing the complex field of design. The most effective, and also the simplest techniques, to 'grow' a shared language is to make joint trips to as many buildings of a similar purpose as possible, supplemented by images and descriptions of others. Helping users properly to visualise their future environment is perhaps next in importance in achieving effective consultation. Working on a community centre for an estate in the East End of London we designed and built a carousel which at the turn of a handle brought up alternative strategies for development to be visualised in context. During the design of recent schools we worked with a colleague who has adapted computer games software that allows students to explore all parts of the proposed building giving a far better picture than the conventional 'fly through'.

During the opening event of the Rollercoaster Young People's Centre in Sydenham, Bridgwater, Somerset, two of our architects stepped forward at the due time to take the visiting Minister of State on a tour. But the group of young people we had been working with swept us aside and took the Minister round the building themselves, expertly pointing out all the architectural features as if they had designed them. Initially surprised, we soon realised that this was the best tribute to effective consultation that one could imagine: our young clients fully owned the design of the building. They may not have known very much about architecture but they had helped decide a number of key elements: for example moving the building away from the site proposed by the council, which they thought was too near the school and would therefore stigmatise the building for potential users from outside the area. There was a three fold advantage from their involvement: their knowledge had helped make the project a success; they had learned a lot from participating in the consultation sessions; and their ownership of the design would mean that they were likely to help look after the building.

Functionalism

From the day of opening a building must be able to perform as required. Vitruvius, the first century BC architectural writer thought that buildings should have three qualities 'commoditas', ie. convenience in use or operability; 'firmitas', ie. build quality or durability; and 'venustas' ie. a stimulating impact on the senses and mind, or delight.[9] Colin St John Wilson, identifying architecture as a "practical art" wrote that its practical character is inherent in its purpose and the conditions of its creation:

> A work of architecture is called into being to serve the cause of innumerable and unpredictable patterns of operation in day-to-day life. Its conception can therefore never be immaculate. It has a concrete historical provenance growing from a whole complex of competing aims that are themselves grounded in initiatives and agencies far removed from the discipline itself: and when completed it has to stand in real spaces and time in defiance of all that nature and the whim of man may bring to it.[10]

'Serving patterns of operations' broadly equates to operability and 'standing in real space and time', to durability. Together these are the 'functions' in Functionalism and are qualities that can be objectively measured. Although St John Wilson was not arguing that they determine everything, the most militant Functionalists, such as the Swiss architect Hannes Meyer, 1889–1954, did believe that the whole form of a building could be derived objectively, championing science and social purpose and denying any role for art.[11] As it happens Meyer was a very talented architect and in his hands the doctrine produced some handsome buildings. Though the palette of materials may have been selected with a severe objectivity, it is evident in Meyer's architecture that, despite his rejection of art, aesthetic judgement has been tacitly exercised in composing the physical forms of the buildings.

At a pivotal period of early Modernism a quasi-scientific method served as an aid to countering prevailing aesthetic norms and liberated architects to explore forms beyond conventional boundaries. In the event, deriving form wholly from function in a linear process came to be the great goal of much modern architecture as generally practiced, especially after the Second World War. In public sector architects' departments, as well as in most private practices and schools of architecture, the design method was primarily focused on the literal and precise fulfilment of a well formulated and detailed brief, which had to come first. All architectural moves had to be justified in functional terms. Any departure was derided as 'formalism', which became a pejorative term. The more complex buildings, such as hospitals, attracted the most dedicated functionalists. For the 500 or so government architects in the UK NHS, in the Ministry of Health's 1960s and 70s heyday as a knowledge centre, the real test of the quality of a design lay in how well and with what clarity it accommodated medical and surgical processes. The locus of the design effort was therefore above all the plan. This is not to say that architects were not conscious of three-dimensional spatial qualities or of grace and order in elevation; but these came second and always had to be justified operationally. When I started work for the first time in a large health practice in 1973, the huge hospital that had been on the drawing board for months had never been drawn in elevation. It had a repeating module and a facade a third of a mile long. The issue is not whether this was good or bad but whether the authors of the work were conscious of what the work would communicate, and wished to have a relationship to form other than as a mere consequence of process. The client's programme, ie. patterns of use as enshrined in the brief, was almost the only concern of design, an approach better described as 'utilitarian' rather than functionalist.

Some people argued that the solution to solving the problems of the functionalist position was to make the definition of function more inclusive: for example, to say that it is a function of the design to provide an emotional experience, to be innovative, to tell a story, to inspire, to help create urban places. But this now seems to be a semantic trick, the substitution of 'function' for 'purpose'. The act of creating a building that is functional in the sense of operability and durability is not the same as that of creating a building that communicates in a premeditated way.

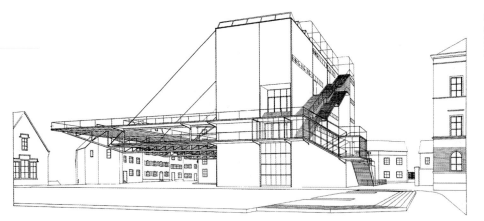

Preliminary perspective sketch study from the northwest of Hannes Meyer's Petersschule Project, 1926.

Iteration

An attraction of concentrating on operability and durability as the only determinant of form is that they can be captured by calculation and deduction, a process enshrined in most engineering disciplines. In contrast, the act of creative design, embracing also the intent to communicate, proceeds as much by induction as deduction. The artist or architect often thinks of an answer and then tests it to see if it is right. Alvar Aalto described this eloquently in his essay "The Trout and the Mountain Stream":

> … architectural design operates with innumerable elements that internally stand in opposition to each other. They are social, human, economic, and technical demands that unite to become psychological problems with an effect on both the individual and the group, on group and individual movements and internal frictions. All this becomes a maze that cannot be sorted out in a rational or technical manner. The large number of different demands and sub-problems form an obstacle that is difficult for the architectural concept to break through. In such cases I work — sometimes totally by instinct — in the following manner. For a moment I forget the maze of problems. After I have developed a feel for the programme and its innumerable demands have been engraved on my subconscious, I begin to draw in a manner rather like that of abstract art…. I eventually arrive at an abstract basis to the main concept, a kind of universal substance with whose help the numerous quarrelling problems can be brought into harmony.[12]

Most designers will recognise how the demands of the programme, or brief, eventually become 'engraved on (the) subconscious' and how, by a process whose course is difficult to predict, one might have an epiphany about the design as a whole: a glimmer of a solution. In practice we do not have to go through this every time. As architects we develop a repertoire of conceptual solutions and in particular when working again and again within a certain type it is common to develop a set of potential formal typologies.

In our practice we try to make sure that the brief in all its richness has been engraved on the subconscious. We call this "understanding the inner life of the building" and it is achieved through immersion as described above.[13] To internalise the brief is the first step to transcending it, to allowing a period of 'play' in the sense employed by a diverse range of theorists and designers including Colin St John Wilson, David Gann and Will Alsop.[14] It is through 'playing' with a number of evidently plausible and apparently implausible design solutions that one avoids the deterministic trap inherent in a narrow utilitarian view of design.

The crucial step in the process is always the leap of imagination that produces a potentially effective and perhaps powerful concept, Aalto's "universal substance with whose help the numerous quarrelling problems can be brought into harmony". Such a concept is like an armature that will generously accommodate the imperatives of operability and durability and from which will spring the communicative, expressive character of the building.

This first step may throw up more than one possible concept, but whether there is one or more the next step is to rigorously test it (or them) in terms of function (operability and durability); more subjective values like 'place making', 'distinctiveness', 'elegance'; and constraints such as budget, time, regulations and resources (natural and human). The third step is a reprise of the first with a new level of understanding where a deepening knowledge of the universe of possible formal solutions to the underlying facts of the project is added.

The non-linear design processes informed by series of successive approximation — an iterative process — cannot, of course, guarantee quality of outcome, any more than can a linear process. The outcome will depend on how deeply the designers understand what is called for, how imaginatively they produce potential concepts and how rigorously they test them. The shift of focus from the particularity of each project to the search for universality, informed nevertheless by particularity, is a natural consequence of such a process: the learning from each project is fed into the wider pool of knowledge about the building type and about all buildings regardless of type.

Long life loose fit

A focus on purpose and use, and on operability and durability as a way of generating form may seem to be an approach driven by social concerns but it has an equally strong aesthetic impulse arising from the relationship between function and form in machines and in nature. Starting from considerations that have nothing to do with appearance machines often assume forms that we find compelling or beautiful. Planes, hot air balloons, watch movements and bicycles are classic examples of a perfect fit between function and form that we, as architects, would love to achieve. Human beings find very many natural forms even more beautiful, and even repellent ones have impressive power, presumably all because of evolution. The extent to which function, appearance and manner of coming into being are inextricably linked in nature is awe-inspiring and instructive.[15] It may be impossible (as yet) for us to emulate nature but it is a wonderful ambition.[16] Some of the most beautiful machines do get close to assuming natural forms, such as aeroplanes, camera shutter irises

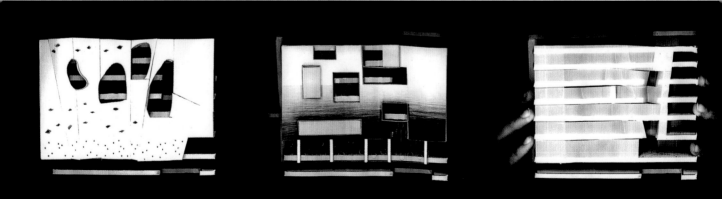

and ball and socket joints but, as yet, whenever architecture takes up natural forms it seems that artifice rather than function is at play.

The limitation of functionalism as a design process is that it depends on a precise and detailed description of purpose. Unlike the use of machines, the use of very few buildings can be fixed in this way for any length of time; even where the general purpose remains the same — such as, school, office, clinic, bar. There are some types of buildings that may have a more functional determinacy, such as theatres, concert halls and prisons, but even they are subject to changes in culture and technology. The mechanical analogy cannot be taken literally, but that elusive perfect reading of function, which thereby yields up a perfectly fitting, wholly objective and yet mysteriously beautiful form remains a tantalising idea.

The history of buildings and settlements tells us that only a minority of buildings go on being used for the purpose for which they were intended. Noting this, Aldo Rossi described the attempt to fix form rigidly to use as "naïve functionalism". And as Rem Koolhaas recently said "the city is a triumph of improvisation over foresight".[17] In a city's political economy, function actually seeks out potentially appropriate forms in its fabric to adapt and inhabit. It appears that to say that "function follows form", the visionary architect Paolo Soleri's dictum, is at least as valid as the common "form follows function". Some historic forms seem to have extraordinary versatility: the Georgian house, the industrial warehouse, the market hall, the garden pavilion, the palazzo, the terrace, and the courtyard house, which is found in all the temperate to hot dry regions of the world. More than their use as replicable types, these forms show that it is possible to discover formal solutions that accommodate but also transcend the specifics and immediacies of the brief to achieve adaptive design.

A past president of the Royal Institute of British Architects, Alex Gordon, contrasted "short life close fit" and "long life loose fit" as alternative design strategies (presciently adding "low energy") back in 1972.[18] He noted that close fit almost inevitably led to short life because it inhibited change and growth, which were a part of the natural order of things. There may well be projects where such a tight strategy is appropriate, but if practised as a general principle it will eventually lead to waste. The deceptively simple formula "long life loose fit" remains the most succinct principle relating function to form.

Study models for the facade for Moorfields Eye Hospital, 2003.

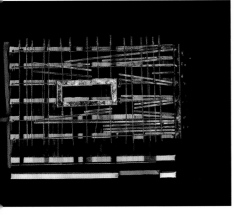

Rollercoaster Young People's Centre,
Bridgwater, Somerset, 1995–1997

On the opening day of this Centre the young clients showed visitors around as if they had designed it. A consistent group aged between 12 and 20 had participated in the project from site selection through to completion and the contractor's work force included people from the local estate.

According the young people's wishes the Centre was sited away from the school and the previous burnt down youth club. It provides a range of specialist and flexible spaces to accommodate a variety of activities, from fitness training and disco to study and building hovercraft.

A two-storey rectangular block parallel with the road runs east/west, housing a workshop, recording studio, group workroom, gym, offices, and wcs. In mid-block a wall making a backdrop for the entrance reception and bar cuts through this orthogonal volume and leads into a wing-shaped extension at the rear. This incorporates a tall day-lit activity space and cafe with a dance area that can be separated off by means of an industrial roller shutter. Set back from the street edge, the rendered two-storey block gives the building a street frontage and acts as an acoustic barrier between the main activity space and the street. Its load bearing blockwork construction has a secure and robust feel, while the steel and timber construction facing the playing fields is open and light.

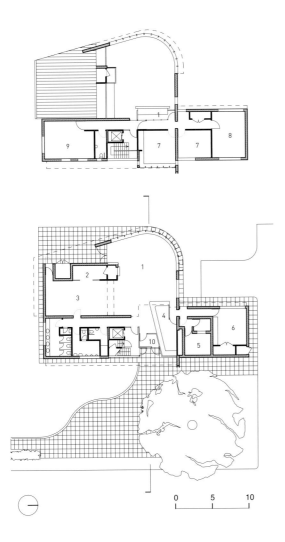

Opposite top: The structural aluminium-clad pitched roof spans the cafe area to make it column-free and flexible. The cafe space connects visually with the grassy playing field.

Opposite bottom left: From the street entrance a yellow wall guides the visitor through to the main space.

Opposite bottom right: The cafe is orientated away from the road and its curved glazed wall reveals the social activity within the building. The building was christened the Rollercoaster Centre by the users because its unclad steelwork was reminiscent of the structure of the fairground ride.

Top and middle: Ground and first floor plans showing the curving wall leading through the front block to the social spaces. Circulation is minimised and kept at the centre of the plan. On the first floor this gives access to a small 'cyber' balcony with computers overlooking the cafe.

1 cafe
2 DJ booth
3 disco/aerobic area
4 servery/kitchen
5 recording studio
6 workshop
7 group workroom
8 gym
9 office
10 entrance

Bottom: Section through the building showing the porch-like overhang of the of the first floor meeting room and the double-height space of the cafe.

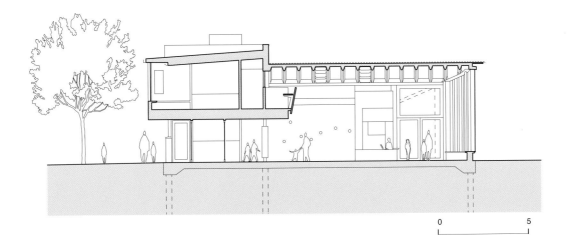

Adaptive design

In the years we have been in practice there have been great changes in the way people work and live, and in the way public services such as education and health care are organised and delivered. These are affected by changes in society, developments in technology and the expectations of the performance, now especially environmental performance, of buildings and public space. Plato's aphorism "change is the only constant" seems more relevant than ever. Design must therefore be able to adapt to changing use and circumstances; and to do so we have to muster the power of all the methods described above: a close observation of purpose and use, an understanding of typologies, and a facility for iterative design to devise buildings and places that work and communicate through architectural form.

Paradoxically, in order to devise effective generic solutions we have had to understand deeply the specifics of use. The Rushton Street Medical Centre embodied the ambition of the local Health Authority to create one of a new generation of local health care centres that would provide a much wider range of services than the usual family general practitioner while just as near people's homes. But the funding had to flow through four separate existing individual practices, which were not prepared to merge. Our brief was therefore to design a building with four front doors to four separate practices in such a way that if and as they merged, or were replaced by larger practices, the building could adapt easily to the new arrangement. Through our immersion in designing for doctors we had found that primary health care required spaces of just four different scales and 'atmosphere' — one: arrival and reception; two: waiting; three: consulting and treatment rooms and four: storage and wcs. Diagrammatically we saw this as a multi-strand ribbon of which we could 'call off' as much 'length' as we needed to establish a GP surgery of a particular size. This length could then be demarcated with a partition that could in the future be removed to make a surgery of a different size, or to combine adjacent surgeries. The cross-section through the building shows how the four scale/atmospheres of spaces work. On the ground floor of the building the waiting area constitutes a central 'mall' flanked by the entrance/reception spaces on one side and the consulting/treatment spaces on the other. The storage spaces and wc are tucked into appropriate positions in plan. The internal walls of the building are not load bearing and so can be moved

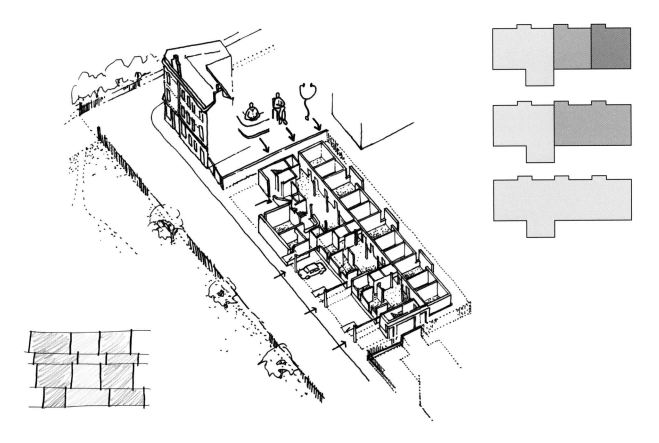

Opposite left: "My office, my desk": a still from the film *Metropolis*, Fritz Lang, 1927.

Opposite right: Children playing hopscotch on a London Street.

Left: The Rushton Street Medical Centre, diagram of the planning principle. Four types and scales of space are represented by four strands of a ribbon, each of a carefully calculated width so that a certain length can be called off to make a certain size of surgery, 1992.

Right: The ground floor plan showing the ability to accommodate one, two or three surgeries.

without affecting the structure. The lighting, heating and ventilation services are designed to make it easy to reposition or remove the key internal walls.

Over the years exactly what was planned really happened. For many years the four GP surgeries functioned separately. In year six a fifth GP practice came into the building and was accommodated on the first floor with a straightforward repositioning of the internal walls and minimal impact on services. In year nine Shoreditch Park Practice (SPP), on the ground floor, absorbed the patient lists of the other two practices and a single extended surgery was created, again with minimal change. The larger premises enabled a much wider range of services to be offered and made a whole clinic available for use by other teams, both in the building and the locality. SPP were already using their waiting area for art exhibitions and now have a 30 metre long top lit gallery for this use.

In preparation for the huge programme of rebuilding of English schools, the Department for Education and Skills commissioned a number of 'Exemplar Designs' in 2004 from different design teams, one of which we led. Our brief was to design a secondary community school for a restricted inner city site, which meant that the building would have to be five or six storeys high. Pedagogy was rapidly changing, bringing a shift of emphasis from teaching to personalised learning assisted by information technology.

The Rushton Street Medical Centre, Hackney, London, 1991–1996

The initial brief was to separately house four small local GP practices but to design in adaptability for future options in line with new thinking about primary health care — a potential that has now been realised. To achieve adaptability the spatial needs of primary care were analysed into four types of space conceived as zones of increasing privacy working back into the site from the back edge of the pavement. The steel framed building is organised about the central zone, a top-lit mall running the length of the building that acts as circulation as well as waiting space on the ground floor. On one side are the consulting and treatment rooms and on the other the administration and service spaces. Four separate entrances from the street allowed the space to be divided to create various sizes of practice premises, three of which have now been united to make a single large practice offering a range of services.

Abundant natural light, high insulation standards and a warm air system with heat recovery conserve energy and reduce fuel bills. The design consciously creates a civic presence responding to long views across the park with a double-storey colonnade allowing the ground floor to set back for car parking. The facade of first floor consulting rooms hang like a wavy curtain within the colonnade.

Top: The parkside facade steps out as it rises and an undulating wall of consulting rooms, banded by Iroko frames is held between the blue rendered facade at second floor and parking bays for vehicular access at ground.

Bottom left: A GP at work in a typical consulting room.

Bottom right: The cramped and cluttered conditions from which the surgeries moved.

Opposite: The height and mass of the design reflects that of the surrounding buildings. A band of London stock bricks makes a solid base from which the lighter cladding of insulated render rises. The surgery on the first floor has its entrance, stair and waiting areas glazed to make access legible from the street.

Top: The height and mass of the design reflects that of
the surrounding buildings. A band of London stock bricks
makes a solid base from which the lighter cladding of
insulated render rises. The surgery on the first floor
has its entrance, stair and waiting areas glazed to make
access legible from the street.

Opposite bottom left: The waiting space is top-lit and served by an open reception desk. The plywood joinery and beech slat surrounds of the steel columns contrast with the painted plaster surfaces.

Opposite bottom right: The bright interiors are well-lit with natural light. Timber stair treads, handrails and screens soften the clinical environments and are hard-wearing for constant use.

Top and middle: Ground and first floor plans.

1 waiting area and reception
2 consulting room
3 office
4 nurses' room
5 treatment room
6 common room
7 multi-purpose room
8 entrance

Bottom: Cross-section through the building showing the stepping facade to the park and the roof light to the waiting area on the ground floor.

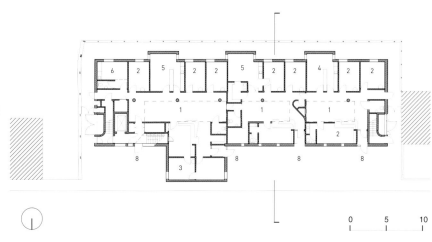

0   5   10

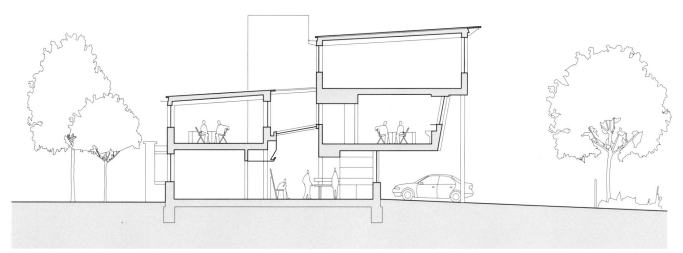

0   5

The future of the idea of the classroom itself was uncertain but for the time being the majority of teachers would still need them. We proposed that the formal teaching areas be regarded as an experimental 'rig' that the school could adapt to anything from conventional classrooms, through any range of alternative sizes and shapes of space to complete open plan. All the heating and electrical services were either on the external walls or in the floors and few structural columns intruded into the floor plates. However, not all the parts of the schools needed to be so adaptable. The ancilliary spaces, such as toilets and prep rooms, were attached to service and staircase cores in order to be unobtrusive. Key cultural and social spaces, like the main hall, the dining spaces and library, were designed as special forms in the general matrix of adaptable space, mostly on the ground floor. Though this 'exemplar' has not been built we have incorporated many of its principles into other built school projects.

In our primary care projects in London, procured through the Public Private Partnership LIFT programme, there has been a requirement to maximise the value of the building at the end of the 25 year lease period. At that point the building may become offices or flats. We have discovered that without forcing the design we can devise planning grids that work for a range of building types. We also devised elevations that had compositional coherence regardless of the location of windows. Clearly, it is useful during design to ask, from time to time, what if this was not an office/school/ health centre? What if these were flats? Provided that the structure and servicing strategy is thought through with the potential for adaptability in mind, it is quite possible to ensure day-to-day flexibility, medium term adaptability, and long term potential for changes of use.

As one meditates on a succession of projects and their large number of different demands and sub-problems, as Aalto put it, one become as conscious of the operational similarities, as of the differences between them. This applies most obviously within a type such as office, housing or school, but extends wider. All buildings accommodate people and their activities, all buildings require conscious manipulation of space and of connections and separation of spaces, and all buildings are located in particular physical and cultural contexts. It is likely that in its life-cycle a building will be called on to serve a purpose other than for which it was created. In architectural form-making, understanding use is a potent combination of underpinning and springboard just as in playing music mastering the instrument is utterly essential but only the beginning. If you go no further than playing the notes correctly you get a boring, uninspiring recital; in communicating powerfully a musician transcends the mechanics of playing.

With a strong consciousness of the resources available to construct and operate buildings, we want to create an architecture that with no apparent effort offers functionality and durability. The sensual experience of the building can then come to the fore in its many aspects: making places as a part of its setting; an object or composition of objects in its own right; and an environment or a set of spaces to be in and to move through for pleasure — a building as a customisable, adaptable and effective tool in the hands of its occupiers and owners, and a thing of beauty.

1 One consequence of this change is a deep lingering confusion in the public about what it is that architects actually do. It was perfectly obvious well into the twentieth century that the architect's main job was to orchestrate the appearance of the outside of buildings together with some interior design. They did this using a vocabulary of forms that was more or less familiar. The compositions followed trains of thought that were mysterious to the non-cognoscenti and had nothing to do with the physical use of the building. These buildings, still all around us, look completely different from what is being built today.

2 Adrian Forty in *Words and Buildings: A Vocabulary of Modern Architecture*, London: Thames & Hudson, 2000, analyses the changing meaning of functionalism as well as many other words whose meanings are taken for granted, often wrongly.

3 For example: "Unfortunately, in many buildings there was no effort made to create amenities in the public areas. Instead, a mean functionalism reigned, providing only cramped spaces and mundane materials." From the Pittsburgh Department of City Planning website: www.city.pittsburgh.pa.us/wt/html/historic_interiors.html. The term is not restricted to architecture, eg. "Unfortunately he is a puritanical control-freak who has encouraged and enforced the dismal functionalism that now passes for literacy teaching." From a review by Pam Harwood in *Books for Keeps*, no. 126, January 2001.

4 The term postmodern, whose origins are in literary criticism, appears to have been first applied to architecture by Charles Jencks. He used it as a tool of analysis embracing a number of diverse architectural movements united by their rejection of modernist verities, chiefly functionalism. However, it soon got attached to an unruly extrapolation of classical forms.

5 Mumford, Lewis, *The City in History*, London: Secker & Warburg, 1961 and Jacobs, Jane, *The Death and Life of Great American Cities*, New York: Random House, 1961.

6 Venturi, Robert and Denise Scott-Brown, *Complexity and Contradiction in Architecture*, New York: Museum of Modern Art, 1966; *Learning from Las Vegas*, Cambridge: MIT Press, 1972.

7 The members of Team 10 were: Jaap B Bakema and Aldo van Eyck (Holland), Georges Candilis and Shadrach Woods (France), Alison and Peter Smithson (England), Giancarlo De Carlo (Italy), Jose A Coderch (Spain), Charles Polonyi (Hungary), Jerzy Soltan (Poland) and Stefan Wewerka (Germany).

8 See chapter "Care".

9 Sir Henry Wootton translated these in 1624 as "commodity, firmness and delight". The currently used *Design Quality Indicator* (Construction Industry Council, UK) uses the expressions functionality, build quality and impact.

10 St John Wilson, Colin, *Architectural Reflections: Studies in the philosophy and practice of architecture*, Oxford: Oxford University Press, 1992, p. 31.

11 Saint, Andrew, *The Image of the Architect*, London: Yale University Press, 1983.

12 Quoted in St John Wilson, *Architectural Reflections*.

13 Extract from "Our Architectural Values", Penoyre & Prasad Practice Plan 2002: "A deep commitment to discovering the essential nature of the building as an organism.... This means taking the inner life of the building as the starting point for all design. In contemplating and researching this inner life we have on the past dwelt almost entirely on function – no detail of it was too ordinary or profane. But function was to be understood generously – to include emotional and sensual needs, not just the mechanics of organisation.... The phrase "inner life" is not to be taken to mean the life within the building – it is akin more to 'essence' or 'raison d'etre'. So consideration of the surrounding and context is entirely congruent with the search for the inner life."

14 In *Architectural Reflections* St John Wilson describes Aalto's approach as involving 'play' as one of the stages of design and expands on the concept in "The play of use and the use of play." David Gann with Mark Dodgson and Ammon Salter explored innovation technology in *Think, Play, Do*, Oxford: Oxford University Press, 2005, and identify play as a crucial step in generating innovation. Will Alsop's working method has consistently used making a free work of art, a painting or a sculpture, as a starting point even before assimilating the brief. He has called the product of this activity a "sacrificial design", an example of the use of inductive logic.

15 Thompson, D'Arcy, *On Growth and Form*, Cambridge: Cambridge University Press, 1961. Thompson's book, originally published in 1942, has been a key text in architectural education and theory.

16 The principle of Functionalism is popularly attributed to nineteenth century American architect Louis Sullivan and his invariably misquoted dictum "form follows function". He actually wrote "form ever follows function", and in context it is clear that he was inspired by the eternal, sublime fit between form and function in nature, not proposing a method: "Whether it be the sweeping eagle in his flight, or the open apple-blossom, the toiling work-horse, the blithe swan, the branching oak, the winding stream at its base, the drifting clouds, over all the coursing sun, *form ever follows function*, and this is the law. Where function does not change form does not change. The granite rocks, the ever-brooding hills, remain for ages; the lightning lives, comes into shape, and dies in a twinkling.

It is the pervading law of all things organic and inorganic, of all things physical and metaphysical, of all things human and all things superhuman, of all true manifestations of the head, of the heart, of the soul, that the life is recognizable in its expression, that form ever follows function. This is the law." Sullivan, Louis H, *The tall office building artistically considered*, *Lippincott's Magazine*, March 1896.

17 Presentation (unpublished) at CABE's annual conference 2006.

18 Gordon, Alex, "The President Introduces his Long Life/Loose Fit/Low Energy Study," *RIBA Journal*, September 1972.

Building Schools for the Future,
Secondary School Design Exemplar, 2003

In preparation for the biggest school building programme since the war the Department of Education and Skills selected a number of architects to prepare theoretical designs on a set of notional sites with different contexts and briefs that would serve as future exemplars. We were asked to take on a very restricted inner city site for a secondary community school that would necessitate a multi-storey solution.

In multi-storey buildings the ground level, the most accessible and visible of all, has a nature fundamentally different from the others. This suggested the principle that all the facilities shared with the local community should be at ground level, to create a 'civic ground', with the formal learning areas lifted up above and easily separated. The shared facilities, sports hall, main hall, cafeteria, performance spaces are also the most tailored in design, whereas to deal with changing pedagogies, the learning areas need to be highly adaptable. We conceived the latter areas as a 'learning rig', a set of floor plates with only two or four internal columns that can be planned as cellular rooms or open learning areas. The design team devised an innovative facade that provides very low energy heating and ventilation to each class space and employs glazing with light bending technology to bring daylight deep into the spaces. The vertical circulation was organised as a set of 'light links'— mini atria connecting the rigs with circulation and services as well as accommodating resource areas, social spaces and terraces. The landscape design was of crucial importance to make the most of the relatively small amount of external space, and incorporated signage and information to reinforce the urban presence of the school. A garden was proposed on the roof. Together all these components made a kit of parts to be used to create variety within a set of standards.

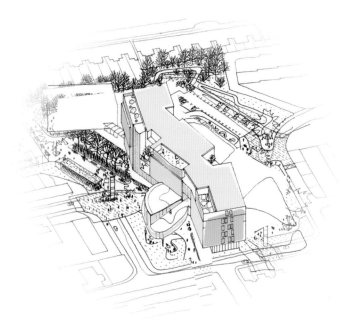

Top: Landscape designer's sketch.

Bottom: Cross-section A-A through the hall.

Opposite top: External view showing the solidity of the 'rigs' contrasting with the transparency of the 'light links'.

Opposite bottom: Cross-section B-B showing the double-height foyer.

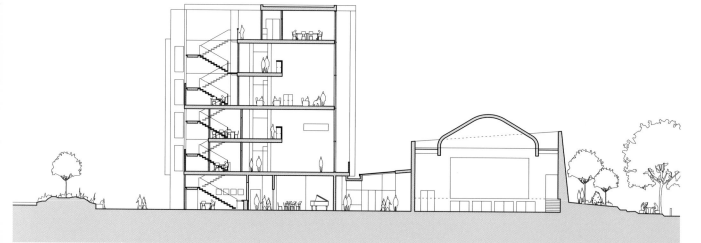

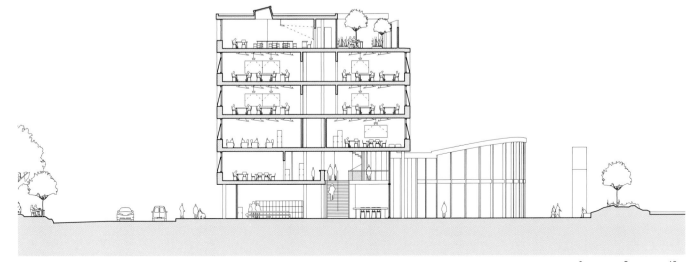

0   5   10

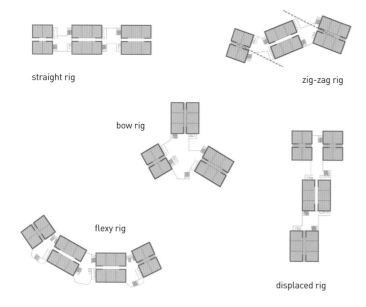

straight rig

zig-zag rig

bow rig

flexy rig

displaced rig

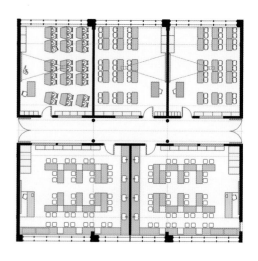

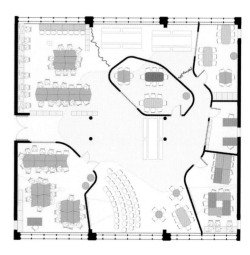

Top left: Diagrams illustrating the various arrangement of rigs with light links between.

Middle left: Study model of the components to demonstrate adaptability on different sites.

Bottom left: Facade study of the south elevation showing the main entrance adjacent to the dining area.

Top right: Adaptive plans. Currently schools are moving away from 'formal' classroom teaching arrangements (top) towards structured learning patterns increasingly tailored towards individual students (bottom). The size of the rig allows flexibility in the layouts both by using moveable walls or by occasional reconfiguration.

Ground and second floor plan.

1 teaching space
2 staff administration and communal
3 wcs/changing
4 circulation
5 storage
6 informal/social
7 entrance

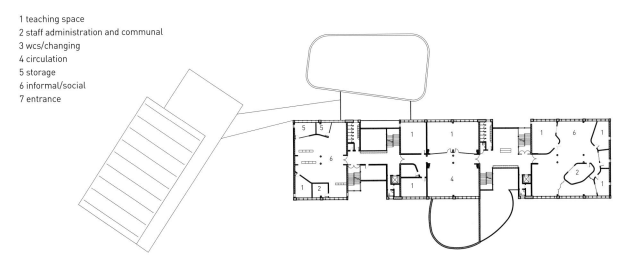

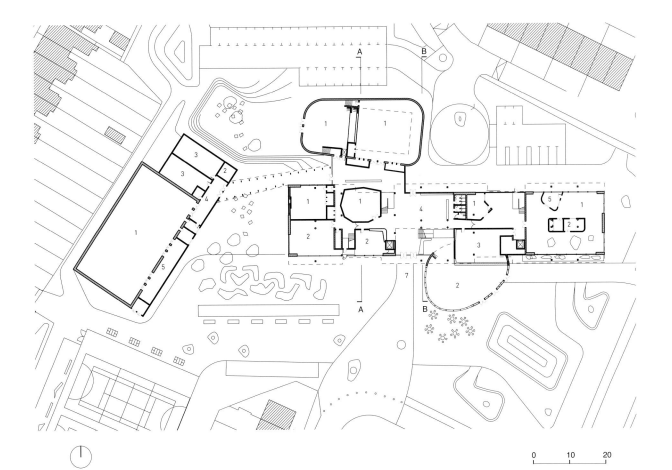

0   10   20

CONSTRUCTION

This chapter explores the internal logic of construction, which has played a large part in the appearance of our buildings, and how contemporary design and construction practice requires a new approach.

Communication is a prime function of a work of architecture but, intentionally or not, every building communicates something through its appearance; nobility, welcome, exuberance, banality, hostility or, perhaps, confusion. While the overall sculptural form, the treatment of surfaces, the handling of the setting, are major components of architectural language, detail, ie. how the means of construction are revealed or hidden can speak volumes. In traditional architecture applied decoration and motifs provided an autonomous narrative that suppressed the everyday facts of construction. In contemporary architecture, devoid of extraneous decoration, the chosen construction techniques at all scales become major determinants of appearance.

Showing and hiding

Construction is almost always layered and by its nature contains both hidden and revealed elements. Amongst the most important acts of an architect is deciding what to show and what to hide. Many hidden elements of construction can be things of beauty in their own right, like the ribs of boats that get covered over with ship-lap boards or steel plates. Often during site visits members of the practice inspecting half constructed buildings, frames and slabs exposed, yearn for their elemental qualities to remain exposed in the finished item. This does not arise simply from a fascination with the exposure of inner complexities as in the fashion for transparent watch or radio cases. It comes rather from a strong attraction for directness and simplicity of expression, a wish for the architecture to quietly tell the story of its own making.

Projects such as New Maltings, 1989, Walworth Surgery, 1991, and The Rushton Street Medical Centre, 1996, display our preoccupation with a first principles approach to construction and the articulation of detail. To take a later example, The Pulross Centre, 2000, in its overall organisation has two major components: the regular orthogonal bed bays and treatment, consulting or work rooms; and the curving circulation spaces. The former are made of concrete, the latter of timber. The large pine mullions that carry the glass and timber boarded curved front facade are expressed within, as is the concrete frame as pilasters and lintels. At the top of the facade, just under the roof eaves is a strip of glazing with no visible beads to hold it. Seen from the upper floor corridor we wanted the ceiling to flow uninterrupted from inside to the big overhanging eaves outside. The glass is clamped within the thickness of the plasterboard of the ceiling and rebated into the mullions. The aim in the detailing was

Fairfaced blockwork facade design drawing for Olney School, near Milton Keynes, 2007.

to express the major constructional and spatial elements as clearly as possible and to place against them carefully crafted accessories like the combined handrail and wall protection. Not all of the details have been equally successful. The exposure of the concrete frame is somewhat haphazard because of the position of partitions and openings, and its impact is lost. The rigid division between timber and concrete structure means that the corridor floors feel less robust than those in the concrete rooms, creating a slightly unsettling transition. But the feeling of space in the corridor is generous exactly as intended; and the stainless steel and beech handrail/protection is a long way from the institutional high impact plastic bumpers you find in hospital corridors. Articulation of constructional detail can be eloquent, but so can its suppression.

Articulation

Even the simplest buildings require the assembly of several materials and of many pieces of the same material. The joint between elements, at many different scales, is a major focus of attention in design. It essentially determines the constructed appearance of a work of architecture, its tectonics (from the Greek *tekton*, builder), as opposed to its layout and spatial arrangements. Just as design may be directed to bringing out, showing, telling of, speaking about, 'celebrating', the essential qualities of a material, so it may be directed to doing the same for the essence of the act of jointing. Even something as simple as connecting two similar lengths of timber can be done in many different ways, each with its own expressive possibilities. Here (opposite) are a few of the ways of making a rigid right-angled joint between two lengths of wood.

Ease of construction, economy and strength may be reasons for choosing one technique over another, but each method also expresses something different about the nature of timber and of jointing. A to D reveal the method of jointing to different extents. E and F conceal it. The mitred concealed tenon, E, hides all end grain and turns timber into a substance that can simply flow round a sharp corner, which architects of an earlier generation would have considered to be dishonest, an illustration of the intriguing nexus between aesthetics and ethics to which we will return later.

Left: The skeletal timber frames of fishing boats being built on a beach in Portugal before completion of hulls with steel plating.

Right: View along the first floor corridor of The Pulross Centre, Brixton, 2000.

The easy to make bolted joints, G and H, with their hidden shear connectors, make the pieces seemingly independent of the other. In G each pieces is cut flush with the edge of the other, whereas in H they pass each other nonchalantly. Joint I, inelegant, direct, and the strongest, speaks of security and robustness, the gusset clamping and trapping the timbers. Joints J and K show a subtle combination of steel and timber. Steel really can flow around a sharp corner without losing strength, and a small L-shaped piece of steel unites the two lengths of timber visibly but discretely, subtly expressing the nature and beauty of the joint. There are additional nuances: should the steel sit flush with the timber surface or just below it? Making it flush requires better workmanship and dimensional control. Is it neater, and in some ways more expressive to create a recess? Then again such a recess may collect dirt and be difficult to finish. Considerations like these are essential for refined and sophisticated detail design but the synergy between detail and the bigger picture matters more.

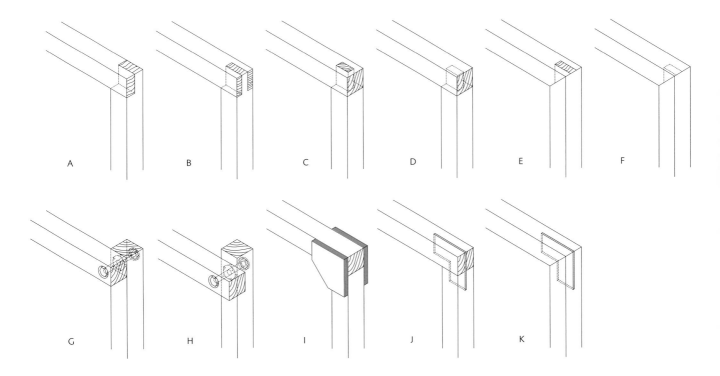

Joinery techniques
A half housed
B tenon into slot
C tenon into mortice
D tenon into mortice with mitre
E and F concealed tenon into
mortice — mitred or butted

Engineering techniques
G bolted with shear connector flush
H bolted with shear connector projecting
I gussetted
J & K flitched — butted or mitred

The Pulross Centre, Brixton Intermediate Care Centre, 1995–2000

The Pulross Centre, embodies the shift away from the hospital to a primary care led National Health Service. Located in an area with a high index of economic deprivation and with associated health problems, its declared and positive philosophy is to regard health as "a state of mental and social wellbeing, not merely the absence of infirmity". Serving as a hub for 23 local GP practices, it provides specialist day clinics for patients in the neighbourhood as well as in-patient beds for people needing 24 hour medical care.

At the end of Pulross Road the building is marked by the lantern window of the dining room. The ground slopes down gently to make an ellipsoidal forecourt with a mature plane tree at its centre and the curving glass and timber facade of the building making an edge. The main entrance leads into a double-height foyer from which almost all parts of the centre are visible and accessible. The cafe and social spaces here are designed for open access to local people with the rest of the building able to be secured. The ground floor houses the clinics and a day room with a garden while the three four-bay wards on the first floor have level access to a raised garden built up with the demolished and excavated material. Most of the patient and visitor circulation has views out into the landscaped and well treed forecourt and its walls are protected from trolleys with a specially designed beech and stainless steel handrail and wall guarding system. The four high dependency bedrooms are nearest to the strip of staff spaces and have generous projecting bays giving side views from their beds.

Top: While the scale of the building is domestic, its formal vocabulary is modernist, with a virtually flat roof and oversailing eaves, masking the sweep of the glazed curtain wall that encloses the foyer and circulation galleries. Daylight penetrates throughout. External materials are principally stock facing brickwork, Douglas Fir weatherboarding and metal framing for sun shades.

Bottom: Cross-section of the building indicating the timber criblock retaining structure for the raised garden and the bridges that connect it to the first floor.

Opposite: The double-height space at the entrance is overlooked from the first floor nursing station to help night time security. The foyer is used for a variety of community functions, including evening yoga classes. The in-patients can also watch life in the foyer and their dining/living room faces out onto the entrance courtyard.

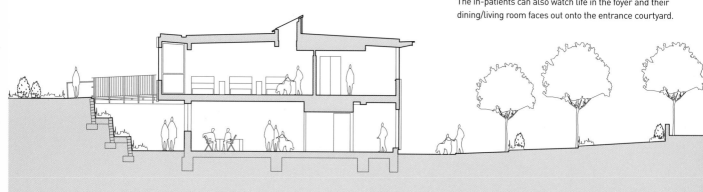

0   5

Top: The short stay four-bed wards and individual rooms for 20 in-patients are on the first floor overlooking the secluded terraced gardens to the rear.

Bottom: The facade curves around the forecourt; a terraced garden with areas for sitting out in good weather and for physiotherapy exercise. A blue metal strip to the edge of the canopy identifies the entrance.

Opposite: Ground and first floor plans.

1 waiting area
2 reception and office
3 quiet room
4 office
5 treatment room
6 utility
7 social space
8 meeting room
9 cubicles
10 gym
11 staff base
12 staff room
13 one–bed rooms
14 four–bed rooms
15 entrance

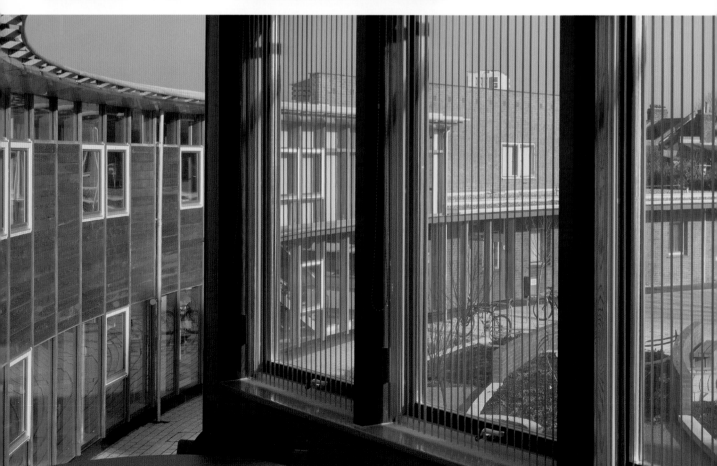

0   10   20

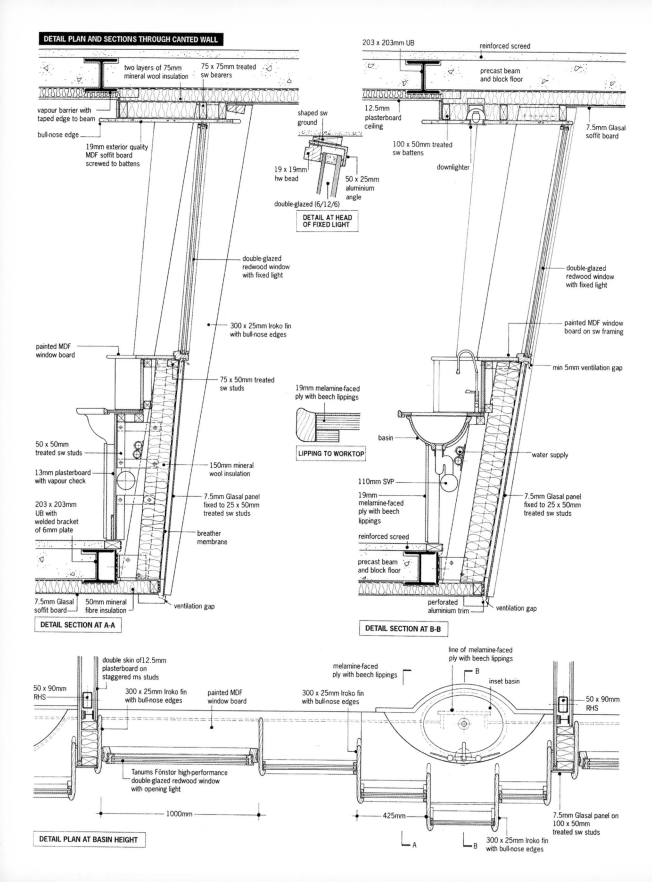

DETAIL PLAN AND SECTIONS THROUGH CANTED WALL

two layers of 75mm mineral wool insulation

75 x 75mm treated sw bearers

vapour barrier with taped edge to beam

bull-nose edge

19mm exterior quality MDF soffit board screwed to battens

203 x 203mm UB

reinforced screed

precast beam and block floor

12.5mm plasterboard ceiling

100 x 50mm treated sw battens

downlighter

7.5mm Glasal soffit board

shaped sw ground

19 x 19mm hw bead

50 x 25mm aluminium angle

double-glazed (6/12/6)

DETAIL AT HEAD OF FIXED LIGHT

double-glazed redwood window with fixed light

300 x 25mm Iroko fin with bull-nose edges

painted MDF window board

75 x 50mm treated sw studs

50 x 50mm treated sw studs

13mm plasterboard with vapour check

203 x 203mm UB with welded bracket of 6mm plate

150mm mineral wool insulation

7.5mm Glasal panel fixed to 25 x 50mm treated sw studs

breather membrane

7.5mm Glasal soffit board

50mm mineral fibre insulation

ventilation gap

DETAIL SECTION AT A-A

19mm melamine-faced ply with beech lippings

LIPPING TO WORKTOP

double-glazed redwood window with fixed light

painted MDF window board on sw framing

min 5mm ventilation gap

basin

water supply

110mm SVP

19mm melamine-faced ply with beech lippings

reinforced screed

precast beam and block floor

7.5mm Glasal panel fixed to 25 x 50mm treated sw studs

perforated aluminium trim

ventilation gap

DETAIL SECTION AT B-B

double skin of 12.5mm plasterboard on staggered ms studs

50 x 90mm RHS

300 x 25mm Iroko fin with bull-nose edges

painted MDF window board

melamine-faced ply with beech lippings

300 x 25mm Iroko fin with bull-nose edges

line of melamine-faced ply with beech lippings

inset basin

50 x 90mm RHS

Tanums Fönstor high-performance double-glazed redwood window with opening light

1000mm

425mm

7.5mm Glasal panel on 100 x 50mm treated sw studs

300 x 25mm Iroko fin with bull-nose edges

DETAIL PLAN AT BASIN HEIGHT

Tectonic culture and DIY

Different schools of thought in architecture concern themselves to different degrees with tectonics and different approaches to concealing and revealing. Minimalism amounts to control by editing details to direct full attention to a few select elements of form and function considered to be the core of the work. Its opposite, which has been called 'maximalism', or 'structural expressionism' revels in letting it all hang out, in showing or 'celebrating' junctions and functions. The majority of modern architecture lies between these poles and deploys innumerable approaches to expression of detail. The delight in the articulation of simple construction in the architecture of Edward Cullinan was an early influence in our design approach.[1] The inherent beauty of the physical elements of which buildings are made captivated us, and we were dedicated to revealing this beauty through the articulation of the distinctiveness, one might say the 'personality', of these elements. Our approach to construction has been influenced by traditional Japanese building, English vernacular architecture, the French architect Violet-le-Duc, the major figures of the Arts and Crafts Movement such as Philip Webb and William Morris, Californian architects Maybeck, Schindler and Green & Green, Scandinavians Sigurd Lewerentz and Alvar Aalto and the Australian Glen Murcutt.

Our feeling for the elements of construction has been nourished through DIY on a large scale. Many members of the office have been engaged in hands-on construction, whether in connection with their own homes, building schools in tsunami hit Sri Lankan villages or putting up exhibitions and art installations. Greg Penoyre and I were inducted into building at an early age, helping fathers with building work and making furniture. At architecture school I was amongst a group that formed a construction company and carried out a refurbishment contract. Later, as part of a self-build housing co-operative friends and I built our own house. Greg has rebuilt parts of a number of houses and outbuildings. The ability to build was highly valued in the early years of the practice and we admired Scandinavian architectural education, which at that time required every architect to master a building craft as part of her/his training. This is in stark contrast to UK architectural education today, which has much reduced technical, let alone practical, content. An architect immersed in practical construction, learning through making and physical exploration, views the design project very differently from one that is not so immersed. This is not necessarily, of itself, a good thing; because such familiarity may promote

Opposite: Detail of the construction of the 'ripple' windows at The Rushton Street. The hardwood fins, and the glass panes are all orthogonal and repetitive but produce a curved surface, the recesses of which house wash handbasins.

Left: Ted Cullinan's own house at Camden Mews, London, 1963–1964.

Centre: Greg Penoyre and his son constructing a garden studio, 1997.

Right: Front elevation of self-build house, Sunand Prasad and friends, Shepherdess Walk, 1985.

the repetition of a narrow range of familiar techniques and inhibit one from stretching possibilities. But we did design our early buildings as if we were going to build them ourselves and we enjoyed expressing their construction rather than subjecting it to a different ruling aesthetic.

Construction and ethics

The layered nature of construction makes it possible to design buildings as one would a stage set. The architect can design and describe the surface envelope of the building together with the interior spaces and their boundary surfaces and leave it to others to work out how they get built. This is architecture as artifice, free of the concern with authenticity that so occupied Modernism and continues to inspire us.

The relationship between architecture and construction has always been complex. We find in Greek temples and Buddhist chaitya halls carved decorative motifs that are true to scale representations of timber construction: joist ends, ribs of vaults, pegs. These stone buildings, some assembled of blocks, others carved out of single pieces of rock are literally models of earlier sacred buildings made of timber. The tectonics of timber construction have been turned into pure representation, preserving the meaning that timber architecture had acquired through its use for sacred ritual; a meaning that it did not have the durability itself to carry for long. Some centuries later motifs of Greek classical architecture were skilfully copied in stucco, and now they can be rendered faithfully in plastics: plastic imitating stucco imitating stone imitating timber; a brilliant play with meaning, inexcusable fakery, or just a cheap and harmless way of capturing the nobility of an ancient tradition?

The Architectural Association's motto "Design with Beauty, Build with Truth" was coined in the middle of the nineteenth century, when the so-called 'Battle of Styles' was in full swing. The motto was a rallying cry for authenticity, for the idea that simple expression of construction was morally superior to dressing up buildings with surface embellishments. In the 1960s and 70s, when some of the older members of the practice were at their studies, 'honesty to materials' was taken as a self-evident good. But was this a moral position or a pragmatic approach, a sure and practical way of making the best looking and most functional buildings? Was it at root a purely mystic belief in the value of revealing served up as a moral

imperative? The title of Henry-Russell Hitchcock's book on Frank Lloyd Wright, *In the Nature of Materials*, 1942, told it more like it is. Wright had a deep understanding of materials and was able to work with them, revealing their nature when he chose to, but adding decoration at will. In the practice of modern architecture applied decoration has not always been considered to be wrong, or pointless but has been used sparingly.

Another, quite different ethical dimension to the rise of modern architecture was fed by ideals of democracy, equality, openness in public affairs and more recently the wise use of the earth's resources. But what explains the visual form(s) of modern architecture is a new way of seeing things that arose around the turn of the nineteenth century. Within architecture the Viennese architect Adolf Loos was the first to crystallise the new principles. In his 1898 essay, "Principles of Building", Loos argued that the true vocabulary of building lies in the materials themselves.[2] "Excessive decoration" was wrong because it obscured their essential beauty. In 1908, in "Ornament and Crime", he equated an absence of ornament with spiritual strength. Ornament was a characteristic of a primitive society. Excessive ornamentation, which he thought had prevailed (in European architecture) since the early eighteenth century amounted to a crime, because in an industrial economy it represented a waste of labour and materials, containing the danger that a large number of products would rapidly go out of style. In his essays we can see how an aesthetic view, materials properly used are by themselves beautiful enough, segued into an ethical one, excessive decoration is therefore a waste and thus a crime. Loos went on to say that as decoration was no longer an essential component of culture, a worker could never be paid a fair price for it. This was prescient, for the biggest reason for the mass of modern buildings is surely cost rather than a universal embrace of abstraction or purity of form.

Le Corbusier described Loos as having performed "an Homeric cleansing" of architecture and himself polemicised the essential beauty of materials. "Unfinished concrete is as beautiful as a warrior, a soldier or an athlete. He has no need to grin like an actor, and be made up with marble", he wrote in his sketchbook in 1955, about the surface of the High Court in the Capitol Complex at Chandigarh.[3]

We could find a variant of these sentiments underlying the work of most great Modernist architects. It was not until 1966 with the publication of Robert Venturi and Denise Scott-Brown's book, *Complexity and Contradiction in Architecture*, that a coherent argument emerged to counter the powerful, simple credo of Modernist conviction.[4] The postmodern view, introduced to architectural culture by this book, with its embrace of ambiguity and of the relativity of truth, sidestepped issues of morality in art.

Despite postmodernism and the challenges of late twentieth and early twenty-first century culture, the thread of, let us call it 'essentialism', keeps running strong in architecture: the idea that materials and their assembly are in themselves capable of producing a strong emotional impact on us and that such impact is superior to that produced by narrative methods such as decoration or reference to previous forms. We don't consider applied decoration, artifice and concealment in themselves to be unethical but they are unlikely to be anything but secondary themes. The primary means of giving form, texture and surface to the work remains direct, orchestrated expression of materials and their interplay.

Opposite left: Chaitya-Hall, Ajanta Caves, India c. 150 AD, carved into a single stone mass and depicting the details of earlier timber construction.

Opposite centre: The classical columns of a domestic porch made of glass reinforced polyester by Stevensons of Norwich.

Opposite right: Minster School under construction, 2006.

New Maltings, Private House, 1987–1989

In Ted Cullinan's 1963–1964 design of the original house the principles so successfully adopted and imaginatively interpreted in his other houses had been compromised by the complexity of the brief. For example, although there was a clear plan with a strip of service rooms along the northern edge of the house, instead of large living spaces facing south with glass to the floor, there were a series of quite small bedrooms with high cills. To accommodate the previous owner's growing family the Cullinan office had designed additional bedrooms at a lower level, ingeniously dug into the hill and reached via a spiral staircase.

Our clients saw the potential of this quirky house on the south-facing slope of the river Stour and we saw our task to be restoring the clarity of planning and accommodating their hospitable and expansive lifestyle. In our design the north facade of the house has been re-built to make a generous and striking entrance hall from which all parts are directly reached. A new dressing room extension to the first floor master bedroom is cantilevered out over the entrance to make a port cochere. Most internal walls on the ground floor are removed to make an almost 30 metre long gallery with large sliding glass windows to the garden. The fabric of the house was upgraded to contemporary standards and the new roof given generous overhangs for better protection from the sun and rain.

Top: Perspective drawing of the entrance.

Bottom left: The garden facade.

Bottom middle and right: The living/dining room and the entrance at dusk.

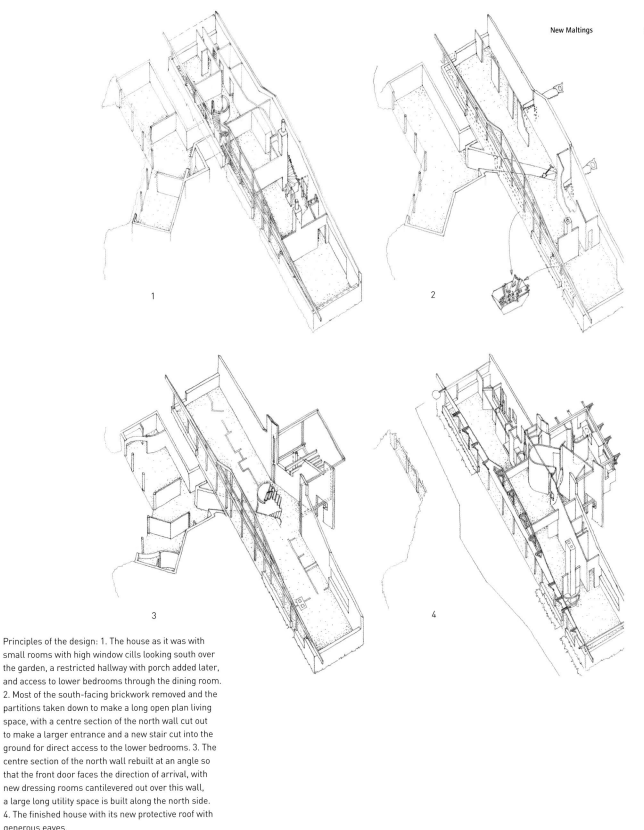

Principles of the design: 1. The house as it was with
small rooms with high window cills looking south over
the garden, a restricted hallway with porch added later,
and access to lower bedrooms through the dining room.
2. Most of the south-facing brickwork removed and the
partitions taken down to make a long open plan living
space, with a centre section of the north wall cut out
to make a larger entrance and a new stair cut into the
ground for direct access to the lower bedrooms. 3. The
centre section of the north wall rebuilt at an angle so
that the front door faces the direction of arrival, with
new dressing rooms cantilevered out over this wall,
a large long utility space is built along the north side.
4. The finished house with its new protective roof with
generous eaves.

From DIY to PFI

A preoccupation with how the logic of construction and the character of materials can be synthesised into a formal language takes many and hugely varied forms. The expressionism of 'high-tech' architects, for example, is in its results a diametric opposite of the work of other contemporary British architects such as Tony Fretton, Caruso St John or Sergison Bates who in their different ways intensely explore a studied, refined simplicity. What unites both these sets of architects and our practice's approaches, whatever other difference, is a belief that the expression of a building is to be derived from the facts of its making. The form is not to be conjured up from other sources and then rendered expediently via whatever materials and techniques serve the purpose. However, putting this belief into practice is becoming harder due to profound changes within the construction industry and its associated professions. A brief reflection over the years since the formation of the architectural profession helps explain how contemporary construction techniques and procurement regimes make it increasingly difficult, except in small scale projects, for architects to craft constructional details.

Architecture was one of the new professions that formed in the first half of the nineteenth century and broadly adopted the ethical formation of the old professions of the Clergy, the Law and Medicine: independent and above commerce. The classic ideal of the nineteenth century profession had already been enunciated by Sir John Soane, 1753–1837, who described an architect as "the intermediate agent between the employer, whose honour and interest he is to study, and the mechanic, whose rights he is to defend…". He asked: "With what propriety can his situation, and that of the builder, or the contractor, be united?"[5]

In 1834 the British Institute of Architects was formed gaining the Royal Charter in 1837. Although the RIBA has sustained professional ethics and excellence for 175 years, in hindsight it is at least questionable that creative experts involved in physical production should have formed restrictive associations modelled on those of lawyers and doctors. The result was an increasing separation between the intellectual conception of design and its physical implementation as a building. Notably the two activities were under the control of different sources of finance, the first, the clients and the second, the contractors, a commercial entity that emerged in the mid-nineteenth century to employ all

Left: Studio in the Centre for Visual Arts, Sway, Hampshire, by Tony Fretton Architects, 1996.

Right: Glass staircase in a Mayfair apartment, by Eva Jiricna Architects, 1994.

the building trades under one command. The design professions divided increasingly throughout the nineteenth century with the formation of various engineering and surveying institutes.

Traditions of craftsmanship, tried and tested techniques, and the scientifically validated contributions of engineers ensured that buildings continued to perform satisfactorily under this division of labour. Although there were significant technological advancements in construction, the industry could not match the innovations in manufacturing processes and the way they exploited technology in the controlled condition of factories. Construction was to remain substantially craft and site based until the late twentieth century.

After the Second World War building science took over from traditional craft knowledge and architects and other designers took on ever increasing responsibility to specify construction down to the last detail. In the 1960s and 70s there were sometimes disastrous failures in performance of buildings as an emergent building science proved insufficiently mature to fill the vacuum left by the loss of traditional techniques. Increased regulation and byelaws and higher expectations of performance of buildings required ever greater quantities of information to be supplied to a contractor, who, under prevailing building contracts, bore little or no responsibility for such information. Inevitably this split of responsibility came to be identified as the major cause of cost and time overruns, which, although far from universal, had come to be seen as the norm in construction. This perception ultimately led in the 1990s to the rapid growth of the 'Design and Build' (D&B) form of contract in which the contractor is responsible for both the design and the delivery of the building; whereas in so-called traditional procurement the usually architect-led design team, is responsible for producing all the design information under a separate contract with the client, and the contractor is responsible for the construction. In the meantime contractors had almost entirely become middle-men with only a small directly employed work force and employing numerous separate trade sub-contractors. This led to a huge reduction in training and apprenticeship systems that previously prevailed in craft-based construction companies.

The last 50 years of the twentieth century has seen the final decline of an industry based on crafts. There have been great advances in the understanding of structure, fabric and services and improvements in the performance of buildings. However, construction has only haphazardly embraced industrialised methods such as prototyping and automation that have been common in other manufacturing sectors for decades. D&B places design and construction under a single management and finance regime, which introduces organisational disciplines that improves certainty of cost and delivery. While this promises reintegration of the intellectual and the physical aspects of building, in practice there has so far been little such integration. Architects and engineers are seen by most contractors as another set of subcontractors to be controlled. Although progressive elements in the industry are committed to 'integrated supply chains', as exist in manufacturing, only a few of today's project management oriented contractors have the capability and training to be true process integrators. Patterns of education and recruitment have caused too much of the total brainpower in the industry to migrate to the design end, which has a poor grip on cost and process issues.

The University Library, University of Portsmouth, Hampshire, 2004–2007

The new Library has more than doubled the size of the well-loved 1976 original by architects Ahrends Burton Koralek, and made a new gateway and heart for the University Campus, located as it is in a prominent position in Ravelin Park between the University's North Campus and student lodgings in Southsea.

Accessed off a new piazza to the west and from the park to the east, a covered street runs right through the building open to students and the public during working hours. From this thoroughfare are accessed IT, seminar spaces and a cafe, arranged around a planted courtyard, and also the turnstiles and main issue desk situated in the three-storey main entrance hall. The ground floor, containing the intensively used IT and seminar rooms forms a base for the building, its battered walls and concrete details taking their architectural cues from the naval fortifications from Napoleonic tomes, fragments of which still exist in Old Portsmouth. Two storeys of book stacks and study space in an internally exposed concrete structure rise above this base. The southwest elevation facing the park is designed as an echeloned series of solid fins and windows such that the windows face due south, making it easier to mitigate solar gain, and making triangular study bays alongside the stacks. The facade flanking the entrance is clad in stone with a series of vertical slot windows making for transparency and acting as a giant sign at the end of Burnaby Road. This facade curves internally towards the street, leading the visitor into the building and terminating in a main stair.

Designed to achieve a BREEAM rating of 'Very Good' the building incorporates strategies for reducing energy use and environmental impact using its high thermal mass with an assisted natural ventilation system with heat recovery.

Top: Study of facade treatments.

Bottom: Detail of a map of Portsmouth in c. 1835, showing naval fortifications, or 'ravelins', which gave the area its name.

Opposite: View from the bridge across the 'street' that passes through the Library.

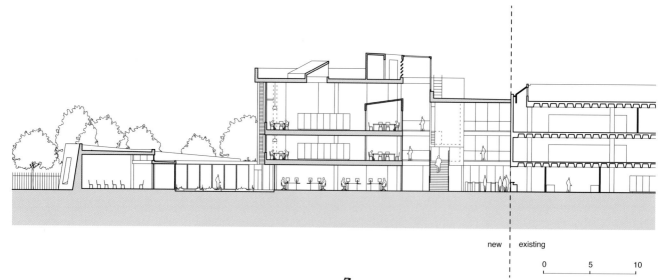

new | existing

0   5   10

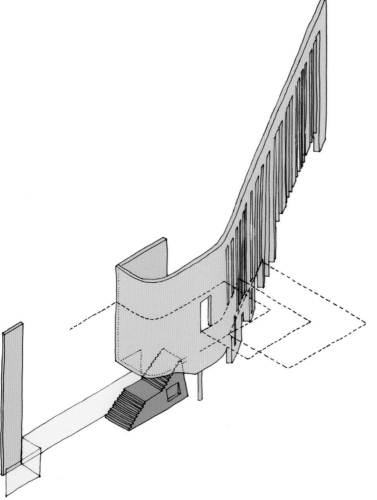

Top: Cross-section.

Bottom: The wall flanking the entrance leads the visitor into the foyer and then wraps around the upper flights of the main stair.

Opposite top left: The life in the reading areas and the ground floor cafe animates the main urban facade.

Opposite top right: The second floor with its five metre high ceiling and angular north lights. The echelons on the south elevations create study carrels.

Opposite bottom: View from the park. The timber-faced study carrels on the upper Library floors overlook the courtyard, the sedum roof of the seminar rooms and the park beyond. The Portland stone frame of the Library floors sits on a dark brick base, an arrangement reminiscent of the way ravelins made an upper level where buildings could be more securely situated.

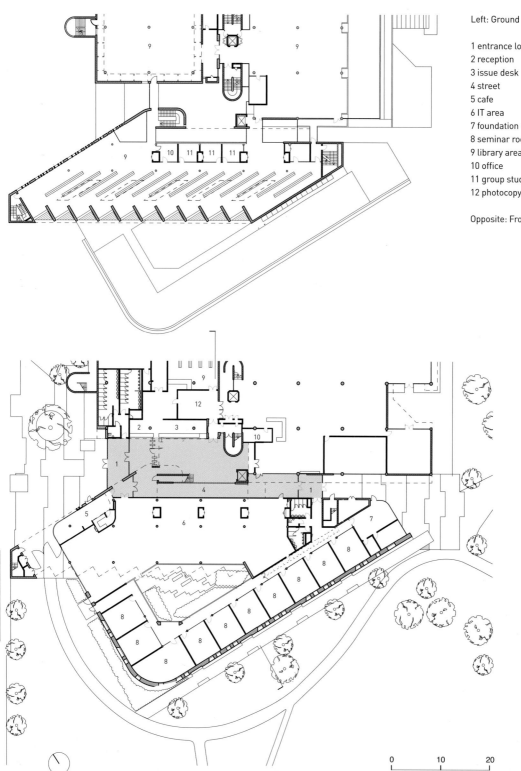

Left: Ground floor and second floor plans.

1 entrance lobby
2 reception
3 issue desk
4 street
5 cafe
6 IT area
7 foundation direct
8 seminar rooms
9 library area
10 office
11 group study room
12 photocopy room

Opposite: Front entrance at night.

0   10   20

The industry is, as a consequence, slow to adopt the extraordinary possibilities of Building Information Modelling (BIM), that can allow a virtual building to be fully designed with every detail integrated prior to being built by Modern Methods of Construction (MMC) whereby much of the manufacture is carried out off site in safe, dry and decent working conditions at higher and more reliable quality and speed. A leading architect/academic blithely said to us not so long ago, "Surely construction is to an architect as printing is to a writer...", perfectly illustrating how out of step with the current concerns of the construction industry professional attitudes can be.

The integration of design and construction is a highly desirable goal, but the nature of the construction contract is only one aspect of achieving it. Even under traditional contracts architects and engineers frequently collaborate on the design with specialist subcontractors ensuring that the design is fully informed by the physical and financial realities of construction. Many engineers and some architects send construction information electronically direct to the machines of fabricators. The real motive behind vesting the responsibility for both design and construction in middle-men was to avoid the client carrying the higher risks associated with split responsibility; it was not to achieve a better ratio of quality to cost. Cost and time over-runs have become less frequent in the industry, though it is difficult to say what effect this has had on overall costs, let alone long term value. The quality of the outcomes, however, has become highly dependent on the ability or willingness of the main contractor, too often acting as the middle-man, to understand and promote design values especially when they come into conflict with profitability, as they inevitably do from time to time.

Our construction ethos outlined in the first half of this chapter arises from a love of the art, science and craft of building and an enjoyment in finding solutions from first principles. Now design for construction has to be guided as much by the management of risk. As the client transfers as much risk as possible to the main contractor, so the main contractor transfers it on to subcontractors and suppliers, including consultants. A key element of managing risk is maximising the clarity of the package of goods and services to be provided by any one supplier and reducing its overlap with other packages; for example supplying and installing the roof structure as distinct from the roof covering as distinct from the safety equipment for roof maintenance. Designing and managing the interface between packages then becomes a key task of design. The attention that we focused on the joint between two components we now focus on the interface between two packages.

The drive to simplify interfaces and reduce packages can result in buildings whose facades and interiors are big inarticulate expanses of one thing, as can be seen in any number of commercial developments, as well as hospitals and some schools procured through the Private Finance Initiative, for example.[6] In D&B contracts, not all the subcontracts are let at the same time, and it is not uncommon for there to be a prolonged period of competitive tendering of subcontractor packages as the main contractor searches out the best deal. This can lead to compromises in appearance and interfaces as the new subcontractor brings building systems and assemblies different from those initially envisaged. Main contractors prefer the production design of the services' installations to be by the heating ventilating and electrical subcontractors rather than carry the risk of the responsibility being split between a consultant engineer and a subcontractor. This can lead to poor integration of pipes, wiring and fittings with the rest of the design, a commonly observed fault in D&B.

Our response to a changed environment for design is to shift focus where necessary from the careful contemplation of detail to the making of fewer, bigger and bolder moves that can survive the process. Whereas in our earlier buildings we would design a balustrade or stair down to selection of screw heads, we now often do not know what balustrade system the contractor will choose. Our design for the Ashburton Learning Village relies on the simplicity of the main teaching spaces combined with strong forms, such as the dramatic shape of the main hall, the large bank of coloured sunshades on the library, and the three-storey high school 'street' with its curvaceous upper galleries and sheer scale of the sports hall underscored by a mezzanine and large roof lights.

A true integration of Design and Build will bring greater rigour helping to prioritise what brings most value, in terms of quality of environment as well as cost. This should lead to clarity, eliminating potential fussiness and fuzziness. D&B need not rule out an intense engagement with tectonics. In our projects for the University of Portsmouth Library, the Moorfields Eye Hospital Children's Eye Centre, and Minster School the main contractor was selected carefully after the basic design had been established and was engaged on the basis of fully 'buying into' that design. The 'what' having been established, we worked with the main contractor to devise the 'how'. In these projects the full design team, including the environmental and structural engineers, as well as, where relevant, a landscape architect, remained engaged on the project with evident benefit to quality.

Designing to build

While we have rejected a crude equation of construction aesthetics and ethics we cannot entirely separate architecture and construction from ethics. With the advances in structural engineering and, now, Computer Aided Design and Manufacturing (CAD/CAM) modern technology has reduced constraints on form to a point that virtually any imaginable shape and height of building has become

Left: The sports hall at Ashburton Learning Village, Croydon, 2006.

Right: Stair detail at New Maltings, 1989.

possible. Modern materials and jointing and sealing techniques promise (though not always yet deliver) smooth 'skins' with high transparency. Cheap energy and the science of environmental control has made it possible to make comfortable and functional open plan buildings in any climate with fewer and fewer internal walls, thereby providing yet greater freedom of shape and size. One result is a plethora of so-called iconic building projects from Leningrad to Lima, as cities compete to attract global property investors. The main concern for the design of these buildings is for their form to be as different as possible from each other. With very few exceptions, such buildings are energy hungry and simply unsustainable in the context of climate change. When built they will add a quantity of greenhouse gases to the atmosphere that must be regarded as unacceptable. In many cases their impact at ground level on the public realm, and the demand of their populations on the transport infrastructure has not been thought thorough.

A major attraction of high-rise construction, well handled, is greater density, offering potential reduction in transport needs and a concentration of human talent and energy that can be very productive. The challenge is therefore to offer such densities with sustainable, energy minimising construction harnessing the best technologies to designs tailored to locality. In our practice's work we see ourselves as reinterpreting earlier craft concerns in a modern constructional context to embrace and reconcile the complexities of sustainability, local response and efficiency while rejecting the idea of the architect as a stylist who leaves construction to others.

The sloping brick base and stone clad upper floors at the University of Portsmouth Library, 2007.

1 All three Senior Partners of our practice worked at Edward Cullinan Architects at various times, as did a number of other people that have passed through our office.
2 Loos, Adolf, *Spoken into the Void: Collected Essays by Adolf Loos, 1897–1900*, trans. Jane O Newman and John H Smith, Cambridge, MA: MIT Press, 1987.
3 Prasad, Sunand, "Le Corbusier in India" in the catalogue of the exhibition *Le Corbusier Architect of the Century*, London: Arts Council of Great Britain, 1987, quoting *Le Corbusier Sketchbooks, Volume 3, 1954–1957*, London: MIT Press, 1982, pp. 24–25.
4 Venturi, Robert and Denise Scott-Brown, *Complexity and Contradiction in Architecture*, New York: Museum of Modern Art, 1966.

5 Saint, Andrew, *The Image of the Architect*, London: Yale University Press, 1983. p. 58.
6 Under the Private Finance Initiative a single commercial entity takes on the responsibility of designing, building, financing and operating a facility for typically 30 years; a DBFO Contract. Devised in the UK under the Conservative government in the early 1990s it was implemented by the Labour government that came into power in 1997. Over 600 such contracts are currently running and have cost more than £50 billion to construct. The system allows public infrastructure to be built without a government having to invest capital, and has now spread to many other countries.

CONTEXT

In the last two decades there has been an explosion of interest in city planning and design typified by the establishment of urbanism as a discipline. This chapter explores how the various currents in urbanism and their relationship to architecture and culture have influenced the work of our practice and the development of our particular approach to the spaces between buildings.

Urbanism

That the design of a building should acknowledge its context is today widely recognised as a fundamental consideration of good design. But it was not always so, and even now 1,000s of buildings built every year show too little understanding of their physical or cultural context. Modernism in architecture tended to emphasise the autonomy of a building, its 'object nature', and modern town planning concentrated on infrastructure, transport, zoning of uses and protection of amenity rather than the nature and quality of public spaces. Critiques focusing on this neglect of the public realm and its everyday use slowly gathered pace from the 1960s onwards and became widely accepted by the late 1970s. But change in practise to reflect a new respect for context proved more elusive. 'Contextualism' and 'urban design' entered the planning and architecture lexicon 30 years ago but only in the last 15 years have some of the fractured urban public spaces of European and North American cities begun to be revitalised. The word urbanism is said to have been coined in 1867 by Ildefons Cerda, who devised the remarkable grid plan for Barcelona, but Urbanism as a distinct discipline is only as old as our practice.[1]

The principles of urbanism are fiercely contested, and contextualism has its critics. Some theorists and practitioners want urban planning and design to return to nineteenth century European patterns of streets and squares. They wish to see these typologies enshrined in regulatory codes, citing their success as protectors of the quality of public space. At the other extreme some believe that the modern city's unpredictable, apparently chaotic and market-driven character is exactly what makes it work and argue for less regulation and more convention breaking. Both these poles, one believing in a return to a past model of harmony and order, the other fascinated by the edgy realities of the contemporary metropolis are a long way from the Modern Movement's positivist belief in scientific and social progress and its often utopian vision of the future.

The physicality of a city, including its public space, is a result partly of chance, partly of negotiation, often of brute force, and sometimes of planning. Such disorderliness was intolerable to twentieth century Modernist architects and planners, for whom utopianism was axiomatic:

The Arches Health Centre,
Belfast, 2005.

Parrock Street Masterplan and Housing with Mixed-use, Gravesend, 1999–2007

This scheme started as a masterplan for the regeneration of a seven acre car park with 1,200 spaces near the town centre, balancing through extensive consultation strongly held contradictory local opinions about retention of car parking on the one hand, and on the other, its replacement with town centre housing and other uses. The consultation started with establishing common points of reference through diagrams and drawings and proceeded via a series of smaller and larger meetings. The plan finally adopted proposed a series of self-contained 'steps' after each of which the local authority could decide not to proceed further. In the full plan the multi-storey car park at the south end of the site would be replaced (step one) by a residential courtyard development over car parking, with a corner tower and other uses on the ground floor; and the north end would be built over (steps two to five) with terraces of family housing, clusters of flats and seven-storey residential towers on the axes of neighbouring streets, all round a new public landscaped square.

After its adoption the masterplan was expanded with an outline specification containing explicit sustainability targets and bids for the land were invited for the land and the implementation of the plan. Steps one to three were then undertaken to our designs, providing 148 dwellings which include winter gardens to the flats achieving Ecohomes 'Very Good' ratings. The developer agreed to raise two of the houses to Ecohomes 'Excellent' and achieved almost instant sales.

Top: The winter gardens on the South Street flats.

Bottom: The operations of the winter gardens originally devised for the CASPAR housing competition, 1998. In cold weather the inner doors are closed and the winter garden helps insulate the kitchen and living space, warming up if the sun is out. On spring or summer days the inner door can be opened up to extend the living space, turning it into an open balcony.

Opposite: The first of the series of small towers at the ends of the existing Victorian streets.

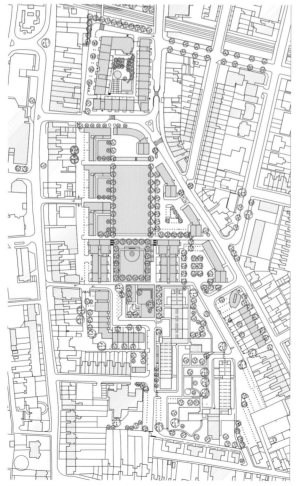

Top: Looking north along Parrock Street, the Lord Street site is at the end of the street.

Bottom left: Plan showing all the steps of the development completed.

Bottom right: The Parrock Street site with car park and the proposed phases or 'steps' of successive development.

0   30   60

Urbanisation cannot be conditioned by the claims of a pre-existent aestheticism; its essence is of a functional order... the chaotic division of land, resulting from sales, speculations, inheritances, must be abolished by a collective and methodical land policy.

CIAM La Sarraz 1928[2]

These sentiments were to become mainstream in post-war European city planning. The magnitude of the power they require to be vested in the state, whether at national or local level, is nowadays inconceivable, as is non-existent any public faith in any one agency's ability to create a desirable future. Real planning, ie. proactive and deliberate decision-making about the futures of land use, resources, communities and built form, has full purchase today only where there are tracts of empty or redundant land. A far more common development context in the UK is for areas of town to be a patchwork of different ownerships, historic uses, accrued rights and vested interests. With the diminishing power of local authorities since the early 1980s, and in particular the reduction in their ability or willingness to use compulsory purchase powers, regional and local planning has become reliant on negotiation and deal making.

Amongst the 100 plus recommendations of the UK government's Urban Taskforce's, *Towards an Urban Renaissance*, 1998, was the idea of the 'spatial masterplan' to guide the development of localities and of larger sites. It recommended that planners should no longer rely on two-dimensional land use maps but should fully consider in three dimensions the optimum strategy for any development, including its urban design. Almost at the same time we started work on just such a study at Lord Street in Gravesend, for the borough council, to consider the future of land adjacent to the city centre occupied by seven acres of car parking including an underused 600 place multi-storey car park. The land was in council ownership; however, strong vested interests were at play: the councillors representing the surrounding rural area whose residents liked handy parking places close to shopping; local traders who thought they would suffer if nearby car parking was lost; a progressive leadership that wanted to see greater residential density to create a more vibrant town centre and to reduce car dependency in the interest of sustainability. Extensive consultation was essential but we had to start with establishing a common language for conducting it, confronting the fear of change, hostility towards articulate professionals; enabling people to take part. After several months of consultations, presentations, and public meetings a strategy was adopted of a development in five phases, or 'steps', leading towards the complete development of the land including a major green space. Each step would, however, be self-contained and further steps could be aborted or postponed if the council chose. The first step was then put out to tender to private developers with a detailed specification for the development incorporating high standards of sustainable design and we were 'novated' to design the houses, flats, some mixed-use and civic spaces in detail. Opportunities to plan and build at the scale of the Lord Street masterplan are not uncommon but the greater part of our work is what has been described as "urban dentistry": inserting new buildings here, remaking a street

Left: The elliptical entrance
court of The Pulross Centre,
Brixton, 2000.

Opposite left: The rear gardens
of The Pulross Centre.

Opposite right: The Schröder
House, Utrecht, The Netherlands,
Gerrit Reitveld, 1924.

there, in a way that reinforces the best in the existing fabric. However, what we do is as much osteopathy or acupuncture: correcting misalignments, releasing blockages, strengthening nodal points to improve interchange between people. Every act of constructing a building amongst existing ones has the potential for improving or diminishing its setting, both aesthetically and in terms of its capacity to support activity. It is impossible, therefore, to separate urbanism from architecture at almost any scale. What brings the two together most emphatically is the objective of making *places*, rather than merely *spaces*.

Place

'Place' has come to have such currency in the built environment disciplines that some define urban design as "the art of place-making". However, the imprecision of the meaning of place parallels that of 'sustainability': tending to multiple definitions based on what people want it to mean rather than a consensus on what it is.[3] But, also like sustainability, the concept works fine in practise.

     The title of Siegfried Gideon's classic book *Space, Time and Architecture*, 1941, has come to represent the powerful if abstract preoccupations of the Modern Movement in architecture. A place, in contrast to space, has human attachment, whether through use, memory or meaning, as the Dutch architect Aldo van Eyck put it with typical eloquence in 1961:

> I arrived at the conclusion that whatever space and time mean, place and occasion mean
> more, for space in the image of man is place, and time in the image of man is occasion....
> A house should therefore be a bunch of places — a city a bunch of places no less.[4]

More recently place has been defined in opposition to 'non-place': transient environments burdened with bureaucracy, lacking in identity, history and urban relationships.[5] The car-dominated suburb, found in cities all over the world is a typical non-place, where most of the public realm has just one function: to accommodate motor transport. So is the typical hospital corridor with its utilitarian and mechanistic character; a space just to pass through as quickly as possible. A place by contrast is a space with a significance beyond the utilitarian. The physical attributes of a space, not necessarily through conscious design are crucial to making it a place. A patch of neglected ground appropriated by kids playing football, marked with improvised goals acquires 'place-ness'. The natural landscape is also full of highly evocative places, an inexhaustible source of inspiration for designers.

Though physical attributes are an essential component there is no place without activity. The very idea of place-making commits architecture and urban design to a seamless synthesis of physical form and human activity. The footballer's patch would be better if easily accessed and well overlooked, perhaps lined with trees for shade. It would be even better if it had another use when the kids were not there. In our work we have sought such multiple use and overlapping value. For example, The Pulross Intermediate Care Centre, 2000, is designed around a semi-private piazza opening off the street with an enfolding oval form made by the facade of the building. Formed around a mature plane tree, it can be used by the local people, serves as a space for physiotherapy exercise and provides vehicle access, standing and turning space. The facade is transparent to make the public spaces within the Centre, including the cafe, visibly part of the urban realm. A raised bay window in the first floor dining area picks up the axis of the approach road and signals the centre from a considerable distance. Not all these uses were given in the brief; some were proposed as part of the design, tested for viability and incorporated in the completed project. The rear of the building, by contrast, is secluded, private and of a domestic scale as befits a place for rehabilitation.

Public space

Architecture is a spatial art. That is not all it is, but in the twentieth century architecture's concern with the manipulation of space came to be widely thought of as its unique and distinguishing characteristic.[6] In arguing for a focus on space rather than the matter of which buildings were made Frank Lloyd Wright used to quote Lao Tzu the founder of Taoism: "Clay is moulded to form a cup. Yet only the space within allows the cup to hold water."[7] Wright's pioneering open plan houses were immensely influential and in some of them, like the Robie House, 1906, he began to dissolve the boundary between inside and outside in pursuit of his mission "to break open the box". The Dutch de Stijl movement in art and architecture explicitly sought to abolish any distinction between outside and inside space, seeing space as an infinite continuum. However, one gets the feeling in the architectural works of de Stijl, most famously the Schröder House, 1924, that this continuum is perceived, or perhaps *felt*, from the point of view of the occupant; that is, from inside to out. Perceived from outside the house and garden there is less sense of the continuum, although one may see that parts of the external wall seem to be removable. 1,000s of modern buildings, greatly aided by the invention of the sliding patio door, have external spaces within the curtilage of the house designed as a seamless continuation of internal space. Within the territory of the building the open plan and flow of space inside and out was related quite tangibly to human activity and pleasure. Outside the building the modernist conception of urban space was rather abstract; for example looking on paper like a de Stijl composition, but only loosely related, if at all, to people in its dimension and configuration. A true integration of the design of an individual building and urban space in modern architecture had to await a new appreciation of traditional street networks, with their rich interconnectivity and interaction between functional public space and buildings.

      In Le Corbusier's design of the Carpenter Center at Harvard, 1963, a ramped public route crosses the site, bisecting the building. Though the entrance is not from this route the glazed flanks of the ramp provide a feeling of passing through the building during everyday journeys through the area. The Economist Building, 1964, by Peter and Alison Smithson, is organised around a plaza on a route modelled on the street network of old London and connecting two roads. These two buildings

Left: The Carpenter Center, Harvard University, Le Corbusier, 1963.

Centre: Model of the Economist Building, St James, London, Peter and Alison Smithson, 1964.

Right: Kunsthal, Rotterdam, OMA/Rem Koolhaas, 1992.

Opposite left: View of The Rushton Street Medical Centre, 1996, from across the park.

Opposite right: The 'street' through the University of Portsmouth Library, 2007.

demonstrated a new conception of the relationship between buildings and urban space in modern architecture in contrast to the prevailing emphasis on a building's object-like nature, and therefore the characterisation of the urban realm as a mere means to serve buildings as a destination. There is an inspiring generosity in the way these two buildings give up privately owned land to the urban public realm to make functional urban connections, thereby increasing the permeability of the city fabric. At the Kunsthal in Rotterdam, 1992, Rem Koolhaas achieved an even greater integration of urban public space with an individual building. The town literally flows through the gallery, at one point becoming a part of the building's internal circulation, with the auditorium opening off it, like a stepped plaza.

In a similar manner, our extension to the University of Portsmouth Library, 2007, is designed around the well-trodden thoroughfare between the North Campus and the student digs in Southsea. An internal street runs through the building from which seminar rooms and IT spaces are accessed, as well as the turnstiles to the library spaces. Compared to the time when patients in beds were wheeled out to take the air in the semi-public square within St Bartholomew's Hospital, a truly permeable city fabric is difficult to achieve in today's security-conscious climate. Many of our schools are organised around a main 'street' but this has to be strictly separated from the urban domain.

We can conceive of public space as a network of nodes, connected by streets, that physically bind together a city, town or neighbourhood. A school, a work place or a health centre can play a role in making the public space of a city as well as a ceremonial square, market plaza, shopping centre or park. The lofty atria of our health centres, for example in Belfast or Hounslow, like that of The Rich Mix Arts Centre in Bethnal Green, all indoor public places, are just such nodes.

A city as a building, a building as a city

Whenever we construct an external wall of a building we potentially define urban space and influence its character. The wall helps make an external space, an outdoor 'room' no less than it helps define the internal space(s). It contributes to the image of the city as well, expressing the personality of the building, ideally representing its owners, its users and what they do – acting as a sort of billboard.

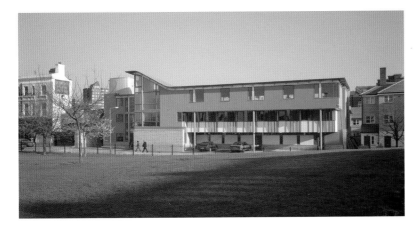

At Portsmouth, the north facade of the Library, scaled deliberately to be visible from a distance down Burnaby Road is intended to welcome students travelling from the North Campus, revealing its inner life through strips of glass as you approach. In addition to giving views deep into the building, and through to the park beyond, it forms one of the bounding elements of a new public forecourt off the road.

Situated in the denser urban fabric of Belfast, the scale and colour of the facades of our Community Treatment and Care Centres (CTCCs) mark them out as civic buildings. The specially created three-storey high glass works by the artist Martin Donlin signal the entrances. The design of The Rushton Street Medical Centre, an element in the regeneration of a run down locality on the edge of a public park in Hackney, makes a conscious civic gesture with a double-height colonnade at the edge of the park, using the elevation to magnify the scale of the building. The large glazed first floor waiting area overlooks the park and is, in turn, visible as a destination in the manner of a terrace cafe.

The analogy of the spaces of a city with the rooms of a building is also effective in reverse: the relationship of a building's internal circulation to its rooms and spaces can be seen as analogous to the relationship between the street and square of a town and its buildings. The power of this idea was convincingly demonstrated at Florian Beigel's influential Half Moon Theatre, 1985. This many layered design, now much altered, played with the ambiguity of the real and theatrical, inside and outside, public and private. The forecourt opened off the street and its surface flowed straight into the auditorium and stage. The rehearsal, changing, and administrative rooms opened off circulation that was conceived as analogous to an arcaded street. Seen from the street the building had the air of a stage set.

In the unbuilt project for a Multi-cultural Arts Centre (MAC) in Cardiff, 1998, the foyer, main auditorium and performance stage were conceived of as being part of a street either side of which were 'houses' which accommodated a number of ancillary functions. In places, by sliding away their facades, the street could also expand into the houses to accommodate much larger events. At Neptune Health Park, Tipton, 1998, a mall runs through the building around which are organised health-related shops, a Citizens' Advice Bureau, a cafe and lettable community function rooms, as well as the health centre and doctors' practice. At our more recent health centres in Belfast, such as the Carlisle Centre, services are similarly organised around the large-scale public space of the atria that are connected

Analytical diagrams, Multi-cultural Arts Centre for Wales, 1998.

Opposite left: Detail of Giambattista Nolli's map of Rome, 1748.

Opposite centre: Early sketch illustrating the axis between two churches that informed the organisation of the Neptune Health Park.

Opposite right: From the atrium, one of the churches is visible beyond through the canalside facade.

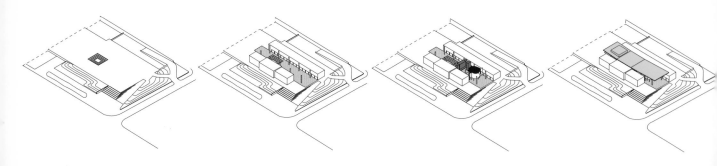

directly to the street. The visitors can find their way easily but at the same time the scene is not dominated by health care.

The Ousdale School Campus at Olney, completed in 2007, occupies what was once a sloping wheat field on the edge of the village. The building is designed as two wings slightly out of parallel connected by a glazed link, which also forms the entrance. The first view for the visitor is the space between the wings, which retains the slope of the original land with ramps, steps, plants and seating areas. Although in a rural setting this court is analogous to an urban public space: for use by the citizens of the community 'school'.

A more literal example of the house/city analogy is that of our design for sheltered housing for older people at Collier's Gardens in Bristol, 2006. The design is based on a village street that connects a set of alternating gardens and lofty top-lit hallways giving access to flats on two levels. Facilities such as the resident's lounge, offices and consulting rooms also open off the street. The flats, the administrative areas and the public spaces are given distinctly different architectural forms to reinforce the village analogy; a cluster of buildings and spaces making for an engaging variety.

Typology and topography

In areas of towns and cities built in the 1960s and 70s one can frequently see what used to be called 'sloap' – space left over after planning. Following Lao Tzu's logic, if what matters is urban public space then perhaps such urban spaces should have been designed first and the form of the buildings simply allowed to be whatever is left over in between. Something very like this is found in many pre-industrial cities, most famously as recorded in Giambattista Nolli's 1748 map of Rome. Nolli surveyed and drew, apparently, every inch of the whole city leaving all public space white on the map and shading in black all private space. Either the white or the black can be seen as the figure or the ground. In some instances the built mass is geometrically regular, leaving irregular public space, but in others the public space is regular, making squares, piazzas and thoroughfares; shaped voids in the built mass which you can immediately identify as places.

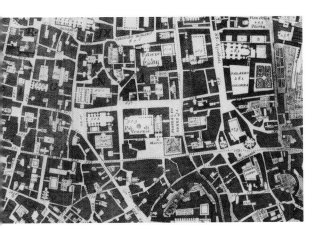
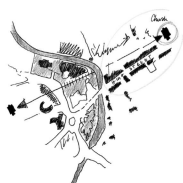

Collier's Gardens, Extra Care Sheltered Housing, Fishponds, Bristol, 2003–2006

Housing for elderly people with a level of care and support graduated to suit need and preference is an increasingly sophisticated business, requiring new kinds of environments. In this scheme we developed a 'garden village' model offering a versatile combination of private and communal, indoor and outdoor spaces. The site is a leftover piece of backlands behind suburban houses, with a plan shaped like a flask with a single point of access and a narrow neck before the main body of the land is reached. The relaxed plan form in which a ribbon of housing zig-zags either side of the main circulation spine makes the most of the available area while maintaining overall coherence.

The main circulation is an internal 'high street' either side of which garden courts alternate with lofty top-lit indoor hallways leading to flats. In addition to the formal lounges there are many incidental spaces for sitting, meeting and chatting. As well as independent flats, the building includes a residents' or communal lounge and restaurant with commercial kitchen, residents' laundry, assisted bathrooms, hairdresser, kitchenettes, IT room, shop, therapy room, overnight guest suite, administrative offices and electric buggy garage. The use of external materials along the high street helps banish any sense of institutionalism. To reinforce the village analogy the component parts are built of different materials: brick and large painted bay windows for the flats; white rendered blockwork for the support spaces and timber louvred glazing for the social spaces.

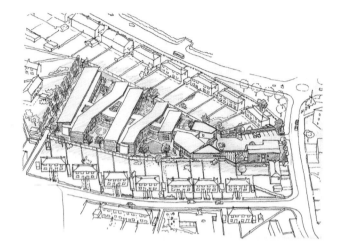

Top: A bird's eye sketch of the scheme.

Bottom: Sunshade louvres of the communal lounge.

Opposite: Large windows on both ground and first floors make strong connections between the interiors of the flats and their gardens.

0   10   20

Top: Ground floor plan.

1 communal lounge
2 kitchen
3 ancillary spaces
4 flat
5 therapy room
6 assisted bathroom
7 laundry
8 entrance

Bottom left: Day-lit hallway between flats.

Bottom right: Interior of the communal lounge.

Opposite: Main entrance.

Space does not have to be enclosed for it to be palpably a man-made place. Obelisks, totems, cairns or just markings on the landscape can be powerful makers of place. But enclosure, or 'bounded-ness', is a characteristic of urban space. When such enclosures are geometrically regular with clear and well dimensioned entrance/exits they seem to become more powerful as places. The evident centredness of these kinds of urban spaces, for example London's Georgian squares, or Rome's piazzas, seems to banish transience. Their deliberateness signals the presence of purpose and use. Scaled up, such spaces create civic monumentality; scaled down they can be charming neighbourhood housing courts. These urban typologies were eloquently championed by Leon and Robert Krier and more recently taken up by the New Urbanists.

In the work of some urbanists the underlying assumption that an ordered and harmonious physical environment will lead to greater harmony and order in social relationships may be nostalgic and naïve at best and deterministic and fascist at worst; but this should not mask the many other highly practical, topographical lessons of pre-Modern urban spatial relationships: clarity of ownership of territory; mixing of uses, and designing for mixed-use; creating networks of active public space; the quality of the pedestrian experience and what use is placed at the back of the pavement; natural supervision of public space without CCTV. These have great relevance to the design of dense and 'walkable' city neighbourhoods with local services; all essential components of sustainable architecture, urbanism and planning. However, they do not have to follow a rigid, or geometrically simplistic pattern of streets and squares to be successful. Urban Syntax, the theory and methodology developed by Bill Hillier is an example of an alternative more open-ended approach.

In our competition entry for housing at Newington Green, rather than strictly adhering to the existing street edge we set some of the houses back to make a public forecourt; but at the corners of the site the buildings came forwards to relate to the older pattern. This enabled the building on the most prominent corner to stand as a strong tall independent object as befitted its position, while also allowing a convenient and space-saving arrangement of car parking and front doors.

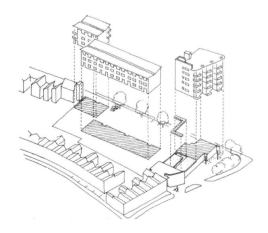  

Left and centre: Sketch and model of the competition design for housing and mixed-use development for The Peabody Trust at Newington Green, London, 1998.

Right: The Brick Lane Mosque, London, built in 1743 as a Huguenot Protestant Church has also been a Methodist Chapel and a Synagogue with almost no alteration.

Culture and design

We can learn a lot from traditional urban form without limiting ourselves to a narrow idea of community and place. In today's cosmopolitan cities, with their movement and mixing of a hugely diverse range of people, transience is a defining and even attractive characteristic. It gives them a unique dynamism and an exciting openness to possibilities. The communities that coalesce and dissolve are no longer necessarily centred on the neighbourhood; they can connect across geographical space, through the Internet and mobile telephony. We have to be continually conscious of the myriad physical and non-physical attributes of settlements, and particularly the contemporary city, that are outside the field of architecture. Drawings of masterplans by architects and urban designers often show orderly streets and squares with equally orderly citizens and bustling cafes. These images seem to suggest that a thriving urban realm can be brought into being simply through design. The reality is more complex and far more interesting.

Cities and towns are products as well as producers of culture; culture conditioned by economic and social realities and relationships within its physical geography. In this complex mix, design has been shown to have a significant and sometimes profound impact. The famous success of post-industrial Bilbao following the building of Frank Gehry's Guggenheim Museum is the greatest recent talisman of 'design led regeneration'. Cities around the world want to replicate the 'Bilbao effect'. However, the city's radical transport strategy, its clever marketing as a tourist destination, and new facilities targeted to service industries have all made as large a contribution. These have their own design aspects: the new metro system, with stations designed by Foster + Partners means more to residents than the flagship Guggenheim; not only helping them to get around quickly but also helping to transform the self-image of the city at an everyday level. Design led regeneration is open to criticism for putting form before content, a triumph of hope over experience perhaps. But as the anarchist writer Colin Ward put it, "economics is as likely to follow civics as civics to follow economics". For Ward the realm of civics includes the physical environment as well as social and cultural qualities.[9] The reality is that physical space constantly interacts with economics, culture and society such that prime cause and effect cannot be confidently attributed.

In 1993 we completed "Accommodating Diversity", a study of housing design in a multi-cultural society whose original brief had included a 'dos and don'ts' checklist. We found only one pair: do talk to the people from the communities who will live in the houses you are building, and don't follow a 'dos and don'ts' checklist. We found that there were indeed innumerable special requirements of different cultures but that there were as many exceptions; and anyway a handful of sensible improvements in existing practice took care of the basic housing needs of most cultures. The rest would be up to good briefing and the chemistry between architect and developer.

Over half of the world's people now live in cities. The multi-cultural nature of contemporary urbanity is manifest in the distinctive neighbourhoods and myriad lifestyle choices of 100s of cities

Patients in their beds taking fresh air in the square of St Bartholomew's Hospital — a compelling example of a truly permeable use of the city fabric, c. 1926.

Opposite: Atrium of the Carlisle Health and Wellbeing Centre, Belfast, 2007 (with Todd Architects).

round the world. But stripped of the superficial, the fabric of a city like London has few traces of 'multi-culturalism'. The filmmaker Udayan Prasad recounts how he spent six weeks in the English terraced houses of Bradford Pakistanis, making a documentary about their kite flying tradition. In that time he never met a woman, though occasionally a bangled hand would pass a meal through a kitchen hatch. The residents had easily adapted house and lifestyle with little alteration of either. Culturally specific motifs in the design of modern religious buildings have powerful meaning for not only their but also other communities, however the looseness of the connection between culture and built form can also apply to sacred functions. The Brick Lane Mosque in east London has been a Protestant Church, a Methodist Chapel and a Synagogue for extended periods since it was built in 1743. In our design work, whenever we find the need for a culture specific design requirement, we try to make it into a solution of wider use and value.[10] Form can express cultures but equally culture can appropriate form.

A healthy city

In the words of the Belfast Declaration signed by the mayors and leaders of European Cities attending the World Health Organisations Healthy Cities conference at City Hall in October 2003 "... the key determinants of health lie outside the direct control of the health sector". Professor Dr Richard Jackson of the School of Public Health, University of California, Berkeley, tells of how he once saw a black woman struggling with heavy bags of shopping in the blistering sun along the narrow side verges of a long empty stretch of a Los Angeles highway. Feeling guilty that he had been too inhibited to give her a lift he started wondering what would happen if she collapsed and was taken to hospital. The diagnosis would have been 'heat stroke' but should it not really be 'poor city design'. Cities made for cars with nowhere to walk, with no shade for the pedestrians and no transport affordable by the people who service the city. If the first aim of health care is to prevent ill health, then the design of cities, its institutions and infrastructure have a greater role in health care than surgeries, clinics and hospitals. We need a public health revolution like that of the nineteenth century when clean water and sewage systems dramatically reduced incidence of disease. Now the city, through well located, well designed and well managed parks, footpaths, cycle routes, public spaces and facilities, must positively encourage exercise and other health-giving activities while reducing anxiety and stress.

A number of strands are coming together in the early twenty-first century to map out the task of designing settlements: these include quantifiable matters like public safety, security, access, health and the mitigation of, and adaption to climate change, but also qualitative and less tangible ones like the capacity to stimulate economic activity and social interaction in all its diversity while projecting a strong image of the place. Almost every act of designing buildings or spaces can contribute to this weave. Urbanism is as much a state of awareness as a discipline.

1 Cowan, Robert, *Dictionary of Urbanism*, Tisbury: Streetwise Press, 2005.

2 La Sarraz Declaration of the Congrès International d'Architecture Moderne (CIAM) Switzerland, 1928.

3 Cowan, *Dictionary of Urbanism* gives a number of interpretations, some entertainingly contradictory.

4 van Eyck, Aldo, "The Medicine of Reciprocity Tentatively Illustrated" in Ligtelijn, Vincent, ed., *Aldo van Eyck, Works*, Bussum: THOTH, 1999, p. 89. Article originally published in *Forum*, vol 15, nos 6–7, 1961.

5 Auge, Mark, *Introduction to an Anthropology of Supermodernity*, London: Verso, 1995.

6 Forty, Adrian, *Words and Buildings: A Vocabulary of Modern Architecture*, London: Thames & Hudson, 2000, p. 256.

7 Lao Tzu, Verse 11 of the *Tao Te Ching*.

8 Other architects had previously made the street/corridor analogy in their work, for example Peter and Alison Smithson at Robin Hood Gardens, London, 1964, but in most of these projects the circulation system of the building did not openly connect with the surrounding streets.

9 Discussion at the Architectural Association, London c. 1995.

10 *Accommodating Diversity: Housing Design in a Multi-cultural Society* has a number of examples; such as in houses for Orthodox Jewish people, meeting the need to have a Succoh, a space that can be temporarily opened to the sky, by creating a single-storey bay that makes a valuable addition for any household. National Housing Federation, 1997, 2nd edition.

The Rich Mix Arts Centre, Bethnal Green, London, 2002–2005

The area around Brick Lane in London's East End epitomises the multi-cultural mix of the modern metropolis, the idea of the 'world city'. In the seventeenth century Huguenot people fleeing persecution settled in this poor quarter, followed later by Jews, then Bangladeshis and, at the end of twentieth century, by Somalis. The overt racial tension prevalent from the 1970s through to the 90s gave way by the end of the century to a bustling mix of Bangladeshi shops, restaurants and workplaces together with an earlier market tradition and an energetic and younger creative arts and cafe/bar scene. The aim of the Centre, housed in redundant cloth trade premises, is to provide a resource and showcase for new art and cultural practices in which crossing traditional boundaries and mixing media is both common and increasingly easy to achieve and disseminate through digital means. To reflect the ever-changing nature of culture much of the Centre is conceived as a framework that can be adapted to changing uses. The various spaces are organised around a central 'town square' from which can be reached three cinemas, music technology training studios, an arts gallery and a rooftop venue and performance space heavily sound proofed to 100 dba and provided with a panoramic window framing views of the city. Distributed in between are managed work spaces initially left as a shell for fitting out.

The interior of the building was stripped back to its concrete frame and two large volumes carved out by removing areas of floor — to make the central square/cafe and the art exhibition space. To deal with solar gain and to provide daylight control in the interior the south facade has a bank of adjustable aluminium louvres which form a giant ever-changing billboard that transforms the image of the building and onto which images can also be projected. The silver and gold louvres and four coloured caps of the window mullions form a weave-like pattern reminiscent of fabrics. On the north side the trapezoidal shape of the site plan has been exploited to make the stack of three cinemas over a kitchen serving food in the 'town square'. The cinema stack is clad in a silvery aluminium carapace that provides an unexpected shift of scale at the end of Montclare Street.

Top and bottom: Early sketch and visualisation of the front facade.

Opposite: Front facade on Bethnal Green Road.

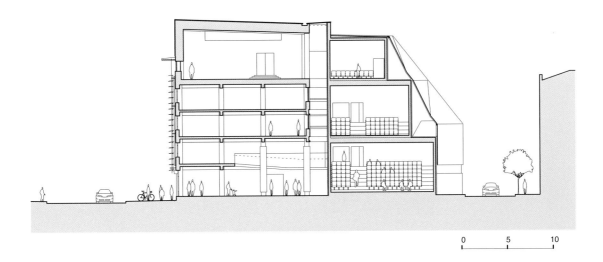

Opposite: The rear facade with aluminium cladding to the cinemas.

Top: Cross-section.

Bottom: The main stair in the top-lit slot between the old building and the new cinemas.

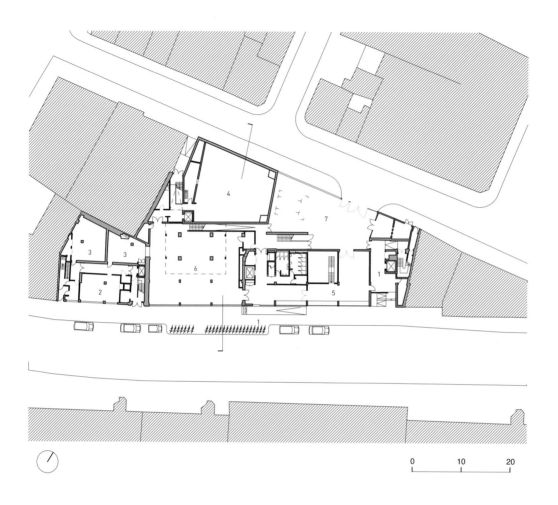

Top: Ground Floor plan.

1 entrance foyer
2 office
3 studio
4 cinema
5 visual arts gallery
6 cafe/bar/meeting space
7 service pod

Bottom: Simple interiors have been decorated using artist-designed wallpapers.

Opposite: The central 'square' with cafe.

ART

The involvement of artists in our buildings has ranged from installing works in the building to true collaboration in the design. This chapter asks whether there is a gap in the ability of contemporary architecture to communicate that which a practising artist can fulfil.

The Necessity of Narrative

The sculptor Sokari Douglas Camp collaborated with us in our 1998 design of the Multi-cultural Arts Centre (MAC) for Cardiff. She noted in our joint report that although she knew she had made a contribution, "telling stories", she was unsure whether it would be recognisable in the finished building. Was this an indication of the success of the collaboration or a reflection of the tyranny of a design process where practical considerations weigh so heavily as to eclipse the concerns and practice of a fine artist?

Architecture has sometimes been called "the Mother of the Arts", but in everyday practice its relationship to art goes no further than 'family friend'.[1] Public authorities in many countries have had 'Percent for Art' policies recommending the allocation of up to one per cent of a capital project budget for art. Buildings funded with the Arts Lottery in the UK all followed this policy to ensure inclusion of pieces by artists. Occasionally there was greater engagement of a practising artist's imagination with the architecture. Architects are generally content to be excluded from being considered as artists, and indeed many would be embarrassed to be called artists for two quite opposite reasons: some because they do not feel worthy of such a title and others because they consider it to be somewhat frivolous. Notable exceptions from very different realms of the profession include John Outram, Quinlan Terry and Zaha Hadid. Architecture itself occupies an uncertain position in contemporary culture. UK governments have always located it in their culture departments, but departments of environment, local government and industry influence its practice far more. In academia it may variously be located under arts, humanities or technology faculties.

Outram considers that it is an indignity to be required to work with artists to ensure there is art in his buildings and wants to continue a tradition in European architecture that has its roots in the work of largely anonymous Romanesque and Gothic master builders. The tradition was thereafter carried by the known individual architect/artists of the Renaissance and continued in this way through subsequent periods, declining in the early nineteenth century with the emergence of engineering as a determinant of architectural form. In pre-industrial cultures the unity of the visual arts and architecture prevails, as in contemporary Hindu and Jain temples built by the temple master builders of the Sonpura family.[2] In the nineteenth century architects in Europe began to be called on specifically to add 'style' to buildings. This is perhaps most evident in exhibition halls and railway stations, such as

Moveable sunshade and light control louvres of The Rich Mix Arts Centre, London, 2005.

London's St Pancras, where a large span space is fronted by a 'head building' of deliberate and quite separate architectural composition. However, adventurous engineering was not, in itself, thought to be capable of communicating the right message to the public, and versions of either Gothic or Classical architecture were pressed into service to give such buildings appropriate civic status.[3] In reaction, a number of brilliant architects embraced the new possibilities offered by engineering and harnessed them to create unified works of architecture, laying the foundation for what came to be known as Modern architecture.[4]

Nonetheless, well into the second half of the twentieth century architecture could be typified as the art in buildings as well as the art of building. In their training, architects studied the visual arts, which not only gave them skills but also judgement. This training intensified what Richard Sennet calls the "conscience of the eye", a continuous visual awareness coupled with the facility of reading meaning into what you see.[5] In times of change, the advocates of change often do not realise that some of the things they most value are threatened by the change they are advocating. The modernist architectural revolutionaries, from Adolf Loos to James Stirling were steeped in classical traditions and their hands and eyes trained in it. Most of them embraced a scientist and functional approach to

Top: The Peak, painting for the Hong Kong Peak project, Zaha Hadid, 1982–1983.

Bottom: Expression of structure as part of architectural composition: Violet-le-Duc's open-sided market hall from *Entretiens sur l'architecture*, 1863 and 1872.

Opposite left: Oriel Chambers, Water Street, Liverpool, Peter Ellis, 1864.

Opposite right: Corrugated bicycle shelters, Transtation 0, Sakai, Japan, Endo Shuhei Architect, 1997.

architecture, as well as a radical aesthetic directed at giving artistic expression to what they saw as the spirit of the age. However, within two or three generations the training (including the detailed drawing and memorising of the Classical Orders) that had provided the unacknowledged guiding force in the composition of architectural form had disappeared from schools, regarded as unnecessary now there was to be a rational basis for all design.[6]

The public remains confused about the architect's capacities and role. On the one hand, because of the large functional element in contemporary building design, there is a tendency to think that anyone can do the architect's job, or that the architect's job is fundamentally a process-based activity. On the other hand people are all too aware that there is something missing from most modern buildings and would like the architect to have the mysterious power to produce beauty, or at any rate, meaning. Architecture is in danger of losing its mystery. Almost anyone can draw a plan, though many people find it difficult to imagine future form in three dimensions. Few can create beautiful or compelling forms. That should be the special ability of the architect, refined through years of study and practice. But on the whole architects have abandoned this territory.[7] Is this the gap that schemes such as Percent for Art or the RSA's Art for Architecture might fill? If so what would be the role of the artists thereby engaged? To try and understand this it may help to briefly examine the meaning of architecture and art in relationship to buildings.

Nikolaus Pevsner, author of the monumental *Buildings of Britain*, famously stated some 60 years ago that "A bicycle shed is a building; Lincoln Cathedral is a piece of Architecture... the term architecture applies only to buildings designed with a view to aesthetic appeal."[8] However, there would seem to be rather more than aesthetic appeal involved in the design of Lincoln Cathedral. And some bicycle sheds have clearly been built with a view to aesthetic appeal. The philosopher Ludwig Wittgenstein wrote at about the same time as Pevsner's famous definition: "Architecture immortalises and glorifies something. Hence there can be no architecture where there is nothing to glorify."[9] As discussed in other chapters here, the role of architecture is to consciously communicate. The refreshing ethical austerity of Wittgenstein demands to know whether there is anything worth communicating. Perhaps we can have bicycle sheds that glorify the bicycle, human ingenuity or shed-ness. Anything can be designed with a view to aesthetic appeal, but not everything is worth glorifying. In this respect the big monuments,

religious or secular, are not the problem; their hermeneutic intent, their nature as bearers of meaning inviting interpretation, is not in doubt. Most architects, designs teams, clients and constructors operate in the vast gap between Lincoln Cathedral and a bicycle shed, dealing with everyday, if often substantial buildings. The question is: can we, should we, glorify the everyday through architecture?

One of the key strands of the Modern Movement in art and architecture was the exaltation of the everyday, partly as a political act, a reaction to nineteenth century naturalism, which was content to make idealised art objects for wealthy patrons. Now such artistic concern with the everyday is, of course, commonplace. The elusive goal in architecture today is how to take the everyday and represent it in a meaningful way; to make a tangible emotional connection between a building and its customers, users and public. For Wittgenstein's "glorify" we might substitute "speak about": "There can be no architecture where there is nothing to speak about."

In areas of culture other than architecture, speaking about and telling stories is the norm. Its paucity in architecture is illustrated by the telling phrase "the wow factor" that politicians ask for in regeneration projects, and public clients solemnly write into briefs for schools and hospitals. It is not a phrase heard as a critical term in music, paintings, video, web design, dance, theatre, film or literature.

By the second half of the twentieth century it often seemed as if architecture had no vocabulary that spoke cogently to anyone other than architects and cognoscenti. At the same time the design of the majority of buildings came to aspire to little more than being well turned out. It would be fine for a substantial part of the built environment to be simply well mannered and well ordered provided that, set within such a neutral matrix, there were some works that compelled attention, engaged the senses, altered perceptions or told stories. Although all buildings communicate something, relatively few architects make communication a prime mover of design. A work of art by contrast is intrinsically about deliberate communication. An artist involved in a building project could provide the missing voice: at its simplest as an interpreter layering narrative onto the framework created by functional design; or more profoundly through a deeper dialogue with the architect and engagement with the design.

There is a historic pattern of increasing division of labour in the conception of the built environment. Once upon a time, building was driven by a single intelligence, the master builder or Renaissance universal man, whereas it now requires a large multi-disciplinary team: architect,

I HAVE NOTHING TO SAY AND I AM SAYING IT AND THAT IS POETRY
I HAVE TO SAY POETRY AND IS THAT NOTHING AND AM I SAYING IT
I AM AND I HAVE POETRY TO SAY AND IS THAT NOTHING SAYING IT
I AM NOTHING AND I HAVE POETRY TO SAY AND THAT IS SAYING IT
I THAT AM SAYING POETRY HAVE NOTHING AND IT IS I AND TO SAY
AND I SAY THAT I AM TO HAVE POETRY AND SAYING IT IS NOTHING

engineers, cost consultants, specialist consultants, health and safety consultants and project managers, the last being consultants to organise the consultants. It is only a small step for the artist to become part of a team whose diverse tasks range from designing drains to telling stories.

The architect enjoys a unique freedom in this picture, able to choose one or more from a number of roles, including that of artist if the will and capacity are present. A number of our projects, for example Charter School, The Rich Mix and Wolverhampton Library, have elements that might be considered to be art; that have a conscious narrative purpose, albeit only as one layer in the totality of the cultural meaning of these buildings. The entrance hall at Charter School, which was made by roofing over a neglected courtyard, has a giant steel tree as the structure for the funnel shaped roof which itself is part of capturing and displaying the weather as part of learning. The structure evokes the archetypal tree under which a community gathers. The over-cladding of the main teaching block is rendered as an irregular pattern of blue tones getting lighter towards the sky. This pattern absorbs the irregular placing of the windows to create an overall composition akin to a hugely enlarged area of pixellation in an image; reminiscent of chiaroscuro painting technique it also subtly transforms the building's appearance reducing its perceived weight. The south facade of The Rich Mix, a building to showcase and creatively support the extraordinary cultural mix of London and other world cities, has a bank of adjustable solar control louvres in front of the vertical cladding mullions. We rendered the facade as a coloured weave using these two elements as warp and weft: four repeating colours of mullion and alternating silver and gold on the louvres. Weaving is an art form found in all cultures. We had in mind the elaborate borders of Indian saris and the complex patterns of Ghanaian kenteh cloths. A 'weave' itself stands as an apt metaphor for a 'rich mix'. In the design for the extension of Wolverhampton Central Library the facade is generated from the geometry of text blocks; the words being the solid portions of wall and the gaps between them the windows into the Library. The facade is then overlaid with fragments of the text literally encouraging the building to be read.

Opposite: Cladding design for the main teaching block at the Charter School, Dulwich, completed in 2003.

Left: Model of the proposed new extension to Wolverhampton Central Library, 2003.

Right: The proportion of wall and window on the elevations is based on that of words and the spaces between them in a block of text, in this case a poem by Edwin Morgan, "Opening the Cage", which has 14 variations on 14 words. The words of the poem will appear in selected places on the facade.

Collaborations with artists

While there may be no need for someone called 'an artist' for art to be present in a building, a compelling case remains for the inclusion of a practitioner from the contemporary art scene as a part of the multi-disciplinary design team. The pioneering Art for Architecture programme of the RSA (The Royal Society for the Encouragement of Arts, Manufacture and Commerce), which ran from 1992–2004, produced some wonderful collaborations between artists and architects. In contrast to schemes to purchase and install art in buildings, the RSA programme sought for the artist to work with the architects from the beginning of the project, from the conceptual phase, as an integral part of the design team.[10]

From the early years of the practice we worked with artists on a number of projects as enablers of their imaginations. *Civic Monument*, by Marty St James and Anne Wilson, was based on the idea of expanding the traditional repertoire of monuments, of themes such as war, courage and victory, to celebrate themes like love, leisure and work. Working with the artists we devised a travelling stage set that would start as a monumental arch and gradually deconstruct through the performance completely changing in appearance: becoming open and asymmetrical with cantilevering planes onto which performers would emerge.

Rose Finn-Kelcey's installation *Steam*, 1993, started with the artist's idea of filling the entire gallery space, about 10 x 30 metres, with steam, and went through our suggestion of creating a cube of steam, free of the walls and held in place with warm air curtains such as you find at the entrances to department stores. The project was finally realised with the help of the engineer Max Fordham as a machine with a base to produce steam and a hood to extract it and prevent it from spilling into the surrounding space. The steam created a delicate and endless play of movement, opacity and clarity, held within an enigmatic object of an industrial appearance.

Our project for the renewal of Wolverhampton Civic Halls had two main objectives: to accommodate the needs of modern audiences, performers and venue administration, which were very different from those in 1936 when the Halls were built; and to give the building a new presence in the city. Pierre Vivant joined the project after the basic design was complete and noted that although we

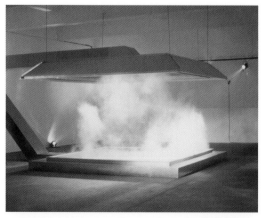

had added external glass boxes containing bars to the flanks of the building, the main facade of this listed building would retain its inscrutable look. To animate this facade and signal the transformation of the Halls into an outward looking place he proposed an installation that would, at the flick of a switch, turn the entire glazed screen behind the classical columns from transparent to translucent and allow images to be back projected onto this screen via "twenty-first century" chandeliers in the foyer. The performance on the stage could thus literally be visible in the public space at the front of the building, fundamentally transforming the relationship of the Halls and the city. Costs proved prohibitive, but we continued to work with Vivant who achieved the original intent with another piece using reflective glass lenses and webcams.

Sokari Douglas Camp joined the design team for our Cardiff MAC project while the three-dimensional form of the building was in development. The building was to accommodate various family oriented cultural practises of minority ethnic communities that existing venues in the city could not cater for. The long-standing community of Tiger Bay, where the building was to be located, had a long history of migration linked with Cardiff's maritime and slave trading past, a subject rich in the stories that Douglas Camp wanted to contribute. Her method was to take part in the design discussion and then make small steel sculptures that captured her take on the evolving design. The eventual design had elements that resulted from this collaboration. One was the small seminar/display space lifted above the entrance doors in the form of a vessel; a reference to traditions of hospitality, to the idea of community and to the ships that brought migrants to the city. Another was the bunch of palm trees that capped the flytower and sign. The project was cancelled after failing to get funding, despite strong advocacy.

We have been discussing art, architecture and their separate and combined capacities to communicate ideas and tell stories. In the realm of health care it has been found that art has a specific therapeutic capacity, not only directly through engaging the patient as artist in art therapy programmes, but also indirectly through making art an essential part of the health care setting. The most extensive example in the UK of the use of art in this way is Chelsea and Westminster Hospital where for many years there has been a vigorous programme of art, which has been subjected to clinical evaluation techniques. The findings of these studies, published in 2003, indicate that the presence of visual art and music

Opposite left: A sketch of *Civic Monument*, 1990.

Opposite right: The installation *Steam*, a collaboration with artist Rose Finn-Kelcey at Chisenhale Gallery, 1992.

Right: Model by Sokari Douglas Camp and sketch by Penoyre & Prasad collaborating in a design for the Multi-cultural Arts Centre for Wales, 1998.

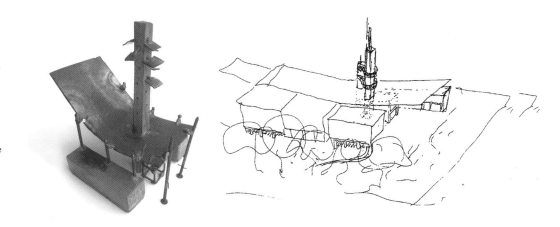

reduced stress, reduced analgesic take up and shortened recovery times.[11] It has now become the norm rather than the exception in our health care projects to incorporate the work of artists.

At the Richard Desmond Children's Eye Centre of Moorfields Eye Hospital we achieved our fullest collaboration to date where an artist took part in the detailed design of the facade as others helped give coherence and richness to the interior. The front of the building has solar shading that we had originally conceived as a flock of birds arrested in mid-flight, or a spray of leaves. The size, fixing system, three-dimensional folding, and total number of the louvre blades had been worked out but there was no satisfactory logic behind the near random distribution of the blades. Alison Turnbull joined the team at this point and found a technique in ophthalmology involving the tracing of the pattern made when orthogonal grids are projected onto curved and irregular surfaces, such as the retina. By bending and twisting paper with a grid and then drawing the result she created a pattern that achieved exactly the appearance wanted, as well as the shading performance specified. Within the building, to visually link five floors, Yuko Shiraishi painted a giant mural on the wall of a light well that zig-zags up the building. Lucy Casson and Samantha Bryan have embedded small surprise sculpture and wall panels to be discovered by the patients.

Peter Smithson once described the work of an American scholar whose research into Piero dell Francesca's painting *The Flagellation*, 1455, had unearthed over a dozen parallel interpretations and narratives, from the multiple identities of the characters to the numerology embedded in the composition.[12] He considered that such layering was a mark of a true work of art but there was a hierarchy in the layers: the top layer was what must captivate the viewer immediately without knowledge of the underlying narratives. The inclusion of artists in the creation of a work of architecture, seeing new things and telling stories seems a logical extension of its intrinsically layered and collaborative nature.

Development of the louvre arrangement for Moorfields Eye Hospital by artist Alison Turnbull, starting with our sketch of flying birds.

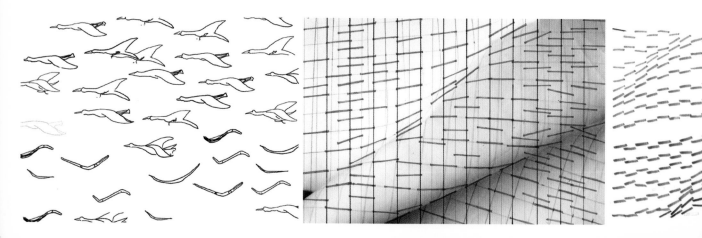

1 This phrase is used so often that one can believe that it literally has a Classical origin. The connection appears to be more tenuous and the usage modern. In Greek myth Mnemosyne (memory) gave birth to the nine muses of the arts, which included some sciences like astronomy, agriculture and geometry. Architecture concretises memory. Painting and sculpture were for a long time, and in many cultures, one with architecture and literally held by it. In Indian classical tradition architecture also included the devising of vehicles. Many things have been called the mother of the arts: theatre, dance, drawing, Paris, Florence and the Catholic Church to name a few. Franceso Goya gave the title to fantasy: "Fantasy, deserted by reason, produces impossible monsters; united with it, fantasy is the mother of the arts and the source of their wonders."
– caption to the famous print *The sleep of reason produces monsters*. Frank Lloyd Wright may have been the first to actually write that "Architecture was the Mother of the Arts."

2 The Sonpuras' best known work in the West is the Neasden Temple in London.

3 The London stations King's Cross and St Pancras provide a striking example of the change of approach. King's Cross Station, 1851–1852, was designed by Lewis Cubitt and its front is a direct expression of the double vault train shed behind. The single vaulted St Pancras train shed, with the world's then largest span, was designed by engineers WH Barlow and RM Ordish and was built 1863–1865. The head building, which gives no clue whatsoever to what is behind, was designed by George Gilbert Scott and built 1868–1874.

4 Architects embracing engineering to anticipate the Modern Movement included Henri Labroust, Violet-le-Duc, Tony Garnier, August Perret and also Louis Sullivan, Antonio Gaudi and Peter Ellis (little known architect of Oriel Chambers in Liverpool).

5 Sennet, Richard, *The Conscience of the Eye: Design and Social Life of Cities*, New York: Norton, 1992.

6 The Orders are the columns and capitals that are an essential part of the composition of Classical buildings and whose parts and proportions were the subject of intense study. They were still being taught at the Moscow School of Architecture in 1980 when I visited.

7 The rarity within modern architecture of the complete architect/artist like Zaha Hadid, Will Alsop or John Outram is telling, but there are many other twenty-first century models of architectural form-making that produce equally or more compelling and functional architecture firmly in the realm of art. Just to name a few from current practice: excursions into free curvilinearity whose realisation has been made possible by computer assisted design and manufacture (Frank Gehry), an intense focus on the display of the poetics of construction (Toyo Ito, Shigeru Ban, Eva Jiricna), a playful engagement with popular taste overlaid on a simple functionalist framework (Piers Gough, FAT), a commitment to graphic sensibility in tune with contemporary fashion (AHMM, Sauerbruch Hutton), a romantic distillation of the aesthetics of technology (Future Systems), an exploration of the power of the most elemental and ordinary characteristics of space, materials and their assembly (Tony Fretton, Caruso St John).

8 Pevsner, Nikolaus, *An Outline of European Architecture*, Harmondsworth: Pelican Books, 1943. p. 15.

9 Wittgenstein, Ludwig, ed., GH von Wright in collaboration with Heikki Nyman, *Culture and Value*, trans., Peter Winch, Oxford: Basil Blackwell, 1980.

10 According to an essay by John Wetenhall, Executive Director of the John and Mable Ringling Museum of Art in Sarasota, Florida, "As a matter of public policy, the percent-for-art concept dates back to the New Deal and the Treasury Department's Section of Painting and Sculpture (established in 1934)", "A Brief History of Percent-for-Art in America", *Public Art Review*, Fall/Winter 1993.

11 Staricoff, Rosalia and Jane Duncan, *A Study of the Effects of Visual and Performing Arts in Health Care*, London, Kings Fund, 2003.

12 Marilyn Aronberg Lavin.

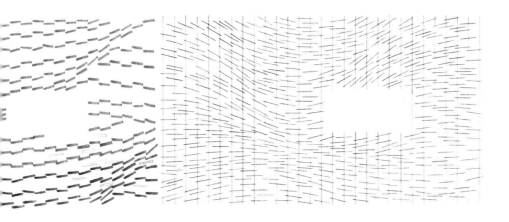

The Richard Desmond Children's Eye Centre, Moorfields Eye Hospital, London, 2002–2006

The Children's Eye Centre makes a bridge between the outstanding clinical expertise of Moorfields Eye Hospital and the research prowess of the adjacent Institute of Ophthalmology to provide a world class facility for treating the eyes of people from six months to 18 years of age. The constricted nature of the site, the internal layout of clinics and the necessary connections to the existing first floor operating theatres and the research floor of the Institute on the second, all contributed to a clear vertical arrangement of spaces within the eight-storey building.

Externally the mass of the building is lifted clear above a largely glazed entrance platform containing a cafe, computer arcade and shops and gives the impression of the street flowing in. Deeper within the building are the arrival and pre-op areas for the surgical patients and relatives with direct access to the surgical first floor. Bridges cross a slot of space running up the building separating the lifts and stairs, acting as a pause prior to entering the clinical areas, introducing a sense of space and scale and enabling the visitors to locate themselves easily. The busy outpatients area has a translucent-coloured 'quiet pod', which breaks through the floor above, making a table there, and creating a sense of scale within. The work of three artists at scales ranging from a four-storey high mural to tiny framed tableau animates the public spaces.

The south facade, facing onto the garden square across Peerless Street, is protected from solar gain by an arrangement of freely placed folded aluminium louvres, held within a large ceramic granite frame enfolding the facade, on tensioned cables suspended in front of glass curtain walling. A projecting bay breaks through this 'net' signalling the most populated part of the building, the out-patient waiting area on the third floor, and signals the building's presence to the main public approach route.

Top: The louvres are occasionally lit up with colour-changing LED lights.

Bottom: The out-patient waiting area with pod on third floor.

Opposite: The main facade from Peerless Street.

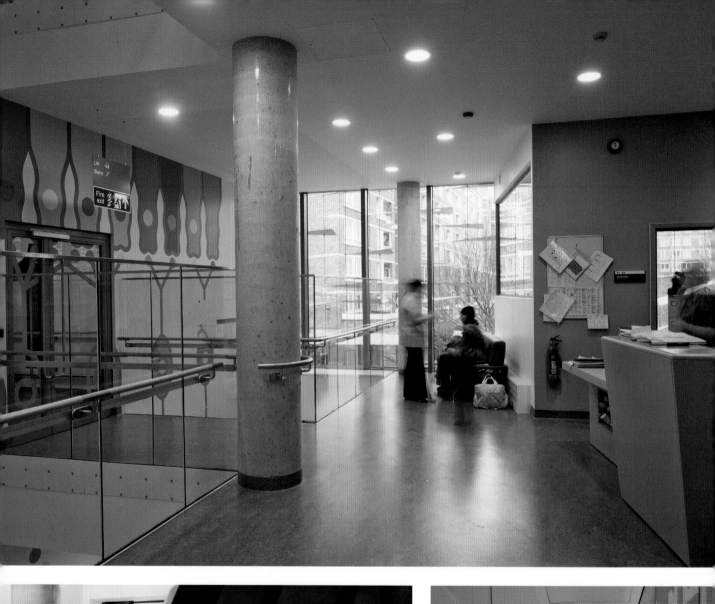

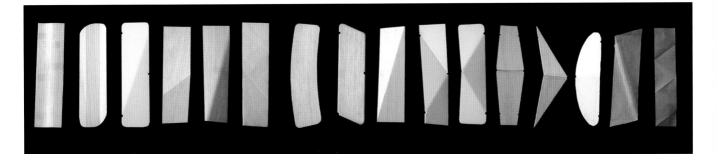

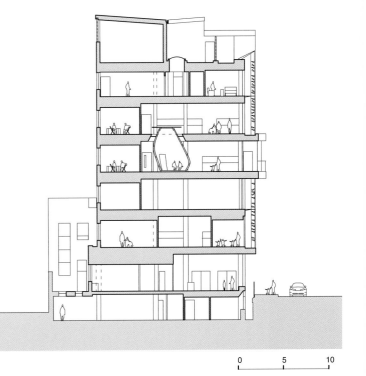

Opposite top: Entrance and reception for the post-operative recovery unit on the first floor.

Opposite bottom left: The walls of the play pod are semi-transparent, revealing the frame within its walls. This element pierces the fourth floor slab and its top is used as a table.

Opposite bottom right: Main entrance foyer with reception and cafe, showing the strong visual connection with the street.

Top and middle: Model studies and detail of the louvres.

Bottom: Cross-section.

Opposite: The lightwell connects the
waiting areas of the two out-patient floors.

Below: Ground floor and third floor plans.

1 reception
2 cafe
3 shop
4 opticians
5 play zone
6 day case reception/lounge
7 private patient clinic

8 ocular prosthetics
9 open air play area
10 waiting
11 pharmacy
12 consulting/clinic
13 patient support
14 entrance

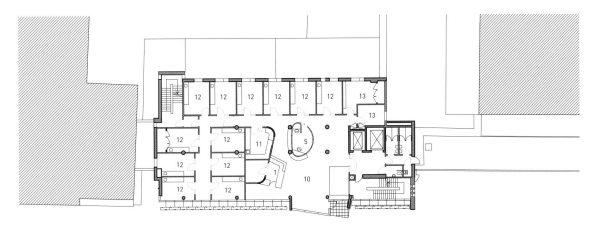

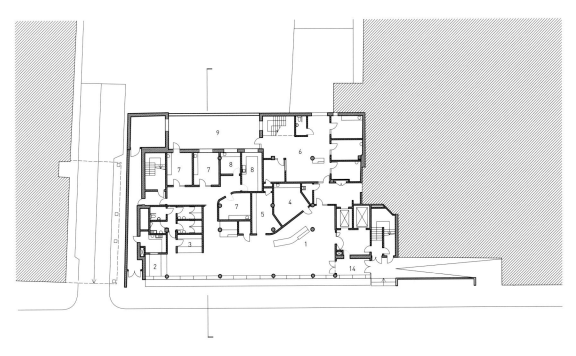

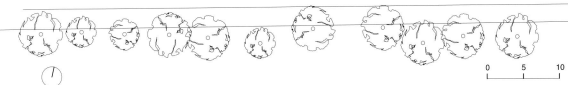

0   5   10

TIME

A substantial portion of all design and construction activity is directly connected with existing buildings, but its results rarely enter the architectural canon. As almost all new development happens alongside old almost all of our work connects to the past. This chapter explores what there is to learn from, and how we might work with the past: the past in the sense of architectural and urban history, as well as existing buildings to be altered, extended or renewed.

The past sure is tense

Looking around at the streets and buildings of towns and cities around the world most people, including architects, would agree that the most admired, best loved, urban places and buildings tend to be pre-modern ones. Why not then just copy them as some architects and urbanists, as well as Prince Charles, has recommended? Because modern architecture can be just as beautiful and performs far better, we could reply. The modernist/traditionalist debate recalls the multiple punning line of Don van Vliet (Captain Beefheart), "The past sure is tense." For the issue is not that modernism despises the past as is so often alleged but that the past is contested territory. Modern architecture is commonly seen as being in simple opposition to 'traditional' or pre-modern architecture.[1] Looking at the shape and surfaces, exterior and interior, of most public and commercial buildings of the last half a century one could easily dismiss the relevance to modern practice of any study of pre-modern buildings. But Le Corbusier himself wrote in 1930, "I confess to having had only one master — the past; and only one discipline — the study of the past."[2] Despite the rhetorical intent here, let no one doubt that a serious study of history informed Modernist convictions.

In our practice, the quest in time is to find the best way to make use of the phenomenal gift that is the past: both as the old building around us with which we inescapably engage; and as recorded architectural history. The passage of time deposits intellectual and physical raw material. It has been our core belief that the twin activities of a study of past architecture and the execution of projects involving existing buildings are not only rewarding but also nourish the quality of all our work, including the design of brand new buildings.[3] In addition to the professional, specialist or academic aspects of such an engagement with the past it seems to us that it is an essential part of understanding our clients; in Winston Churchill's often quoted aphorism "First we shape our buildings and then they shape us."

The past is ever present around us, because buildings last such a long time. But a working knowledge of the past is no longer as embedded in architectural culture as it used to be. Compared to when the older members of our practice were at college, there has been a gradual decline in the teaching of the history and theory of pre-Modern architecture in the training of architects. An architect carries a reference library of design precedents inside her/his head. The libraries of the younger members of our practice are temporally much compressed compared not only with those of the older

Wolverhampton Civic
Halls, 2003.

members, but of their own equivalents 20 or 30 years ago. This seems to be a part of the wider phenomenon of the displacement of a working knowledge of history as an indispensable part of being a cultured citizen. The eminent historian Eric Hobsbawm described young women and men at the end of the twentieth century as "living in a sort of permanent present lacking any organic relation with the public past of the times they live in".[4]

How buildings learn

Our built environment is made mostly of old buildings. In the United Kingdom it is estimated that each year just one per cent of new construction is added to the total of the built stock. Within five years of construction a building will start requiring redecoration and minor repairs, within ten years some components and fittings will need to be replaced, within 25 years the heating and electrics will need replacement or an upgrade. The structure of a building has a much longer and possibly indefinite life-span but its fabric, the roof, walls and floors, is likely to need attention in order to go on keeping out the weather and maintaining internal comfort. Its external envelope may also be replaced or over-clad just to keep up with the times.

The performance of building is also likely to decline relative to prevailing technical standards, which tend to rise continuously. Notably today the performance of heating, ventilating, hot water and electrical systems is being driven upwards by the need to conserve energy and minimise greenhouse gas emissions to slow down climate change. Health and Safety and accessibility for all regardless of their (dis)abilities are another two relatively new drivers for changing ideas about design. So as they age buildings need attention even if their use is to remain unchanged. In practice use rarely remains unchanged: through technological advances and market forces a building may become redundant and be required to be pressed into entirely new service; through evolving circumstances a family may need an alteration or extension of a house, or a business to its premises. While use may change there are many reasons to preserve the old fabric such as an attachment to its character, or insufficient funds for building anew. "Function reforms form" as Stewart Brand puts it in his fascinating and instructive study *How Buildings Learn*, which passionately argues for adding the dimension of time in the design of space and buildings.[5]

Over 50 per cent of the £80 billion plus annual output of the UK construction industry is through working with existing buildings.[6] Much of this is repair and maintenance but a significant portion of this work needs architectural design of two sometimes related but distinct varieties: conversions, alterations and upgrade to change or improve a building's functionality and performance; and conservation of buildings for reasons of historic or architectural value. Despite adaptation and conservation of existing buildings being such an enormous area of work, architectural theory and education has been concerned almost entirely with new buildings.

Snape Maltings Concert Hall, interior
after refurbishment, 2000.

The overriding tenor of twentieth century Modernism was replacement, a conviction that
the new architecture was so superior in functionality and expression that the old would all be swept
away, save a few individual examples of historic importance. When Philip Dowson of Arup Associates
was asked by Benjamin Britten in 1965 to consider converting the old Maltings at Snape in Suffolk
for a new concert hall there was considerable resistance from many within the firm. Surely functional
compromise was inevitable if you used an old building? Why on earth would you not use the best
modern science and techniques to create a superb brand new concert hall? In the event the 800 seat
auditorium that Derek Sugden created within the walls of the Kiln Room of the Maltings has come to
be recognised as one of the finest in the world. Its acoustics have functioned perfectly for a variety of
performances for almost 40 years, something many of the new auditoria of the 1960s failed to do.

From conservation to heritage

Snape Maltings Concert Hall was a turning point in the way old buildings, and in particular vernacular
buildings, have been thought about by British architects. But it was part of the realisation that started
dawning in the 1960s that too much valuable historic fabric had been lost in post-war reconstruction.
Post-war planning achieved what Hitler's bombs could not, as some of the more strident conservationists
of the 1970s have said. Alongside outrage at the loss of individual buildings such as the Euston Arch
or the London Coal Exchange, both in 1962, there arose a new realisation that groups of humbler
buildings often had architectural value that the individual buildings within the group may not have
had, the Maltings at Snape being just such an example.

By the 1970s and 80s the pendulum had swung wholly the other way. 'Heritage' became
a saleable commodity and sentimentalism too often came to displace criticism in the judging of old
buildings. It became commonplace to build replicas of historic buildings, which usually amounted
to no more than pastiche, a crude approximation of the historic form and its details that lost the
proportions and subtlety of the original.

Snape Maltings Concert Hall, Snape, Suffolk, 1996–1999

The great Malt House at Snape was converted to a concert hall in the late 1960s to provide a home for the annual Aldeburgh Festival. Snape Maltings has since become a world famous performance venue, renowned for its acoustics and the beautiful auditorium with its graceful roof trusses, as well as its association with Benjamin Britten who co-founded it. By the end of the century front and back of house facilities badly needed expanding and the auditorium roof had become cluttered with lighting struggling to keep up with developing technology. There were numerous changes of level making access difficult.

The site is fully built up and its eastern edge, looking out over the reed beds of the Alde estuary, runs along the sea wall, which has to be maintained intact. In the design the additional space needed was found by extending the dressing rooms and restaurant block north (all levels) and south (ground floor only) and by raising its roof by 1.5 metres over a new clerestorey window to create an additional level. The horizontal sweep of the clerestory window reflects and gives spectacular views out to the estuarine horizon under a big sky.

New back of stage areas, administrative offices and a service yard were built to allow access for large vehicles carrying stage sets, and strategically positioned lifts were added to give access to all levels. A specially designed lighting rig and winch gallery have enabled versatile modern stage lighting and the auditorium is now cooled using ground water from a borehole. The architecture of the new parts is inspired by the unpretentious directness and simplicity of the existing buildings, with the materials of the structure, fabric and fittings left close to their natural state.

Top: In the Concert Hall itself the stage and auditorium lighting were completely renewed, tripling the available lighting potential and better revealing the elegant roof structure that had become encrusted with stage lamps. Provision has also been made for modern recording technology. Water from a deep aquifer on the site is used to cool the incoming air. Baffles added to the four bluffs on the ridge reduce noise penetration without significantly affecting airflow.

Bottom: The Maltings in the mid-1960s.

Opposite top: The altered buildings in their setting under the vast Suffolk sky.

Opposite bottom: These diagrams show the Maltings viewed from the access road. 1. Indicates the original buildings with the kiln room (auditorium) to the left and the tall barley store now the Britten-Pears School to the right. 2. In the 1970s a few of the 'tumbling bays' (for germinating barley) between the larger brick buildings had been removed and the perimeter penetrated to provide a rear entrance courtyard. 3. Shows the new configuration. The tumbling bays are almost entirely removed, a more permanent loading bay and rear entrance is established with offices/ancillary spaces provided in a building flanking the Concert Hall.

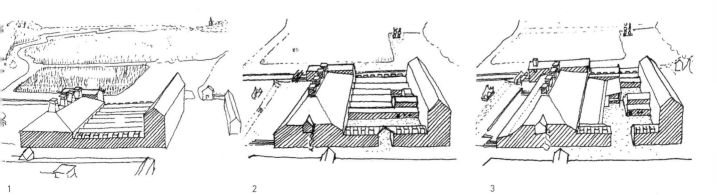

1   2   3

Top: The new floor for dining and hospitality, carried on acoustically mounted steel cradles and separated from the walls to connect spatially with the ground floor.

Bottom: Section through the main concert hall and the refurbished malt store. The ground floor areas accommodate dressing rooms and kitchens.

Opposite: A 50 metre long window inserted under the eaves of the roof gives a panoramic view across the estuary to the east.

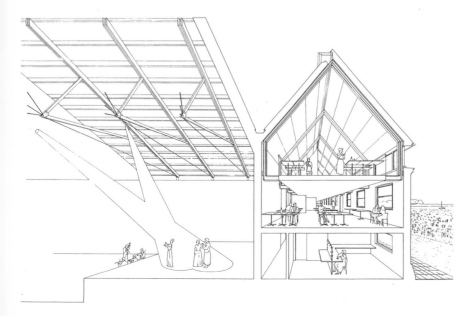

The past as inspiration

As reliable a test as any of good buildings is that they be conveniently laid out, durable in use and pleasing to the senses — the triad of commodity, firmness and delight originally set out by Vitruvius.[7] But how do these three aspects relate to each other? Are they different qualities achieved by different means or are they aspects of an integrated whole? Behind the different answers to such questions lie different attitudes: to the roles and relative power of architects, engineers and builders; to the validity or otherwise of applied decoration; to the nature of architecture itself.

In the post-Classical West as architecture developed from vernacular and Gothic to Renaissance there can be traced an increasing separation between what we now think of as functional aspects (utility, operability, durability) on the one hand and expressive aspects (aesthetics, symbolism) on the other. In the nineteenth century this separation reached a point where the main task of the architect came to be seen as the application of style, the inscription of narrative and representation into the surface and composition of buildings. A contrary ideal animated the Arts and Crafts and related movements that were the precursors of Modernism: an authentic architectural approach required a complete integration of utility, durability and aesthetics. The power of this idea, and its wide capacity for interpretation, is a major reason for the continuing dominance of 'modern architecture' around the world.

While the intellectual, rationalist appeal of Modernism aided its ascendance, cost also played a key role. Cost was a factor even during the celebrated 'Battle of Styles' over the fitness of the Gothic or the Classical for a number of major public commissions between 1840 and 1880. Lord Palmerston, the prime minister at the time of the commissioning of the Foreign Office's new building in 1857, on Whitehall in London, praised his favoured Italianate design as combining "with sufficient beauty and ornament great moderation of expense". Just as the lower cost of the Classical style helped its case over the Gothic in the late nineteenth century, so the lower cost of modernist buildings made them commercially attractive in the twentieth century. Buildings without decoration and complex craftsmanship were cheaper and easier to build.

Technology also played an important part in the demise of traditional architecture but its role is often exaggerated. One of our renovation projects, Sheffield City Hall, was designed by the

Neo-classical architect E Vincent Harris, in 1932, using reinforced concrete technology not dissimilar to Berthold Lubetkin's famous Penguin Pool at London Zoo, built almost at the same time. Long after the invention of reinforced concrete, plate glass, steel framing, lightweight cladding and sophisticated heating and ventilating services, architects and engineers continued to decorate their buildings with versions of traditional architectural languages. The great importance of new building technologies lay rather in the possibilities that they opened up.

Modern abstract architectural forms, with their liberal geometries, fewer rules, and freedom of expression have the ability to accommodate complex modern briefs and their ever-higher performance demands more directly, simply and cheaply than traditional forms. 100 years after their birth these modern languages have proved their ability to move, inspire and uplift and remain full of possibilities. However, they also seem to have produced rather more ugliness than traditional architecture ever could. Traditional architecture offers a standing rebuke to the bulk of modern architecture in the world's towns and cities. This is far more a failure of planning and urban design than of the design of individual buildings, but it also points to a property of the rule-rich systems that underpin traditional architecture: rules and templates limit the damage that mediocre practitioners can do. It was common in the eighteenth and nineteenth centuries for distinguished architects to publish pattern books for others to follow. The rapid growth of London suburbs in the second half of the nineteenth century would not have taken on so ordered, and sometimes gracious, an appearance were it not for the use of pattern books for the designs of facades as well as the application of some simple rules about the laying out of houses and streets. But traditional architectural languages in today's context cut out the high notes as well as the low. They limit the scope for imagination, invention, new ways of seeing and for responding to and expressing new conditions and possibilities of life.

For our practice the answers to today's architectural problems lie in the integration of utility, durability and aesthetics through the exploration of abstract form and its infinite possibilities. However, we can welcome the work of skilled architects who want to keep alive traditional architectural languages, especially when it is accompanied by a nurturing of craft traditions. They face the difficulty that there is very little ability in present architectural culture to discriminate critically between different examples of traditional architecture; for away from the passionate preoccupations of the cognoscenti all pre-modern architectural traditions are seen in contemporary culture as just the one 'traditional architecture', which sits today in contrived opposition to modern architecture, as often uncritically applauded as uncritically rejected. For us the great achievements of the past offer a standard to measure against, to be inspired by and to learn from, and not forms to be copied or methods to be followed. It is therefore essential to be able to discriminate between the quality and character of different old buildings; for example to be able to be moved by the aesthetic daring of Hawksmoor's churches, the spatial inventiveness of Soane, to see how mediocrity and architectural chutzpah sit side by side in Victorian towns.

Opposite left: Photograph of the construction of the cantilevered balconies at Sheffield City Hall, E Vincent Harris, 1932.

Opposite right: Photograph of the construction of the ramps at the Penguin Pool, London Zoo, Regent's Park, Lubetkin, Drake and Tecton, 1933–1934.

In the quest to understand and learn from the architecture of the past, style and language are a small part of the picture. Instead of surface appearance the true appeal of historic fabric lies in two rather more fundamental properties: architectural composition of buildings, and the manner in which individual buildings relate to the whole. Modern architecture has stressed the uniqueness of each work, the expression of the individuality of its designer. At an urban scale this can act against coherence in composition. At the same time, big buildings, say over 50 times larger than an average house, are more common in the post-industrial era and in these a striving for consistency together with an avoidance of embellishment has often produced monotony. We find many examples of historic urban fabric inspiring and instructive for their ability to create endless variety within a calming overall consistency. Such fabric also serves as a backdrop or foil for dramatic individual works of architecture.

The mixture of the old and new, or more accurately the co-existence of several eras of architecture, makes for the richest architectural experiences. Thinking of cities as opposed to the suburbs or the countryside, it is the layering through history that gives a city its soul. It serves to build the folk memory of the city without which the physical environment is just a shell. In an urban context designing a building on an empty site and designing an alteration of or extension to an existing building does call for approaches that are to some extent technically different. But we see no fundamental difference in the nature of the architectural task. There is a brief to be accommodated, the work as a whole has to be coherent as a composition and the resultant forms of the building have to be expressive in the desired way. In most urban contexts the architect is working with existing fabric, even when designing a new building.

Working with old buildings

Architectural and historical values are, of course, not the only grounds for the re-use of old buildings. For buildings constructed since the advent of structural frames independent of external and often internal walls, project economics, timescales or planning context may justify retaining only the structure. This is another type of working with the past, to move it on, without quite obliterating it.

At Charter School, 1999, our designs transformed old school buildings by rethinking the entrance and circulation arrangements, by covering over an underused courtyard to make a grand new entrance hall, and by re-cladding a teaching wing to increase comfort and reduce energy use. At Rich Mix, 2006, 1960s cloth trade premises have been turned into a series of flexible arts spaces and given a dramatic new face of louvres for solar and daylight control.

Reading and learning

Although the techniques, details and the conservationist knowledge required may vary, the principles of design are the same when dealing with a 50 or 500 year old building. The process has to start with uncovering what is there. The Italian architect Giancarlo de Carlo would speak of reading a place. Conducting his celebrated planning study of Urbino, which he started in 1958, such a reading enabled him to decipher the layers of development that had led to the contemporary condition of the city and to gain a profound understanding of the nature of the place. Historic fabric was like a palimpsest onto which each generation could write its own script. In his own design contributions such as the Faculty of Education of the University of Urbino, 1968–1978, he also showed how a modern aesthetic sensibility could be integrated with historic fabric at an urban scale.

The idea of reading a place seems capable of being used in the context of an existing building as much as that of a cleared site or of an urban context. In an architectural project the point of divergence between building anew and extending/altering only comes when the design possibilities get an extra set of limits because of the existing fabric. So the scope for options is quantitatively different in the new and old but the invention and ingenuity required, and the degree of fit demanded of the solutions is not qualitatively different.

In practice, the act of reading existing built form starts with studying the whole and the parts so as to establish the core architectural ideas that produce the best qualities of the buildings. The architect will often find that a number of the elements, most likely those that were added to the original design, either do nothing for the key qualities or positively harm them. She/he may also find hidden, and redundant, spaces capable of transformation to new use.

Opposite left: A typical, though particularly well preserved, haveli in the Walled City of Delhi. The semi-public platform raised above the dust and bustle of the street, the doorway with shady seats either side, the projecting bay above protecting the walls from very hot sun and monsoon rain, make a kit of parts that is repeated with endless variations in detail. Past the doorway there will be a 'dog leg' passage into a shady courtyard with the varied spaces of the house all around. The knowledge of the physical environment built up over time is distilled into a functional and highly expressive architecture with no single author.

Opposite centre: Aerial view of The Royal Crescent, Bath, looking towards the Circus. On the public side there is an ordered consistency — behind there is endless variety.

Opposite right: In working to the masterplan by West 8, many architects were involved in designing individual buildings for the Borneo Sporenburg quarter of Amsterdam, 1993–1997.

Top: Charter School main teaching block cladding before and after refurbishment, 1999 and 2003.

Wolverhampton Civic Halls, Staffordshire, 1996–2001

The Civic and Wulfrun Halls were completed in 1938 on their steeply sloping site to a competition winning design by Lyons & Israel, then only in their mid-20s and later to become among the most respected post-war British architects. Under an austere stripped classical architecture the design embodies an emergent, more open conception of culture where there is little separation of classes and, in principle, even of audience and performer through the 'promenade' plan: the corridor serving the auditorium simply runs on round the back of the stage. The slope is used cleverly to handle deliveries and stage 'get in'.

60 years on, and despite having become one of the top four rock venues in the country, the building was failing in many aspects to cater for modern audiences: there was a lack of adequate bars, women's wcs, administration space and wheelchair access; a series of clumsy additions, suspended ceilings and neglect of the exterior had diminished the spatial quality and the image of the halls.

In our designs all the bar areas are gathered together into two long glass boxes one on each flank of the building, proportioned on the geometric principles of the original massing. A new mezzanine floor level is created under these bars and above the original wc/bar strip to accommodate administrative and support functions. Stage and back stage has been properly connected to suit modern practice. The piecemeal additions have been cleared away, the foyer restored to its original condition and new lifts inserted in the interstices of the original fabric. The glass boxes are detailed to have a smooth 'monolithic' form connected to the masonry of the original with stone louvres that provide screening to back bar and wcs. At night these spaces, lit up, create a new connection between the Halls and their urban setting.

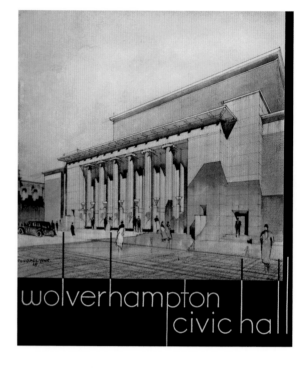

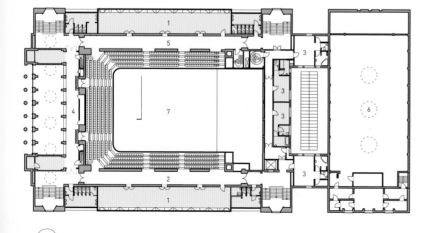

Top: The symmetrical composition of massive brick and stone-clad volumes with a clean lined entrance portico.

Bottom: First floor or gallery plan. Areas converted are shown coloured — the two new bars central to the flank walls with wc facilities at either end, reconfigured circulation spaces and new dressing rooms at the east end of the auditorium.

1 bar
2 north gallery
3 dressing room
4 balcony
5 south gallery
6 Wulfrun Hall
7 civic hall

Opposite: At night, the activity of the bars within the glazed extension is revealed to the town.

0   10   20

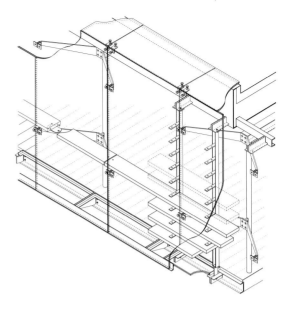

Opposite: The decoration of the auditorium ceiling restored to the original colour scheme.

Top left and right: Interior of the new glazed bar areas. A precast horizontal louvre is bolted into the brackets of the planar glazing to become a counter. This is joined by a series of similar louvres at either end of the glazing. Where the bar stops and service areas begin, the external wall to the building steps in and another set of louvres in the same plane, now external, give privacy to the otherwise glazed facade of the wcs.

Bottom: Cross-section. The new mezzanine level and bar above are shown coloured.

0   5

Such was the case in the 1999 project for the renewal of Wolverhampton Civic Halls. The Halls, built in 1936 to an early, competition winning design by the later highly regarded practice of Lyons & Israel, were described by one of the local councillors as "an old lady in need of a lift". Though our design did involve a face-lift and an image/branding exercise, the point of departure for the design was the functioning of the building as a whole. The very minimal front of house facilities were based on the long outdated view that the mostly male visitors, arrive, go straight into the performance and afterwards leave. In addition to the consequential lack of bars, women's toilets, good access routes and administrative spaces, the building had a somewhat inscrutable architectural expression at odds with its reputation as one of Britain's four best rock venues. But how to add the required several 100 square metres of accommodation to a Grade II listed symmetrical masonry clad building, which appeared to be so complete as to defy addition? A thorough reading of the building revealed a hidden space above the strip of toilets and small bars that flanked the auditorium. At the same time we developed the strategy of making largely glass additions following the geometry of the original building. Some of these would contain new large bars positioned directly above the strip of toilets and small bars. We could thereby adjust the height of the hidden space to be able to house administrative offices with little external impact.

At Snape Maltings Concert Hall there was a similar problem of adding substantial new accommodation to bring the venue up to current standards without damaging the much loved character of the Maltings complex and its powerful presence in the extraordinary estuarine landscape. Site curtilage and tidal defences severely constrained available development land. On studying the cross-section of the malt store, which had been converted to create changing rooms and the restaurant, we realised that by raising the entire roof by 1.5 metres it would be possible to insert a new floor to provide a significant portion of the additional space and that this would have an ideal relationship to bars and foyer. We also knew that in the Arup conversion, the ridge line of the adjacent kiln room had been substantially raised to make the auditorium, so the increase in scale of the changing room/restaurant block would restore earlier relative proportions. In the final design the block is extended by three bays, the roof is raised and a floor suspended in the space created and new changing rooms are added underneath a new viewing terrace. Thus 600 square metres of new space were added with a subtle transformation of the old.

Urbino with the University Faculty of Education, Giancarlo de Carlo, 1968–1978.

At Sheffield City Hall the upper circle, originally being for the lower classes, could only be reached from the street outside. In the plan of the Hall the main auditorium is an oval casket held within a rectangular box, which in turn is enclosed by another such box. The 'squinch' shape between the oval and the corners of the rectangle accommodates service risers and the space between the boxes contains much of the circulation. A detailed reading of the plan revealed that there were empty spaces in the squinches as well as the boxes such that we could insert additional stairs and access galleries to make new connections and circulations routes without harming the spatial qualities of the original.

In the 1980s it became common for local authority planning officers to require new buildings to be 'in-keeping' with adjacent pre-modern buildings, too often regardless of the merits of the existing. In the case of extensions this rule was applied with greater force. If what is at stake here is protection of the irreplaceable qualities of certain historical settings and buildings, then juxtaposing contemporary designs with older forms is surely a more authentic tribute to history. Rather than be in-keeping with historic buildings it seems much more important to learn from them. In our work at Snape the design of the new additions as regards appearance, materials and detail is inspired by the unpretentious and direct architecture of the nineteenth century agro-industrial buildings of the Maltings, which almost certainly did not involve an architect. Their design was led by the requirements of the malt making process and the need to withstand the weather. It used local materials put together with great simplicity, but also skilled craftsmanship. We have tried to retain this spirit as far as possible while meeting the rather higher requirements for comfort, energy conservation, disability access, electronic equipment use and health and safety.

Conservation

Although there is a great deal of building science involved, conservation also requires a large measure of judgement based on historic knowledge and insights. It is easy to 'overdo' conservation, and the conservation architect has to know the point at which the wish to return the work to an imagined original state threatens to destroy what is actually, materially present. Some of our refurbishment and renewal projects such as The Charter School and The Rich Mix have involved buildings of variable architectural merit and of relatively recent origin where re-use rather than conservation is the aim. Nevertheless there were parts of the existing fabric where restoring it to its original state was all that was needed. At The Charter School the staircases, despite their footworn teak treads, and the main hall with its unique, stage arrangement needed only a coat of paint.

At the other end of the restoration spectrum layers added through repeated conversions must be stripped back to reveal the hidden core qualities of a building. False ceilings were often used in the 1960s to hide cornices and lower lofty spaces regarded as wasteful and old fashioned at the time. Sheffield City Hall, 1920–1934, had extensive areas of painting and gilding by local craftsmen, which

St Jerome in his Study,
Antonello da Messina, 1475.

Opposite: Castelvecchio
Museum, Verona,
Carlo Scarpa, 1997.

had decayed, been over-painted or otherwise covered up. These were carefully restored using old records and expert techniques. Suspended ceilings covering up mouldings and cornices, and intrusive fittings were removed and rooms returned to their original scale and proportions. Both at Sheffield City Hall and Wolverhampton Civic Halls the foyers were cleared of accumulated kiosks and restored to their original so as to intensify the play between old forms and new insertions. Conservation may also include improving the climatic and energy performance of buildings.

Juxtaposing old and new

Exemplars of working with existing buildings are rare in the architectural canon. One of the few is the work of Carlo Scarpa, seemingly effortlessly combining archaeology with style; juxtaposing the old and the new so that each is magically made more beautiful by the other, as if to underscore the magnificence of the passage of time. Scarpa's details have a lovingly hand-crafted character and though his aesthetic sensibility is modern the work expresses continuity with the past. The painting by Antonello da Messina, *St Jerome in his Study*, 1475, shows the Saint in a wooden building, which stands free within a church interior. While full of other allusions, the painting endures as an inspiring example of how one might bring new uses to old buildings through insertion rather than conversion.

Alongside the restoration of historic features at Sheffield City Hall, front of house counters, bars, stairs, toilets, auditorium seating and stage fittings of purely modern design were installed in juxtaposition with the old. The best juxtapositions of old and new seem to occur when the essence of the contribution from each period is most intensely revealed. That usually means a light touch restoration of the old elements and the careful handling of their junctions with the new ones. The polished granite bar fronts at Sheffield City Hall are free standing objects in its panelled rooms and columned halls creating engaging reflections and spatial illusions. The delicate stainless steel staircases aim to add new sparkle to domed and arched lobbies with gilt decorations from the 1930s. The new bars at Wolverhampton Civic Halls externally follow the geometric discipline of the stripped Classicism of the original, but in contrast to the brick and stone they are made of smooth structural glass.

1 The common use of 'traditional' in opposition to 'modern' is unsatisfactory, suggesting that the modern era, itself difficult to delineate precisely, is excluded from establishing traditions. Critics have written about modern traditions, notably Colin St John Wilson in *The Other Tradition of Modern Architecture: The Uncompleted Project*, London: Black Dog Publishing, 2007 (revised edition, original date 1995).

2 Le Corbusier, *Precisions: On the Present State of Architecture and City Planning*, trans. Edith Schreiber Aujame, Cambridge, MA: MIT Press, 1991. Originally published in Paris in 1930.

3 Our first brochure in 1990 did rather overstate this "we see no distinction between modern and traditional architecture".

4 "The destruction of the past, or rather the social mechanisms that link one's contemporary experience to that of earlier generations, is one of the most characteristic and eerie phenomena of the late twentieth century. Most young men and women at the century's end grow up in a sort of permanent present lacking any organic relation to the public past of the times they live in." If architects are losing the ability to understand, and discriminate between the quality of different historical buildings, it would be hardly surprising if such an ability were to be lost in architectural culture generally. That such ability should be replaced by an indiscriminate sentimentalism about the past seems inevitable. Hobsbawm, Eric, *The Age of Extremes: The Short Twentieth Century 1914–1991*, London: Abacus, 1995.

5 Brand, Stewart, *How Buildings Learn*, London: Phoenix Illustrated, 1997, p. 3.

6 UK Department of Trade and Industry, *Construction Statistics Annual Report 2006*, Norwich: The Stationery Office, 2006. These data do not fully identify extensions and alterations as opposed to repair and maintenance. The 'Repair and Maintenance' category, which confusingly includes some housing alterations and extensions, accounted for 47 per cent of the UK construction output in 2005.

7 See also essay "Purpose".

Sheffield City Hall,
1997–2005

The City Hall is one of Sheffield's great civic buildings, a memorial to the soldiers who lost their lives in the First World War and now a key part of Sheffield's thriving cultural quarter, with concerts and events throughout the year in its three major spaces. Designed in 1920 by E Vincent Harris but not completed until 1932 the building has a technologically advanced concrete structure and perhaps the UK's first uplit dance floor underneath its Neo-classical exterior. It also had fine examples of gilding and wall painting carried out by the city's craftsmen. As with other buildings of a similar age, like Wolverhampton Civic Halls, which we also remodelled, the building was held in great affection, but frustrated the variable demands of twenty-first century events. Access was limited, the circulation awkward and the ancillary facilities inadequate. Over the years layers of piecemeal alterations and additions had cluttered the interiors.

Following our designs the two auditoria and the dance hall have been refurbished, and associated back stage facilities improved, increasing their flexibility to accommodate a broader spectrum of events. The integrity of the original foyer and other spaces is restored by relocating the box office and recreating original decorations from records. The circulation was completely rethought. New lifts and internal staircases inserted into pockets of space outside the main auditorium to provide internal access to the second floor and the ballroom previously accessible only from outside. A new set of polished granite bars, box office and retail counters was placed within the restored interiors. The exterior of the hall was cleaned and two stone enclosures at the front given glass lanterns to express the new outward facing and inclusive approach. The adjacent civic space has been redesigned as part of a wider programme of city centre regeneration.

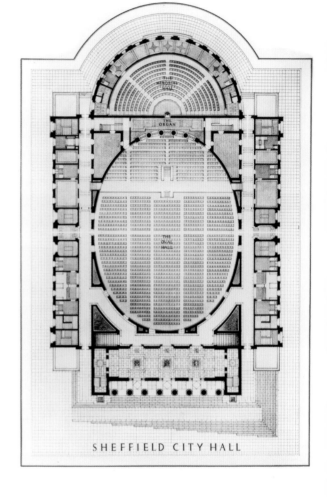

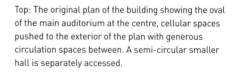

SHEFFIELD CITY HALL

Top: The original plan of the building showing the oval of the main auditorium at the centre, cellular spaces pushed to the exterior of the plan with generous circulation spaces between. A semi-circular smaller hall is separately accessed.

Bottom: This photograph of the City Hall entrance facade in the 1930s illustrates its Neo-classical style typical of civic buildings of the 1920s.

Opposite: Interior of the refurbished auditorium. A number of original features were retained, including the coffered fibrous plaster ceiling and the elliptical laylight. The ventilation strategy is entirely new. Previously cool air entered the space from the roof and was extracted from the lower areas, a strategy that was never effective as hot air rises. This system was reversed in the refurbishment so that cool air was drawn into a plenum beneath a new raised access floor, allowed to naturally rise as it is heated by the activity in the auditorium and exhausted via existing grilles within the cornices at high level.

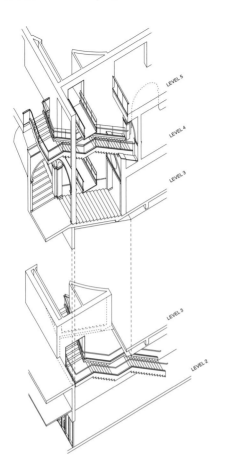

LEVEL 5
LEVEL 4
LEVEL 3
LEVEL 3
LEVEL 2

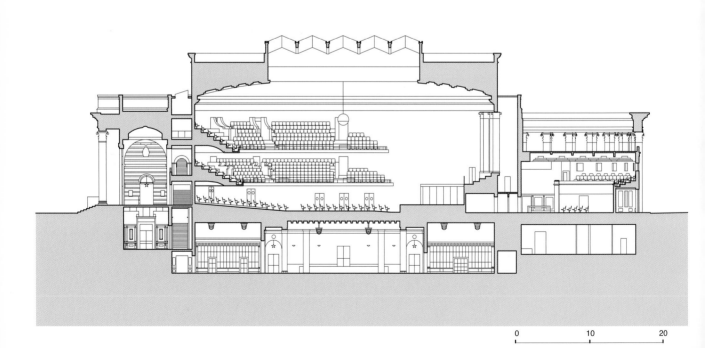

0   10   20

Opposite top left and right and this page top: View of a new staircase giving internal access to the second floor tier of seating. The axonometric drawing shows how this element winds its way up within previously hidden spaces. The reinforced concrete construction of the building meant that some of the structural interventions were complicated.

Opposite bottom: The cross-section through the building shows its three main spaces including the basement ballroom.

Bottom: More playful than the exterior the original interior colour schemes and gilding were faithfully conserved, restored or reinstated in the refurbishment. In the vaulted Arches Bar the shades and pattern were ascertained by carefully stripping back layers of paint and studying contemporary photographs.

CARE

This chapter is based on the premise that the environment in which health care is delivered should be an integral part of that care. It explores how architecture can play a significant role at a number of levels, from the intimate and personal to the urban and public, in the mission to heal and to promote health.

From process to place

The National Health Service, free to all citizens at the point of delivery and provided on the basis only of clinical need is a monument of democratic civilisation. Unfortunately, health care provided in the UK by the NHS, however excellent, tended to be delivered in environments that generally ranged from institutional to shabby. Except in private hospitals and clinics, and sometimes in the local family General Practice, health care and dowdy surroundings go hand in hand. This is true around much of the world with some significant exceptions such as Northern Europe. Just when we are at our most vulnerable, in need of all the support we can get, we are let down by the design and construction of the places where health is to be restored. Happily within the last 15 years the ill health of health care environments has become widely recognised, and effective remedies for this condition have been discovered or re-discovered. The reason for this recognition is that private and public purse holders have begun to realise that people get better more quickly in environments expertly designed with the full range of human needs in mind.

By the 1980s the notion of 'patient focused medicine' and 'patient focused care' was becoming established. In both state and privately funded health care systems these phrases are now part of the marketing lexicon, but they originate in a deeper change in the relationship between the supply side and demand side of health care. This in turn reflects a wider shift in the balance of power between producers and consumers in the manufacturing and service industries generally. In the health services such consumer oriented care can be contrasted to procedures devised purely to suit operational efficiencies as seen by the providers of the care.[1] For too long medical orthodoxy ignored the feelings of the patient and the impact of her/his state of mind on the efficacy of medical interventions. The most obvious change has been the admission, albeit limited, of the 'holistic' view into 'conventional medicine', a view that sees the whole of the human organism in its physical and mental aspects as indivisibly linked. But more thoroughgoing operational changes follow a fundamental change of perspective: from seeing the world from the medic's point of view to seeing the world from the patient's point of view. This may be realised in practice through simple measures such as providing more information to patients or moving staff rather than patients round a hospital for consultation and diagnosis. In time it should inspire the whole culture of care and its delivery to fully support

The Pulross Intermediate Care Centre, 2000.

each person's capacity to be the prime agent of her or his healing, albeit moderated by operational constraints and good sense. American insurance companies and health maintenance organisations like Kaiser Permanente have begun to adopt such practices on the basis of good business sense. The need for private companies to compete has introduced 'customer focus' into general business practice in a way that is harder to emulate in state run systems with monopoly where the patient's custom can all too easily be taken for granted.

Patient-focused care needs patient focused design. Engaged in the design of health care environments for the National Health Service from the inception of the practice, Greg Penoyre and I set out to explore where patient focused design might lead. Our experience at Edward Cullinan Architects working on the pioneering Community Care Centre in Lambeth, 1981, had engendered in us a passionately held belief that the quality of the patient environment profoundly influenced the quality of the outcome for the patient. The key part of this environment was the place where caring and curing happened.

The idea that a place with certain special qualities may cure specific disease or restore health generally is hardly new. The importance of physical surroundings has been a consistent theme in medicine from all cultures before the advent of modern scientific medicine. In Ancient Greece people came to the legendary Sanctuary of Asklepios at Epidaurus because it was just such a place. Though the association with the healer God is what made Epidaurus special and though we don't know exactly what the settlement and buildings were like, it is reasonable to assume that the designer/builders would have reinforced its unique qualities. In Europe and the USA in the nineteenth century physicians and scientists began to reverse the popular theory that night air was bad for you and to promote better ventilation.[2] Florence Nightingale was a strong advocate of good ventilation to counter and cure diseases but she went further and recognised the visual impact of surroundings on the patient. She wrote in her diaries in 1860:

> I mention from experience, as quite perceptible in promoting recovery, the being able to see out of a window, instead of looking against a dead wall; the bright colours of flowers, the being able to read in bed by the light of a window close to the bed-head. It is generally said the effect is upon the mind. Perhaps so, but it is no less upon the body on that account....[3]

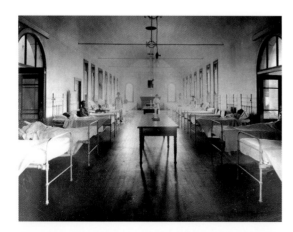

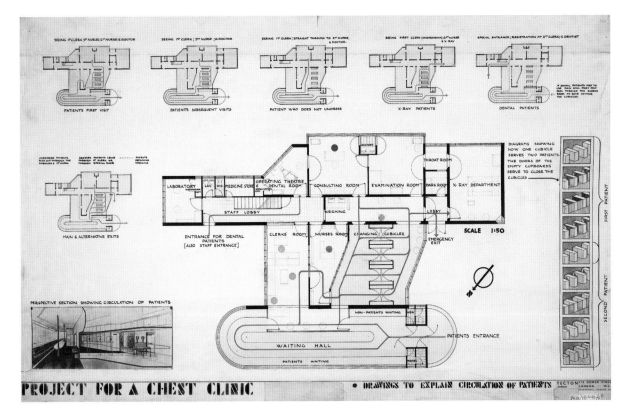

PROJECT FOR A CHEST CLINIC • DRAWINGS TO EXPLAIN CIRCULATION OF PATIENTS

It was 130 years before controlled clinical trials proved that she was right.[4] Fortunately, many had believed her anyway.

Florence Nightingale had already developed what we now know as the Nightingale Ward with its high ceilings and tall windows on both sides. She went on to contribute to the building and design of St Thomas' Hospital when it moved to Lambeth in 1861. The steadily increasing importance given to privacy and changing ideas about infection control eventually made Nightingale Wards obsolete; but a belief in fresh air, light and pleasant surroundings for curing a wide range of illnesses, above all Tuberculosis, animated many hospital and clinic designs of early Modern architecture, most famously Johanne Duiker's Zonestraal and Alvar Aalto's Paimio Sanatorium.

The astonishing achievements of modern medicine, perhaps above all the discovery of antibiotics and advances in surgery seemed to make redundant such strategies based on environmental factors in alleviating and curing illness. The attention of designers turned instead to devising the best arrangement to support the doctors and nurses; to matters like logistics and clinical adjacencies; to operational economy and efficiency. The shift of focus to process is already evident in some designs of the 1930s, including the celebrated Finsbury Health Centre by Tecton. Hospital and health care architects and planners set about developing these aims, convinced that the scientific temper that had produced medical breakthroughs now needed to be applied to the design of modern health care buildings. These buildings were thought of as instruments, not places; as utilitarian devices and not environments shaping the patients' experience. In the UK the creation of the NHS provided a tremendous opportunity for a concentrated programme of developing fundamental principles of good health care design. Between the late 1950s and the mid-70s the architects, engineers and planners

Opposite left: A typical Nightingale Ward in action in the nineteenth century.

Opposite right: Patients on the roof terrace of Alvar Aalto's Paimio Sanatorium, 1933, receiving fresh air and sun.

Design for East Ham Chest Clinic, London, for Dr Philip Ellman by Tecton, 1932. The plan is organised to make the process of consultation as efficient as possible.

at the Ministry (later Department) of Health produced the best technical guidance for this area in the world. This collection of guidance, which has continued to be used and updated, remains a monumental achievement in design research; logical, objective, empirical, quantitative, and above all practical.

Throughout this heady period, when it seemed as if a disease-free future was just round the corner, little attention was paid to the experience and feelings of the patient. In the realm of design, process was everything and place was nowhere. And 'nowhere' is a good word to describe the corridors of 1,000s of modern hospitals around the world. Local clinics, health centres and GP surgeries were often just as dingy and impersonal, however excellent the standards of medical care. The focus on process to the exclusion of the quality of place is evident outside these buildings as much as it is inside. The hospital or health centre, even on city sites, was not seen as a part of the making of an urban public realm. Vehicle movement logistics and highway design determined the design of the approaches to the buildings and hugely influenced the spatial relationship of the building mass to its urban context.

In the middle of all this utilitarian, process dominated thinking, there were individual examples of design that embodied a faith in the power of architecture to uplift us as individuals and ease the connections between us as citizens. The ward blocks of Wexham General Hospital, 1958–1966, by Powell and Moya have been described as the "first example of patient focused design".[5] Philip Powell discarded initial designs based on prevailing theories of logistics and clinical efficiency, and proposed covering much of the site in a low-rise network of courtyards integrated with the landscape. The corridors were generally single loaded, ie. one side had no rooms, just views out and plenty of daylight coming in. The wards, too, had excellent views and daylight. All this was done without compromise to the clinical imperatives. The work of Powell and Moya stands out as a series of inspiring essays in making humane environments that accommodate modern technology without ever losing sight of the needs and feelings of the individual it is meant to serve. In the meantime, Le Corbusier's unrealised design for the Venice Hospital drew its conceptual logic simultaneously from urban context and operational need. The loose structural grid and the scale matched the historic urban morphology, drawing the streets and waterways of the city into the ground floor of the hospital. The simultaneous

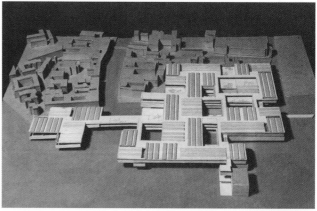

answering of what initially appear as conflicting demands is the profound power at the heart of architecture and is what has primarily animated the work of our practice.

How a healing environment works

The aim of the health care system is to treat and prevent illness but patients', and their companions', parents' or other carers' experience of the system itself often increases stress and anxiety. The ennui of waiting, fear of being overlooked, fear of forgetting to tell doctors all the facts, being in proximity to other ill people all make worse the anxiety and stress caused by being unwell. Those that are the least confident in navigating 'the system' perhaps through socio-cultural background and economic circumstances, or young people afraid of the stigma that may be attached to visiting health centres, such as for sexual health problems, have to deal with additional stress. The fears associated with health care can inhibit the most vulnerable people from accessing it.

The environment can make all this worse: noise, smells, inability to see what is going on, lack of privacy, difficulty in communicating, glare, poor thermal comfort and air quality. These words alone bring many outpatient waiting areas vividly to mind. A well-designed environment can not only eliminate such stress factors, it can positively promote a sense of calm and ease; it cannot, of course, guarantee wellbeing but at least it should make you feel better. We have heard patients say of well-designed buildings, including some of ours: "I felt better as soon as I arrived here." The layout of a waiting area can help people to maintain contact with desk staff and raise the quality of personal space. Well engineered design can create environments with good acoustics, thermal comfort and fresh air to breathe. Signs can be easy to read and un-confusing. We can design the entrances and circulation so that no one other than you and your carers need know why you have come to the clinic.

As we asked in our winning competition entry for elderly care provision at Newhaven Downs House, 1994, (where Philip Powell was amongst the judges):

> What do you see when you come in? Is it as far as possible like home, with the clinical stuff unobtrusive? Does the layout allow patients maximum dignity, ie. freedom with security and privacy? Is there a variety of living spaces? Is it safe and secure for people with a variety of impairments? Does it avoid long featureless corridors?

Patient focused design can go further: it can communicate values, such as "this organisation will care for you personally" or "this is a professionally run outfit that rarely gets it wrong". Quality of finishes, of lighting, the absence of clutter, investment in making a place with its own character, eg. through design and art, can all contribute to making people feel respected and cared for.

Opposite left: A ward around a courtyard at Wexham Park Hospital, Powell and Moya, 1958–1966.

Opposite right: Unrealised design for Venice Hospital, Le Corbusier, 1964. The plan is woven into the pattern of the city's streets and canals and the building's height would have matched that of the historic fabric.

Walworth Road Surgery, London, 1986–1991

Recent rapid expansion had made this surgery for seven GPs severely overcrowded. Determined to retain their strong local ties and their familiar high street presence for the community, the doctors acquired a small builders' yard and house tucked away in the dense urban fabric of this lively area of south London. The yard was landlocked and separated from the old premises by a right of way.

The buildings were converted and refurbished to provide quiet and calm spaces away from the hustle and bustle of the Walworth Road. They are linked by a new building placed in the yard and planned round a small court shielded from the right of way by a massive but delicately perforated brick wall. This new heart of the surgery contains the reception and waiting spaces as well as five consulting rooms, nurse's room, treatment suite and the administrative office. These are linked to the old premises via a bridge that also serves as a waiting space. In spite of the immured, backlands site the design allows daylight into the building's deepest parts whilst creating privacy and mitigating overlooking.

Ground floor walls are faced with pale buff brick, and the first floor wall to the courtyard is of timber frame construction clad in stained plywood. Windows are set within deep timber sub-frames to increase privacy in the rooms and make generous window cills. The profiled sheet aluminium roof 'peels' up to the north to bring glare-free daylight into the consulting rooms.

Top: Ground floor plan.

1 interview room
2 reception
3 waiting area
4 administrative/office
5 wc
6 consulting room
7 nurse's/treatment
8 courtyard
9 public access
10 multi-purpose/clinic space
11 nappy changing
12 stairs to staff and councillor's room

Bottom: A wave shaped profiled aluminium roof lets in daylight from clerestorey windows into a number of rooms and a bridge over the right of way connects the new to the original, refurbished premises leading from the front floor waiting area.

Opposite top left: The secluded courtyard garden around which the consulting rooms are arranged.

Opposite top right: Through the large glazed entrance facade the visitor can immediately see the reception and waiting areas on two levels behind. This is the only part of the site where abundant daylight is captured without creating overlooking and privacy problems.

Opposite bottom: Cross-section. Corridors on ground and first floor run the length of the site against an existing party wall. The upper corridor has roof lights opposite each pair of consulting room doors. Directly beneath each roof light are pavement lights set into the concrete floor slab and a glimmer of daylight in this way enlivens the otherwise buried ground floor corridor and marks the entrance to rooms.

Designing for doctors

The first of a number of GP surgeries that we designed in our early years was at 1 Manor Place, Southwark in south London, where Dr Roger Higgs and a group of radical doctors were running a practice from very cramped high street premises. The surgery had existed there since the 1890s. Not even an offer from the Family Health Services Authority to move the practice to a brand new building on a generous site could entice them to abandon the well-established relationship with the local community underwritten by their high street address. Dr Higgs had been pivotal in creating the path-breaking Lambeth Community Care Centre in 1982 by persuading people to see the world through the eyes of patients: an old lady recovering from a hip operation and waiting to be near her son and family; or a young man whose need for constant care has exhausted his single mum who badly needs a respite. This scheme anticipated by a decade and a half changes in the relationship between acute and primary care.

When a landlocked builder's yard behind their surgery came up for auction Dr Higgs and colleagues turned up in disguise, so as not to alert adjoining owners, and successfully bid for the freehold. Dispiritingly, the advice they then received from experienced health care architects suggested that with all the constraints present on the site it would be impossible to build satisfactory GP premises there. Not only was the site hemmed in from all sides and short of space, it was separated from the existing premises by an intrusive right of way. Working closely with the doctors and with Ann Noble, as specialist health architect, we worked our way through six design iterations to arrive at the built scheme.

Left: A consulting room at Walworth Surgery.

Right: *The Milkmaid*, Johannes Vermeer, 1660.

Opposite left: Consulting room, Coldhabour Lane Surgery, 1991. Dr Puri believed that his patients wanted an impression of calm traditional authority with the clinical paraphernalia hidden away in separate examination and treatment rooms.

Opposite right: Early computer study model for the design of the consulting rooms at The Rushton Street Medical Centre.

Organising the plan of the building around a tiny courtyard garden was the key to unlocking the potential of the site. To make the building easy for patients to navigate despite the complicated situation all the parts are visibly connected. The arrangement reveals itself immediately on entry, with the semi-circular reception desk overlooking the waiting areas. The consulting rooms on the ground floor have large windows onto the secluded courtyard while those on the first floor have smaller windows (for privacy from neighbours) with clerestorey daylight making up the overall light level. Daylight from above is generally effective in creating calm, glare-free environments. Natural light illuminates the figures within the space but bright areas do not intrude into the normal field of vision. The effect is like that in many Dutch School paintings where mysterious light illuminates faces against a darker background. Furthermore, good daylight is said by our GP clients to directly aid diagnosis because it makes it easier to assess pallor and skin condition.

Dr Higgs and many of our early GP clients were interested in making the doctor/patient relationship less one-sided, to empower the patient on both egalitarian and practical grounds. No longer passive witnesses having things done to them patients would be better informed and take more responsibility and control of their health. Most of the GPs made a point of personally fetching the waiting patient and accompanying them to the consulting room. Within the consulting room they wanted to avoid the old arrangement of the doctor behind a large desk and the patient across, separated by an expanse of mahogany, literal or metaphorical. The introduction of information technology in primary care meant there had to be room on the desk for a screen. The doctors, rather than conceal what was on the screen from the patient, saw this as an opportunity to draw the patient in; a contrast to the illegibility and mysterious markings of the traditional doctors script. Finally, it was important that the patient was on the 'non-writing-arm' side of the doctor so that the doctor's arms and shoulders presented an open aspect to the patient, a welcoming body language. The position of the door to the consulting room and the position and design of the furniture in our surgery designs are influenced by these considerations. For example, the normally oblong desk has a triangular 'blip' either side of which sit the doctor and patient. There is also storage space for toys and sitting space for another member of the patient's family.

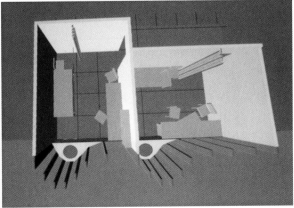

Some GPs feel that the paraphernalia of examination spoils the atmosphere of the consulting room and that having separate rooms for consultation and examination increases throughput and aids privacy. However, the combined, space efficient consulting/examination room has become the norm and, if well designed, allows maximum communication between GP and patient while protecting dignity. At The Rushton Street Medical Centre, working with another group of very thoughtful GPs we noted that undressing for an examination is quick, straightforward and not generally embarrassing; but there is much more potential for embarrassment if you can be watched while getting dressed. As a result we developed an ideal consulting room configuration in which the doctor naturally, in the course of washing hands, turned her or his back on the patient after the examination so they could dress in privacy. This detail may seem trivial to some in the context of the loftier aims of architectural form making; but such engagement with the inner life of buildings (see the chapter "Purpose") seems to us to be the basis of architecture.

Wellness

Over 70 years ago, in 1935, two south London GPs conducted the Peckham Experiment to test the effectiveness of preventive health care as opposed to the orthodox curative approach. Their Pioneer Health Centre, designed by Owen Williams, had huge open plan column free spaces, flooded with light, with a swimming pool at the centre and numerous opportunities for leisure and social activities as well as some medical facilities.[6] 950 working class families signed up at a shilling a week to be part of the experiment to see whether life habits such as diet, the amount of daily exercise and a supportive social network with a limited input from professionals would improve health. The research lasted over 15 years, with a gap during the Second World War. The full results of this sophisticated study are complex to interpret because of its path-breaking acknowledgement of social factors in, and the interdependency of, individuals' mental and physical health. In brief, it was found that the general wellbeing of participants improved, as did their family lives and creativity. Why the Peckham Experiment has not had more influence is difficult to understand, but perhaps the key reason was that in establishing the National Health Service just after the war, the government and medical establishment found it more straightforward to focus its mission around curing illness rather than the less defined idea of wellness.

The goal of universal access to medicine determined only on clinical need and free at the point of delivery without any rationing proved sustainable for 50 years in European welfare economies. Ultimately, the very success of this type of health care system in repairing bodies and prolonging life, rather than focusing on the quality of life itself, brought about a crisis of demand exceeding supply. In the non-welfare economies of the 'developed' world, such as the United States, there is a parallel crisis centred on the health insurance industry, while the un-insured are experiencing a remorseless deterioration in their health and life expectancy.

Pioneer Health Centre, Peckham, London: the library and rest room, Owen Williams, 1935.

Clean water, vaccination and the control of pollution had a dramatic effect in reducing diseases that were once common. But now we have so called "diseases of affluence" such as heart problems, diabetes and obesity, which together with an ageing population are costing billions to governments and insurance companies. The true meaning of Dutch Humanist philosopher/theologian Erasmus' proverb "prevention is better than cure", coined in the fifteenth century, is at last being recognised now that attention is beginning to be focused on making people more aware of and responsible for their health.

In 1999 the UK government launched a programme of Healthy Living Centres supported by grants.[7] Similar centres have been established in the United States and the European Union, often taking shape as networks of services rather than individual buildings. They are generally aimed at tackling some of the root causes of ill health such as unemployment, poverty, lack of education and difficulties in accessing facilities and services. Many also offer a range of health regimes and complementary therapies, but the key element is the spreading of information about health to individuals and families so that they can take steps in their own lives towards greater wellness.

Care in the neighbourhood

Seen from the point of view of the recipients, in particular of the most vulnerable people, joining up the services around the individual rather than maintaining demarcation around specialisms is the key to achieving the best outcomes. The highly medicalised view of health that prevailed through much of the twentieth century had the hospital at the apex of the system. The emerging model of the health system is primary care led.[8] Spending decisions about the majority of the resources of the health system will be made by the primary care service, which will also provide as much of the care and treatment as possible; the hospitals providing what only they can. A patient focused view implies that care pathways should be geographically located to suit patient's needs and that means as near home as possible. In most populations health problems and other problems, such as those with housing and family histories, are inextricably linked and therefore health and social care services also need to be integrated.

The recognition of wellness as an important good, the shift of focus to primary care and the related emergence of integrated care, have now led to a new generation of community based health buildings, halfway between a family GP surgery and a district hospital. Previously disparate agencies are being brought together under one roof so that local citizens can have the most effective access to health and related services.

Our practice has been developing an architecture for this new type since Neptune Health Park, 1995, in Tipton in the West Midlands, an area with one of the highest levels of ill health and social deprivation in the UK. This pioneering Healthy Living Centre houses a GP practice, a diagnostic and treatment centre, a Citizens' Advice Bureau, a community health resource centre, health related shops

Ground and first floor plan of Neptune Health Park, Tipton, 1995–1998.

1 consulting rooms
2 waiting area
3 reception
4 records
5 treatment
6 surgery
7 office/administration/staff
8 diagnostic
9 information
10 community workshop
11 pharmacy
12 optician
13 interview
14 case worker
15 entrance

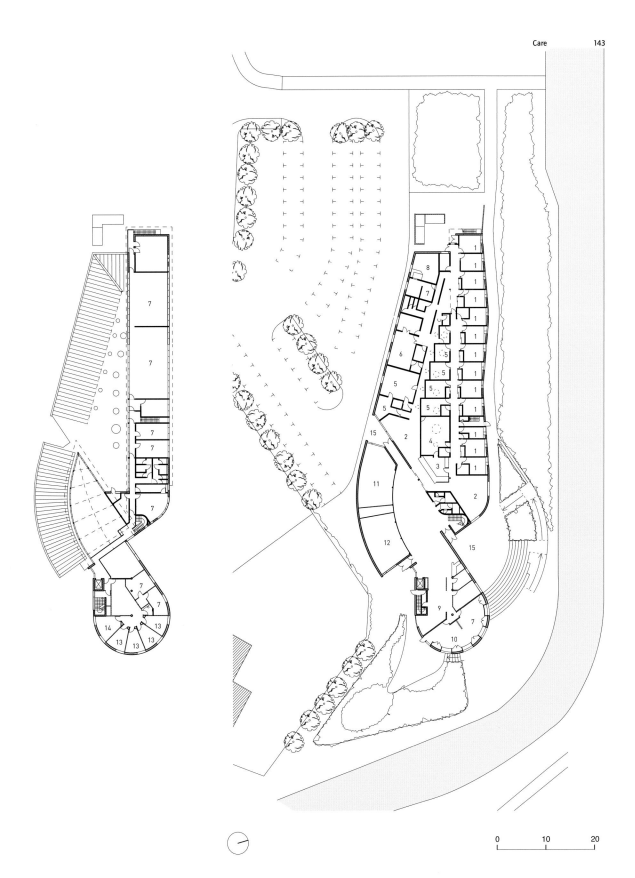

0   10   20

and a cafe. The inclusion of specifically health-promoting facilities, such as a swimming pool or sports centre, recalling the Peckham Experiment, was discussed but funding has not been available. The vision for the centre as articulated by Dr Colin Brown was to raise the level of health awareness and information amongst the whole population to that of a health conscious, Sunday supplement reading middle class person. Unusually for a health building, Neptune Health Park was also intended to help catalyse the regeneration of the parts of the town south of the Wolverhampton Canal, an area that was recovering from the industrial collapse of the 1980s.

The requirement of linking together a number of different agencies and of urban regeneration prompted a design approach in which the centre was viewed not so much as a building but as a clustering of events around a public space. The public realm of the town could be extended into the heart of the cluster as a through route, also giving access to the various services. Accordingly, the centre is organised around an axis that links two churches — one in the northern and one in the southern part of the town. Two entrances opposite each other on this axis lead to a concourse from which the various services are reached in the manner of a small shopping centre. As many of the spaces as possible look out onto the canal, and the cafe in the concourse spills out onto a stepped canalside terrace.

Bringing the urban public realm into the health care environment is a powerful means of dissolving the hitherto hermetic character and institutionalism of health centres and hospitals. This has been a consistent theme in our practice's designs for a number of health centres in Belfast and London, including the Pulross Intermediate Care Centre and the Moorfields Eye Hospital Children's Eye Centre.

A little known side effect of the 'Troubles' in Northern Ireland is that the province's public services have not been undergoing continuous reform as on the UK mainland. As a result they have not experienced the same high levels of uncertainty and rates of change of leadership. This stability has allowed health trusts like the South and East Belfast Health & Social Care Trust (SEBT) the time needed for successful innovation. Innovative practises cannot be implemented without changes in working culture, which requires painstakingly developed support from the staff. The resultant Community Treatment and Care Centres (CTCCs) of the SEBT embody transformations in health care ahead of their equivalents on the mainland and anticipated key proposals of the NHS Plan by two or three years.

View of Neptune Health Park across the canal.

In the late 1990s as Neptune Health Park was being completed, the SEBT was considering how to make more efficient use of its estate. This comprised over 80 scattered properties from which staff from several disciplines provided the full range of primary care, community care and social services. Together with John Cole of Northern Ireland Health Estates, SEBT, in a moment of epiphany, realised that having a clear vision of future models of service delivery had to come before the rationalisation of the estate in the context of a changing NHS. The Trust had been developing a vision of 'joined up service' focused on the needs, including very varied individual needs, of its public. Wherever possible, services currently delivered from hospital would be delivered nearer peoples' homes, and where appropriate in their homes. Health professionals were to be encouraged to work in an interdisciplinary way to ensure that health and social care aspects of their clients' problems were considered and addressed in the round. Such principles suggested a new kind of health centre, one that would be both a place for wide ranging consultation and treatment and also a base for outreach ('domiciliary') staff. The Trust, realising that this meant a profound change in working practises embarked on an extended programme of collaboration with their staff to devise new ways of working. It engaged the pioneering workplace design consultancy DEGW to carry out a feasibility study for the centres, including extensive consultation with staff.

SEBT established that its population of 210,000 people would be optimally served through three centres each catering for 70,000 people. The 80 old buildings would be sold to help pay for the new centres as they came on line. In 2001 Penoyre & Prasad, in partnership with Todd Architects of Belfast, won the commission to design the CTCCs, the first two of which were completed in 2005. These buildings have a range of diagnostic, clinical, therapeutic and social services as well as a cafe, Citizens' Advice Bureaux and health information resources. Almost half the floor space in these centres accommodates outreach staff. The buildings are planned around lofty atria which connect directly to the pavement outside and from which most of the functions can be easily and visibly accessed.

The North and West Belfast Trust's three Health and Wellbeing Centres follow similar principles of integrated care tailored to local culture and need. In England, the NHS LIFT programme has many parallel aims and an additional factor: the procurement method involves a property deal that places a high value on enabling future alternative uses of health facilities. Incorporating adaptability as a future office or residential accommodation has obvious implications for the structure, fabric and servicing of the building. It also suggests a conception of the building as generic urban fabric, extending the public realm of the city into its entrance and circulation design and helping to define and protect urban places adjacent to the building. Whatever the use of the building it must remain a valued part of the urban fabric. At The Heart of Hounslow Health Centre, our design creates a public plaza at the entrance, which leads to the building's atrium much as might be expected of a commercial design in the City of London.

The Arches Community Treatment and Care Centre, Belfast, with Todd Architects, 2001–2005

In the late 1990s the South East Belfast Health and Social Services Trust completely rethought the way it was providing services to its client population and decided to build three new centres providing integrated care, replacing 40 of its previous premises. The Arches accommodates six GP practices, clinical and minor operations suites, a Citizens' Advice Bureau, health information points; family and children's services and a range of others including physiotherapy, dentistry, podiatry and speech and language; as well as offices for domiciliary staff such as district nurses, health visitors and social/community workers. Bringing all these together, and providing shared meeting, training and staff facilities, is intended to create an entirely new working culture where information and understanding can be shared to improve the offer to the Trust's clients.

A new building was built in front of a remodelled existing health centre to create a five-storey atrium between the two. All the waiting spaces on all levels are adjacent to the atrium and can be pointed to from the reception desk so that people can find their way around this large building with ease. The building becomes increasingly private as the visitor goes up, the top floors being entirely for staff, including a staff 'club' on the roof with views of the characteristic Belfast hills.

The external elevations reflect the two main types of spaces within. Consulting rooms have a series of square openings within rendered insulation with subtly offset glazing and coloured panels. The open plan work spaces have glazed curtain walling with vertical silver mullions. Over the entrance the window pattern is interrupted with a four-storey high glass mural by one of a number of artists that were involved in the project.

Top: In the typical consulting room, services are contained over the corridor and bulkheads in the rooms contain the ventilation equipment. The soffit of the consulting room steps up towards the window. The window extends vertically to the soffit with more natural light penetrating the room.

Bottom: Patients waiting in the curved balconies of the waiting areas can always see the receptionist.

Opposite top: The building presents its longest elevation to the southeast and is glimpsed between the shops on Holywood Road. Martin Donlin's glazed banner above the canopy signals the entrance.

Opposite bottom: The old health centre before reconstruction.

Overleaf: The five-storey atrium with its Ficus longifolia tree is the hub. Flooded with daylight, the space is animated by the activity on the waiting balconies, bridges and stairs that protrude into it or line its vertical faces.

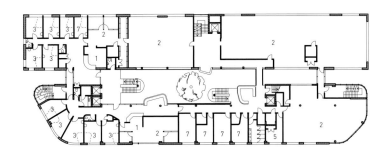

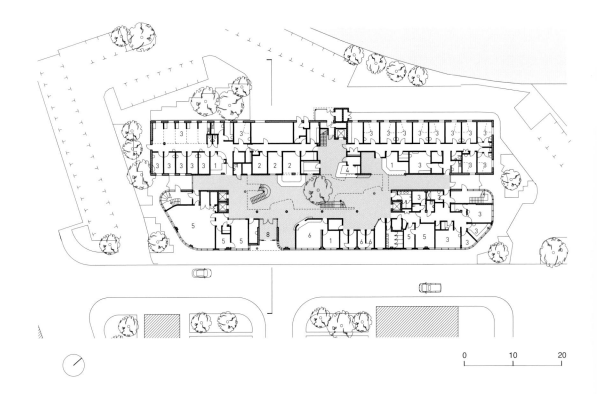

Top: The cellular nature of the third floor plan in the GP areas contrasts with the more open plan staff work areas to the east.

1 reception
2 office/staff
3 clinical
4 cafe kiosk
5 conference/interview
6 health information/Citizens' Advice Bureau
7 meeting room
8 entrance

Middle: The ground plan showing the entrance and main foyer to the building. A canal curves behind the site, separating it from the urban fabric to the north.

Bottom: Cross-section.

The Bradbury Community Treatment and Care Centre, with Todd Architects, 2001–2005

Like the earlier Arches Centre, The Bradbury Centre replaces many dispersed smaller service facilities to make a landmark Centre for health and social services serving a population of 70,000 in South Belfast. The building is on the corner made by the Lisburn Road and the railway that passes under it and has a tadpole-like plan: the head on the road and a tail stretching parallel to the railway. A freeform three-storey volume, taking up the scale of adjacent houses, and a long four-storey rectangular block along the railway, form a top-lit atrium between them. Patients and visitors enter this atrium, with a cafe, health information point, and a Citizens' Advice Bureau adjacent. The sub-receptions and waiting areas of most departments overlook the atrium and can in turn be easily seen upon entry. Corridors to the consulting and other spaces lead off galleries and all have pools of daylight either from the side or from above via light wells. The third floor contains offices and staff areas with fine views over the Belfast hills.

The freeform volume is formed internally with a series of sloping and staggered laminated timber baulks with glazing between and on the road elevation with curtain walling. The brick front of the long block reduces to a base round the corner with insulated render above perforated and large openings containing glazing and coloured panels using a palette reflecting mosses and herbs.

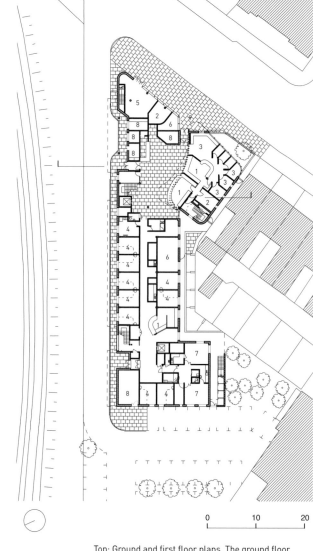

0   10   20

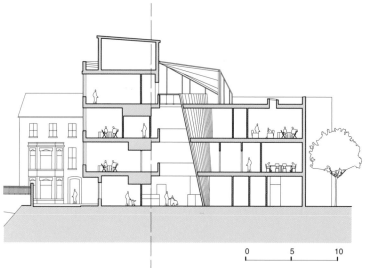

0   5   10

Top: Ground and first floor plans. The ground floor contains a minor surgery suite and consulting rooms for use on a sessional basis. The first floor is dedicated to Children's Services, with a waiting area overlooking the main atrium space.

1 reception
2 office
3 health information
4 consulting room
5 retail
6 conference/interview
7 treatment room
8 share/ancillary
9 entrance

Bottom: Cross-section stepped at the dashed line.

Opposite: The timber housing the reception area with the roof light beyond, bringing natural light into the lobby.

Humanising the health care institution

The patient experience

No single element of design has a greater impact on the experience of a large building than the quality of circulation spaces. How can the architect avoid creating soulless, confounding corridors so familiar in health centres and hospitals and make navigation easy for the visitor? Cost constraints drive down the quantity and quality of circulation space. The specified ratio of clinical space to circulation space is usually based on historical data and relates to buildings of the very kind that patient focused design is dedicated to getting away from. It is helpful at the start of the design to trace a patient's or visitor's journey through the building. We can write different storyboards for visits by different users from arriving to leaving. The moment of arrival and the first impression of the building is particularly important. Wherever possible we organise the arrival space to have plenty of daylight and a view into a green and pleasant courtyard. Often a cafe and information centre are immediately visible, as well as the most important element, a person who will take care of you, or at least direct you.

Despite improvements in appointment booking systems, waiting is and will continue to be a significant part of most peoples' experience of health care: what we term "in-between time" spent in "in-between spaces". Once in a room with a health practitioner, the patient enters a different state of mind. Though it is important for consulting rooms to be well designed, greater scope exists in the in-between spaces, for design to make the patient's experience a happy one. Waiting areas have traditionally been utilitarian and regimented, driven by the wish to pack as many people in as little a space as possible. But why not disperse waiting into smaller clusters with spatial variety and perhaps pleasant views, internal or external. The traditional old copies of *Reader's Digest* and *Home & Garden* can be supplemented with other opportunities for patients to use their time, browsing information at a terminal or listening to music, for example.

The patient's journey is greatly eased if a building's layout is as apparent, or legible, as possible; if the design promotes 'intuitive wayfinding'. Our larger health care buildings are generally planned round a lofty hallway or atrium such that the receptionist can directly point to where the

patient needs to go. Colour is used to further help distinguish different areas. Signage then acts as a supportive layer of information, not the primary method of directing people. Beyond their value in assisting the patient and visitor's journey, the spatial quality, scale and surface character of common spaces have the capacity to raise spirits and communicate care, respect and confidence.

At the Children's Eye Centre at Moorfields, patients and visitors arrive at a lofty foyer and cafe with few overt associations with health care apart from a 'shop' where glasses and prosthetics can be fitted. The waiting children range from six month old babies to over 16s and there is a bank of computers in an arcade-like space for use by the older ones. From here a light shaft runs up four upper floors, on each of which the pattern of arrival is the same, crossing the void via a bridge to find the reception desk and waiting area for the various sub-departments. On the main out-patients floor, a projecting bay juts out over the street and a fibreglass pod offers a private space for older children. The surgical patients have access to a small play terrace while they wait in the pre-op area. The aim of these architectural devices, interpenetrating spaces – bridges, pods, bay window, terrace – is to give a distinct identity to each part and to enrich the experience of using the whole building.

The staff experience

Contact time with health practitioners and carers is the most valued part of patients' and their companions' encounter with a health care institution. Patient focus leads naturally to providing good conditions for staff to do their work; to design for operational effectiveness as well as high environmental quality: good daylight, acoustics, air quality, spatial variety and high standards of finish. In modern health care buildings as much as half the accommodation may be for administrative or for outreach staff, which makes them like offices to most intents and purposes.

In his book, *The New Office*, Francis Duffy of DEGW sets out the huge changes in working methods that have simultaneously brought about, and been enabled by, a complete rethink of what an office can be.[9] Space utilisation studies, for example, show that in traditional offices the drive to demonstrate status meant that the people who use space the least, the higher managers who are often

Typical storyboard to track user experience, 2003.

out at meetings, have the most spacious offices while the people who use space for the most time, such as clerical staff, use much less area, being densely packed into open plan spaces. DEGW have combined this observation with an analysis of different kinds of work patterns, from highly individual and autonomous to collective and interdependent, to create office layouts that use space far more efficiently (doing the same or more with less space) and effectively (achieving greater performance by people).

For many administrative tasks, Information Technology makes it possible to work anywhere that is comfortable, reasonably quiet and equipped with a seat and a ledge for a laptop. However, there are other tasks such as making confidential phone calls and taking notes, which require more dedicated environments. By studying the various tasks involved in providing services it is possible to devise highly flexible and versatile environments that are efficient, feel open and inclusive, and allow for future change. In integrated care centres, with their several services and agencies to deliver them, good social spaces for staff increase the chances of interaction across professional boundaries as well as promoting cohesion within. Such spaces are usefully seen as 'staff clubs' and in our designs we have placed them in the parts of the building with the best outlook where staff can literally turn away from immediate concerns and refresh their energies.

Identity

Except in some emergencies, the family GP is our gateway to the health care system. Preserving the special relationship between the GP practice and its clientele within a large multi-agency and multi-functional integrated care centre presents an architectural challenge: how do you give each component of the centre the right identity while also expressing the unity of the whole? In working with the staff and managers of The Heart of Hounslow Health Centre, in west London, we put forward alternative models to help define the nature of the place. At one end the centre could be conceptualised as a 'village' with different 'houses'; at the other as a single corporate building.

Organisational diagrams drawn on a flip chart during consultation for The Heart of Hounslow Health Centre, London, 2003.

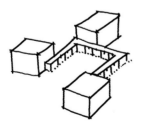

cloister

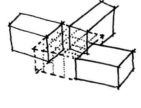

cluster

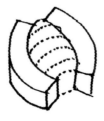

unitary

The village model gives clear identity to each part and relies on the 'high street' and 'green' to bind the parts. The unitary building clearly expresses the integration of services but carries the danger of institutionalism and appearing impersonal. The clients unanimously chose the single building model because they wanted to give out a clear signal of the transformation from an atomised, 'silo mentality' set of services to a coherent and 'joined up' service. While expressing unity and the power of the institution, the architecture must make space for the expression of empathy. The plan form of The Heart of Hounslow Centre is like a pair of hands cradling a space between them. This form creates an elongated internal street, which is wider in the middle, so as to make a 'heart' for the building. Architectural devices such as clerestorey and roof lights, tinted glass casting colour shadows on the walls, bridges animating the elongated space all lift the spirit of this place. Moving around the building people can always relate to this space, and the circulation routes that lead out from it are short, distinctive and, as far as possible, day-lit. Users have described this building as having the feel of a hotel, with the connotations of holidays and the good feelings associated with these.

Expression

Hospitals in towns and cities have always been prominent civic buildings, not least because of their sheer size. Large modern hospitals tend to present a heavily utilitarian aspect. Their techno-medical prowess is much valued but their appearance generally represents just what patient focused care is dedicated to banish. Some nineteenth century hospitals, like Giles Gilbert Scott's Leeds General Infirmary or Hospital de St Pau in Barcelona, display a characteristic self-confidence coupled with a welcoming civic presence that is inspiring in its engagement with the urban realm. Our designs for the new generation of large community-based health centres have a degree of civic prominence that is an expression of confidence in the health system, but without overt branding as health facilities, except for the name board. The colours on the facade of The Arches Centre in Belfast make it stand out as a beacon of renewal in its run down surroundings, while the canopy under the three-storey glass mural signals its entrance. At The Heart of Hounslow Centre the sinuous facade, with coloured panels in the window strip, sets it apart from the mundane offices of the town centre. At the same time, a small urban piazza binds the entrance of the centre to the urban realm. In our design for the Children's Eye Centre at Moorfields in London, the apparent bulk of the building is lifted off the ground floor to allow the street to have a strong visual link with the entrance foyer and its cafe. The facade's distinctive pattern of irregularly placed solar control louvres, and the circular peep holes in the flank facing the public transport route, respond to the demand in the brief for the design to represent the Centre's status as a world renowned institution while also making it easy to find in its back street location.

The Heart of Hounslow Health Centre, London, 2003–2007

This Centre was built in pursuit of a new ambition for primary care in the NHS whereby a large range of services is gathered together in one place so as to better serve patients, develop staff capacities and provide 'joined up' delivery. This ambition needed to be expressed in the civic qualities of the architecture. The building was procured through a Public Private Partnership, which means that possible future uses of the building need to be considered in the design. Together with the constantly changing nature of health services, this makes a compelling case for adaptive design.

The Heart of Hounslow hosts four GP practices, a range of clinical services, physiotherapy, podiatry, dentistry and speech and language services, social care outreach services, special facilities for children, adolescents and people with learning disabilities and a health information/cafe area. Almost half of the accommodation is workspace for domiciliary staff. All these functions are organised around a five-storey high atrium with bridges and galleries, and the parts of the building can be easily pointed out from the reception desk.

The concrete structure of the building is organised on a simple repetitive module that allows areas to be set up as open plan offices or as cellular clinical rooms with non-structural internal partitions. Externally, windows alternating with coloured aluminium panels form horizontal bands. If necessary the window and panel position can be changed to follow internal reconfiguration; but they are positioned in such a way that partition positions can be extensively altered and still permit day-lit internal rooms. The services strategy, with its ducted air heating and comfort cooling, supports this adaptability with the main distribution in a central spine following the corridor zone.

The atrium is painted white so that the coloured glass in clerestorey windows and the entrance screens cast ever-changing patterns on its internal surfaces. The staff 'club' is located on the top floor with panoramic views over London.

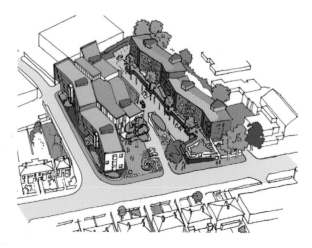

Top: A detail of the coloured glass.

Left: Aerial sketch of scheme showing context and proposed housing on the site of the replaced old health centre.

Opposite: Interior bridges in the main atrium space.

0   10   20

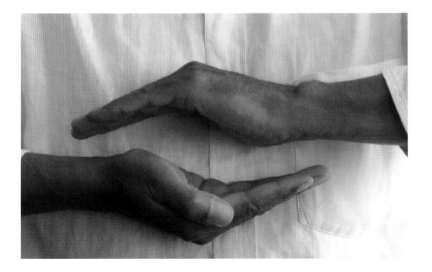

Opposite: Ground and first floor plans. The waiting areas relate directly to the atrium via the reception desks so that patients do not have to wander through internal corridors.

1 reception
2 waiting
3 early years/family
4 office
5 treatment/therapy
6 ancillary
7 testing/observation/assessment
8 consulting room
9 gym
10 training/teaching
11 library
12 entrance

Top: Street facade. Being on the air path to Heathrow this is a sealed building to protect from noise.

Bottom: Interlocking hands—a diagram of the plans.

Opposite: Street facade.

Top: Entrance facade. The main entrance leads from a small new piazza with a tree.

Bottom: Cross-section.

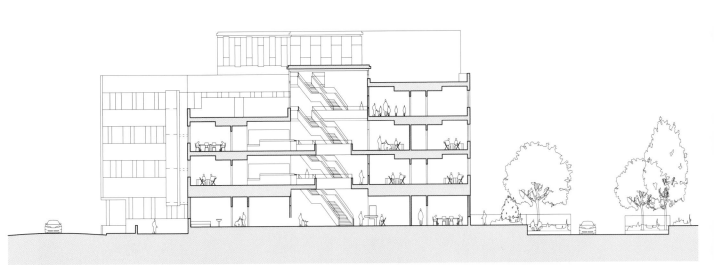

0   5   10

Mental health and the sensory environment

We were short-listed in 1993 for a competition to design a nursing home for 40 people with dementia, then described as "the Elderly Mentally Ill" (EMI).[10] The patients were to be transferred from Tooting Bec Hospital, where they were housed in nineteenth century Nightingale Wards. There could be no starker manifestation of institutionalism: originally the inmates of the mental illness wings of Tooting Bec could have included women whose 'symptoms' were having illegitimate children; even in the 1980s the same institution would have housed people with paranoid schizophrenic conditions, as well as people with mental functions impaired purely through the aging process. In the 1980s such institutions began to be closed down and people with mental illness dispersed under the Care in the Community programme to smaller specialised units. Woodlands Nursing Home was part of this programme.

Our scheme, on the restricted inner city site, was based on the creation of four large homes of ten residents, each with its own garden. The homes were L-shaped in plan with the garden nestling in the crook of the L, its outer boundaries secured by a timber trellised fence. Similar secure gardens had been found to work well by affording residents freedom to wander in safety both inside and outside. We were convinced that such freedoms were at the essence of the dignity that was lacking in institutionalised care and would be a paramount aim in the new home. The key move in our winning entry was the creation of surprisingly large gardens at both ground and first floor level. Their size was enabled by the smaller 'footprint' of the two-storey solution, creating raised levels using rubble and spoil left on the site from the demolition of previous buildings and the foundation excavation for the new one.

In making the transition from a design that satisfies operational and organisational needs to one that also positively affects peoples' sense of wellness, an architect has to engage with their sensory apparatus, and the intuitive and reflexive aspects of their intellect, their memories, their values and curiosity. The obvious way of doing this is to put oneself in the place of the building's users so as to arrive at rough propositions and then to inform, test and refine these through consultation and dialogue. Designing for elderly people with dementia presents a particular challenge: the residents are there 24

Tooting Bec Hospital, SW17

hours a day, which calls for an environment that is as supportive and pleasurable as possible; however it is, of course, extremely difficult to communicate with the residents and to put oneself in their place.

Elderly people in our society are often considered to have few sensual needs. If they are suffering from dementia such needs are further neglected. Our thesis in the design of Woodlands Nursing Home (and the subsequent Newhaven Down House) was that precisely because we cannot accurately communicate with people who have dementia, we must create an environment full of opportunities for stimulating the senses. And this could be combined with clues that may help the person locate themselves in their home. Of the five physical senses, a building's design can address all but taste. Light and colour enrich the surroundings, make places distinctive and animate corridors. Different textures on handrails and doorknobs can offer tactile clues to help locate places. As regards the acoustic environment unwanted noise can be reduced by carpets and absorbent wall and ceiling surfaces, and welcome sounds may be added by wind chimes and birdsong. And the careful specification of floors and other surfaces, together with good maintenance and natural ventilation, helps avoid the twin smells associated with nursing homes: urine and disinfectant. Pleasant smells can be introduced by cut flowers, by scents and by the proximity of a garden.

The two wings of the homes have five bedrooms each, along a corridor punctuated by side lights on the lower floor and by clerestorey windows on the upper floor. The rooms are designed to be places of calm with pipe-work tucked away behind shelves and the boxy safe-temperature radiator concealed below the window cill. Immediately outside the ground floor window is a raised planting bed just below window cill height. This allows people in wheelchairs to touch plants and do gardening while establishing distance from the window for privacy.

At the centre of the L are the dining and sitting rooms with easy access to the garden, and at one end of each house is a small garden room for more intimate social encounters — a visit from a relative, say, or just somewhere to be quiet, in privacy, away from other residents, and an alternative to the bedroom. Notably, such a function was not a simple 'given' of the brief, but emerged in conversation between architect and client.

The design of Woodlands Nursing Home is also an exercise in creating a secluded community within a dense inner city area. The raised gardens act as buffers to the outside making a safe haven for residents, protected from the public realm of the city. The entrance forecourt connects firmly with the surrounding streets and on approach the visitor immediately glimpses the central garden, its design inspired by the Islamic gardens of the Alhambra, with a fountain, a rill and a geometric layout. Of the other three gardens one is of a Japanese style; another, with its spreading tree, like a corner of a Georgian country estate and the third a simple English cottage garden with a rose arbour. The distinctiveness of the four gardens gives identity to different parts of the whole and, with Georgina Livingston, the project's landscape architect, we devised alternative routes that carers and patients could take around each garden, and from garden to garden, to create within this constrained and secluded world a sense of expansiveness and multiplicity of experience.

Opposite left: Historic photograph of the original Tooting Bec Hospital, late nineteenth century.

Opposite right: Model of Woodlands Nursing Home, 1993–1995.

Alongside patients and staff, patients relatives and carers play a crucial part in health care and particularly in mental health care. The positive influence of the environment on the visitor becomes a key factor in the design. The impact of the new home on the wellbeing and morale of the residents is hard to gauge, but its impact on visitors is evident. The husband of one resident was so grateful for the home making his wife happier, that he sponsored the hair salon after she died. At Newhaven Downs House patients in the old wards had few visitors, especially grandchildren. In the new building children felt much more welcome and some would drop in on their way home from school.

We were told that when patients with dementia were moved from one institution to another there was typically a 40 per cent jump in mortality and as many as five or six people could die within a short period. In the event, no patient died following the move from Tooting Bec to Woodlands. The same happened at Newhaven Downs House, which at the request of patients and relatives was built in two phases so that existing patients would not have to move away. Only a thorough research project can establish the reasons for this large reduction in mortality. In the meantime we work on the assumption that a synergy between improved care and a thoughtful architecture saved lives.

This page and opposite: Interior view of a typical bedroom at Woodlands Nursing Home and a design sketch.

1 "Traditionally, Western medicine has focused on a model of disease whereby pathology was regarded as well defined alteration in normal physiology that should respond to appropriate pharmaceutical or surgical interventions. However, in recent years patient focused medicine has become an important aspect of Penoyre & Prasad's work. The concept of health related quality of life has represented an important advance in dealing with these concerns in our treatment of disease." Sauder, DN, "Editorial", *Journal of Cutaneous Medicine and Surgery*, 1;4(1):1, January 2000.

2 The word malaria literally translates as bad 'air', the fear of which, together with the theory that 'miasma' rising in the night air was a principle carrier of diseases caused people to keep windows shut at night.

3 Nightingale, Florence, *Diary*, 1860.

4 The pioneering work by R Ulrich ("Viewing through a window may influence recovery from surgery", *Science*, vol. 224 (27), April 1984, pp. 420–421) has been followed by a number of others usefully gathered together in the following publications by the Commission for Architecture and the Built Environment: *A Bibliography of Design Value*, London, December 2001. *The Value of Good Design: How Buildings and Spaces Create Economic and Social Value*, London, November 2002, and Stowe, Derek A, "Transformation in Health Care Architecture: from the Hospital to a Health Care Organism" in *Changing Hospital Design*, ed. S Prasad, London: RIBA Publications, 2007.

5 Philip Powell played a key role at two points in the development of our practice — he chaired the jury that judged our competition entry for the redevelopment of Newhaven Downs Hospital and was on the selection panel for the works at Snape Maltings Concert Hall.

6 George Scott Williamson and Innes Pearse were the GPs. Owen Williams was a Civil Engineer who also designed the celebrated Daily Express Building in London and the Boots Factory in Nottingham.

7 Around 300 such centres will have been established by the end of the programme in 2009.

8 The NHS Plan published by the UK government in July 2000 marked, amongst other things, the decisive shift in the UK health care system from a hospital led service to a primary care led service. The plan envisaged building 500 new 'one stop primary care centres' and stated "Many GPs will be working in teams from modern multi-purpose premises alongside nurses, pharmacists, dentists, therapists, opticians, midwives and social care staff."

9 Duffy, Francis, *The New Office*, London: Conran Octopus Ltd, 1997.

10 Nowadays many of the patients will have been diagnosed as suffering from Alzheimers disease.

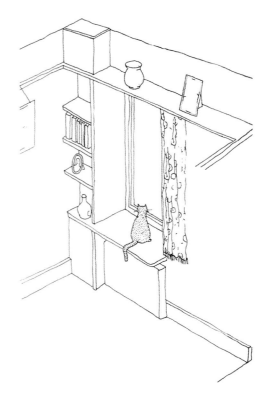

Woodlands Nursing Home, Kennington, London, 1993–1995

This nursing home was built to provide care for 40 elderly mentally infirm people, who were previously in the wards of the huge Tooting Bec Hospital. Whilst ensuring safety, security and privacy the design aims to afford maximum freedom and dignity to the residents, most of whom suffer from dementia. The home's human scale is set by its four houses, each with two five bedroom wings and a secure garden nestling in the crook of the 'L' they form. Although the building is on two floors the sculpted landscape design making use of spoil left on the site from previous demolitions allows level access from the houses to their own gardens, whether on ground or first floor. Each house has its own living, dining, quiet room and kitchenette, as well as staff and ancillary spaces. A central theme of the design has been to aid orientation while stimulating the senses: spaces have different qualities of light, space, colour and acoustic treatment; surfaces, such as support rails, and door handles are of different textures in different places.

The roof construction uses inexpensive trussed rafters in a new way to form clerestorey glazing at the ridges to bring light into the corridors. Walls are of externally insulated and rendered masonry on a red brick base which in places form "crinkle crankle" walls with raised flower beds at wheelchair accessible height that also serve to give privacy to ground floor bedrooms. The houses are joined at the entrance with a glazed link, which gives a glimpse into the central formal garden.

Top: The central courtyard looking back towards the entrance.

Bottom: Cross-section showing a raised garden.

Opposite: At the end of the buildings the cross-section is revealed on the exterior. Brackets help create generous overhangs of the aluminium roof.

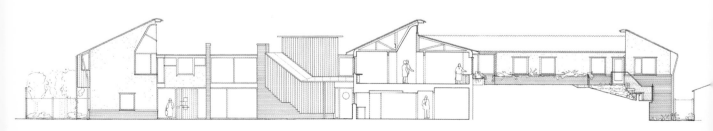

Opposite top: The northeastern house with its large, simple garden.

Opposite bottom left: Corridors are double-loaded and day-lit by clerestorey windows. Textured timber handrails, skirtings and architraves provide warmth and tactility amongst the easy clean surfaces.

Opposite bottom right: The stepped landscape is richly planted, this garden having a Japanese theme. The brick retaining walls continue the construction vocabulary of the building.

Right: Ground and first floor plans.

1 entrance
2 office
3 clinic
4 visitor
5 quiet room
6 dining
7 living
8 staff
9 kitchen and service wing
10 salon
11 seminar
12 reminiscence room
13 laundry
14 plant

Bottom: The landscape architect's drawing of the gardens illustrating the four gardens amongst the houses.

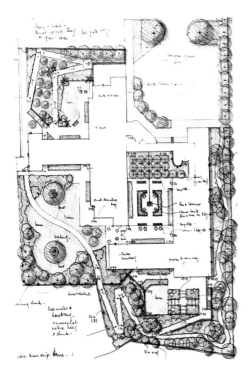

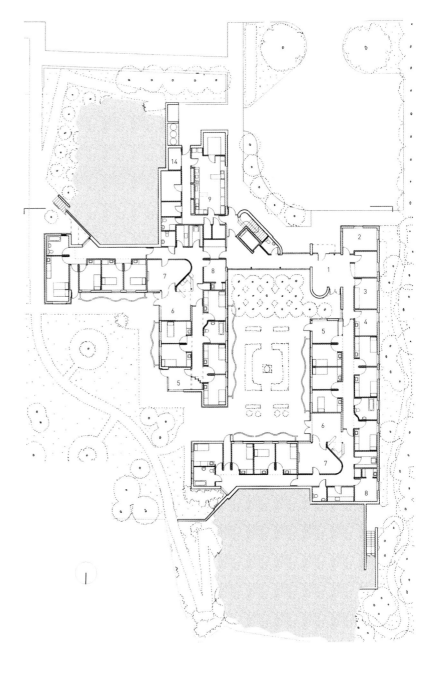

Newhaven Downs House, East Sussex, 1994–1997

The old Newhaven Downs Hospital sat on a strip of land parallel to the contours on a north facing slope above the town between the edge of a wood and a long sward. This project replaced its large clinical wards with more comfortable, dignified, and less institutional environments for frail and mentally infirm residents. By placing the building at the upper edge of the site and nestling it into the steeper gradient of the hill, the fall across the site is used to provide level access from a set of ground and first floor houses into gardens and landscaped areas.

Like that of the earlier Woodlands Nursing Home, the design is focused on gently stimulating the senses, not only for pleasure, but also to help orientate residents with impaired faculties: textured handrails and door handles, coloured wall panels, lofty top-lit corridors, hardwood joinery. Sitting areas have fine views over Newhaven and the Downs to the south, and the main entrance has the air of a country hotel.

Externally the building's architecture takes its cues from the old chalk and red brick field walls that subdivided the site. The load bearing blockwork structure is clad with brick and chalky render on thick insulation under simple concrete tile roofs to provide a high thermal mass energy efficient envelope. A number of artists added works that responded to the design: such as the decals on the high level clerestorey windows which cast beautiful patterns on the walls opposite, and the waiting area carpet in the later Polyclinic, which alludes to herbs and medicinal plants.

Top: View from entrance approach with successive wings.

Bottom: North/south cross-section through the building showing the relationship to the hill.

Opposite: The front entrance at night.

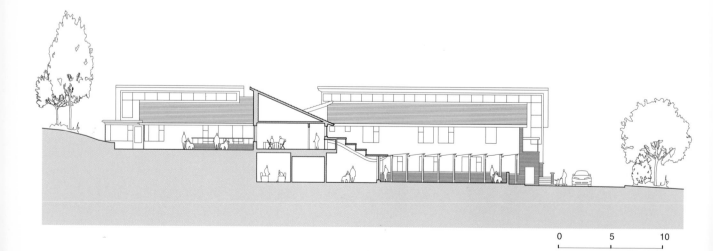

0   5   10

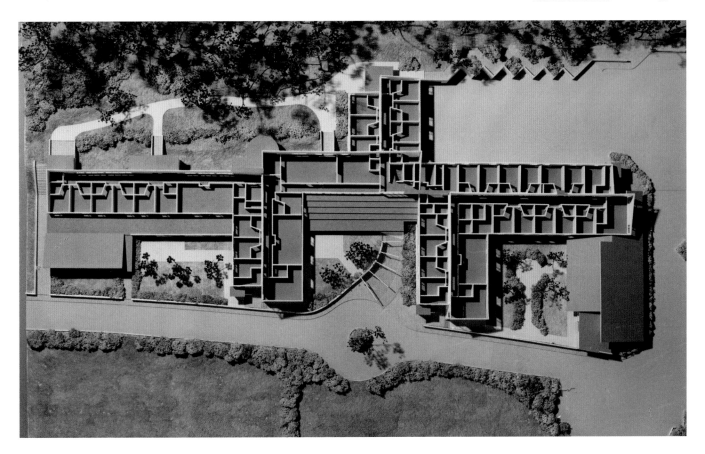

Opposite top left: The tendency of corridors to be dull and institutional is countered with generous height and being top-lit, and by connecting to the outside with views and a sitting place at their ends.

Opposite top right: View of the model towards the entrance, showing the overall arrangement.

Opposite bottom: The residents' day lounge with its secluded garden is intended to have the air of a country hotel rather than a nursing home. The terraced form of the roof reflects the stepped landscape and the strips of glazing allow light to bounce off the roof surface onto the ceiling inside.

Top: Model showing the plan of the home and its gardens in the landscape. The corridors that run the length of the building have offsets to make 'pausing' places.

Bottom: East/west cross-section through a wing of the building.

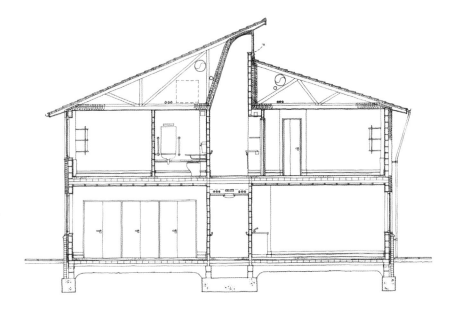

LEARNING

*The purpose of schooling and the methods of teaching, appear in the philosophy and morals of
all civilisations, but have become the subject of a wider and often passionate debate in modern
democracies. School building programmes, such as that in 1950s and 60s, and again in the early
twenty-first century in England, draw attention to the relationship between schooling and school
buildings, between learning and learning environments, a subject we have been closely involved in.*

The hidden curriculum

If schools existed simply to impart knowledge there would be little role for architecture. Indeed with
the advent of ubiquitous Information and Communication Technology (ICT) there might be no need for
buildings at all. Some ICT enthusiasts argue precisely for that, education without specifically created
places, inadvertently illustrating the survival of the idea that a school's main and possibly only purpose
is transference of knowledge or even just raw information. In our work with schools and ICT we have
found the opposite. By taking care so well of the functional aspects of knowledge transfer, and therefore
reducing the requirement for people to be in the same place simply to exchange information, ICT has
crystallised the true role of the design of places: to assist human communication and self-realisation in all
its subtlety, complexity and richness.

At different times and in different cultures schools have consistently represented a far richer
project than imparting knowledge; from the Greek philosopher Plutarch, "The mind is not a vessel to be
filled but a fire to be ignited", to the 1944 Education Act, almost two millennia later:

> ... it shall be the duty of the local education authority for every area, so far as their powers
> extend, to continue towards the spiritual, mental and physical developments of the community.[1]

In many cultures the place of the school, such as the madrasa in Islamic societies, and the high
status of teachers as pillars of the community are inseparable. School buildings have been important
community hubs, representing civilisation through learning and culture, and frequently functioning
as practical resources for community activities. At the same time schools are instruments for the
socialisation of young people; places where fundamentals of social behaviour are learned, personal
strategies developed for dealing with the world, and information, knowledge and wisdom of a variety
not officially on offer learnt from peers.

Education as a process of socialisation is sometimes called the "hidden curriculum", a phrase
coined by the sociologist Philip Jackson in 1968.[2] Benson R Snyder borrowed it for the title of his

Landscaped courtyard at the
heart of the Olney Campus of
Ousdale School, near Milton
Keynes, 2007.

1970 book, which argued that the implicit academic and social norms in educational institutions inhibited independent thought and creativity.[3] Radical thinkers like Paul Goodman, Paolo Freire and Ivan Illich had already been saying that society, and particularly the state, used imparting knowledge through compulsory schooling as a pretext for creating compliant citizens and consumers rather than independent, free and creative thinkers and doers. So the hidden curriculum has sometimes had a sinister cast, rather like a 'hidden agenda', and has therefore been used to support the libertarian case against mass education for 'de-schooling society'.[4]

Whatever its history the phrase "hidden curriculum" remains useful as a catch-all term to describe all that is not formally included in the school curriculum but which nevertheless is recognised in today's educational thinking as being central to the development of the whole individual. The design of the physical environments can greatly influence this relationship. Teachers at the Ashburton Learning Village, 2006, a community school combined with a public library, reported a significant change in the children's attitude after they moved to the building that we had designed. They attributed this to the varied and interconnected circulation and social spaces of the school, together with the open feeling produced by glazing giving views into the classrooms. The building, with its triple-height central 'street' seemed to treat the children with such respect that some in this tough south London area could not believe that it was actually for them. The vandalism that plagued the old library has disappeared and students who would not previously be seen near books are using it. The skills and attitudes learnt in the social space can have a major impact on the learning that takes place in the classroom and laboratory and vice versa. The design of external spaces is crucial for the hidden curriculum to flourish; and variety is a principal quality: places to be quiet, to be noisy, to be with others, to be away from others. The series of interlinked courtyards of the old London County Council buildings that we transformed in our design for the Charter School, 1999, provide just such variety. If a school is analogous to a village or small town then the internal circulation and the external social spaces, as opposed to sports facilities, are the public realm, the social glue that binds the community.

As well as supporting the pedagogy of both the formal and the hidden curriculum, the design of a school has to support its function as a community resource and the school's symbolic value. For state funded schools these wider aims are directed in a number of ways: representing the school as

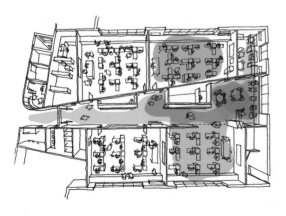

an efficient, attractive and caring business; representing the community and government as a well organised, forward-thinking and democratic entity; representing the state as a force for good. At the time of writing there is a demand, as vague as it is strong, for the design of a school to express something exciting, somehow connected with the future, perhaps as a promise that things are going to be better. In this last respect the task of the architect could not be more different than it was during the first flush of publicly financed school building in the late nineteenth century when dignified and assured architecture such as that of London Board Schools spoke of the reserved might and eternal verities of Victorian culture.

Some people involved in school building programmes today think that buildings are of little relevance and cite inspirational teachers who achieved educational excellence in leaking tin sheds. We totally agree that only people and not buildings can transform education; but well designed buildings will help the best people do their job even better. At the same time, designers need to understand how that job and its aims have been changing and will go on changing.

Pedagogies

Halfway through our design work on a comprehensive school in Essex the head teacher visited the United States and decided on a new organisation of the school completely different from what was in the brief: instead of being divided into five years each with seven classes there would be three smaller 'schools' within the school and a degree of mixed age teaching. In an east London school a new pedagogy, based on a horseshoe shaped layout of all the desks in a classroom, and therefore requiring a room 25 per cent larger than the norm, has been linked with a steep rise in educational attainment. To reduce distractions, the rooms have relatively smaller windows with high cills, and no views to or from the corridor. At the other extreme, an award winning south London school has completely open plan teaching, in part inspired by Danish experiments. Educationalists, teachers, parents and politicians, and of course pupils, have many different views on the best way to educate a child or young person and the educational landscape today looks like a messy collage of old and new pedagogies.

British private education in the nineteenth and twentieth centuries refined effective ways of developing young people from moneyed families to advance themselves and serve as the governing classes of an industrialised and more democratic society. Today, nearly 150 years after the first introduction of compulsory education, and 60 years after the establishment of free universal education, the leadership of the major political parties remains very largely privately educated, as does the membership of the judiciary. In all the professions privately educated people are vastly overrepresented relative to their proportions in society as whole. The teaching practices developed in private schools were initially adopted for publicly funded schools and in particular for grammar schools. The fundamentals of these practises, compulsory attendance, school uniforms, explicit norms

Left: The layout of a teaching wing at Ashburton Learning Village, 2006.

Right: Oban Street School, Poplar, 1881, a typical example of the work of the London School Board.

Hellerup school, Copenhagen, Arkitema, 2003. The learning spaces are all of open plan arranged around a central atrium which also acts as the main meeting space.

Opposite left: Bedales School, Petersfield, Hampshire.

Opposite right: Sevagram Ashram, India, established by Mahatma Gandhi.

of acceptable behaviour, a school's day approximating to the working day, the day divided into lessons, the pupils divided into year groups and then into classes, the classical division and hierarchy of subjects, the teachers mirroring these arrangements, teachers acting in *loco parentis*, and the annual cycles of terms and tests all continue to form the basic armature around or against which changes, from radical to minor, are tried and implemented.

Underpinning these fundamentals of traditional schooling is an assumption about the nature of the similarity and difference between individuals: children within an age group, with a few exceptions, should be taught in the same way using a standard set of instructions which embody desirable goals. Naturally they have individual personalities but these are to be nurtured through specialisation in the later school years and in extra-curricular activities. Teaching is something adults do to children. Although widely disproved, the notion that children are miniature adults has not disappeared from the education system.[4]

Some of the most effective challenges to these assumptions came from Rudolf Steiner, 1861–1925, and Maria Montessori, 1870–1952. For Steiner education was but one part of a bigger theory of existence, anthroposophy, and for Montessori understanding the child was the key to solving problems of conflict on a worldwide scale. Both believed, albeit in quite distinct ways, that the child was fundamentally different from an adult. Steiner believed that the child must be helped to develop her or his own potential rather than be pushed towards goals that adults and society thought desirable. The secret of education lay in understanding the relationship between the physical and spiritual. Montessori believed in nurturing and supporting the child's innate curiosity and superior ability to synthesise experience, through teachers acting as guides and helpers rather than controllers.

Steiner's and Montessori's thinking influenced teaching around the world, sometimes chiming with local philosophies and experiments. Cecil Reddie, 1858–1932, credited as the pioneer of Progressive Education in the UK had already established Abbotsholme School, Warwickshire in 1889, where in contrast to the academic and sport centred regimes of other private schools, the focus was on the spiritual and intellectual development of the individual in close communion with nature.[5] John Badley, 1865–1967, was hugely influenced by Reddie and went on to found Bedales in Hampshire, which Greg Penoyre attended. Badley cited many other influences on his pedagogy including Maria Montessori and John Dewey, who believed in the effectiveness of "learning by doing".[6]

In Mahatma Gandhi's pedagogy *Nai Taleem* (New Education) learning by doing is a key aspect. Children should be exposed to the processes of producing goods and services so that academic abstraction of curricular subjects may be rooted in the life experience of the child. I was brought up in Sevagram in central India in a largely self-sufficient Gandhian community where the mornings at school were taken up by planting, harvesting, spinning, weaving, crafts and so on, very much like the regime at Reddie's Abbotsholme and to some extent at Bedales. Formal lessons took place in the afternoon. Maths and science in particular could be directly related to productive activities. Secondary age students were able to take on specialised studies in agriculture, animal husbandry and many other vocations as well as academic subjects. For Gandhi, and for the poet-artist Rabindranath Tagore, propounding and implementing radical educational philosophies was part of the struggle to liberate the country, and therefore education, from imperial control.[7] Nai Taleem was effective in an agrarian society but the absence of formal qualifications that an increasingly exam obsessed and urbanised outside world could recognise discouraged entrants. With no one to develop it for a changing society this version of learning by doing withered away in the 1960s. Tagore's special combination of education, art and agrarian culture had already hugely influenced Leonard Elmhirst who bought Dartington Hall in Devon and founded a school based on progressive lines and a college with buildings by the radical modernist architect William Lescaze.

Steiner's and Montessori's educational theories in parallel with the work of theorists like Jean Piaget and fringe experimenters like AS Neill at Summerhill School in the UK, helped to establish what came to be known in the 1970s and 80s as "child centred education".[8] The child centred approach had a huge impact on state primary schools which underwent a permanent transformation in the 1970s together with a general acceptance that before puberty at least, children learn and develop in a way that bears little relationship to the way adults process information and stimuli. It had much less impact on state secondary education.

The Charter School, Dulwich, London, 1999–2003

The original 1950s school buildings, designed in the London County Council Architects' Department under Sir Leslie Martin were organised around a series of courtyards and had many fine features, such as the unusual main hall with its two-way facing stage and foyer under the steeply raked second auditorium. However, they suffered with defects typical of buildings of their period: prone to leaks and draughts, too hot in the summer, costly to heat in the winter and riddled with asbestos. After the previous school closed down, the Local Education Authority acceded to local parental pressure to create a new 1,200 place comprehensive school.

Our competition winning design answered the Local Education Authority's brief to transform the image as well as the operations of the school by reversing the previous access arrangements: the original rear entrance on a higher ground level became the new front and the students look out over London when they come into school every day. Through a large opening cut into a corner, they enter a huge new foyer created out of a neglected courtyard, with a tree-like steel structure holding up the roof, which acts as a collector of rainwater and solar energy, to encourage consciousness of sustainability. From this foyer, new glazed routes lead to the other pavilions of the school; its hall, dining block, library and teaching spaces with views into a series of re-landscaped courts between suitable for different activities. All this was achieved within a year and in subsequent phases the main five-storey teaching block has been re-fitted and re-clad with a high performance facade and the main hall has been upgraded with a new audio-visual installation and refurbished with improved access, lighting and a cafe/foyer.

Top: The new school entrance.

Bottom: Model of the school campus. The two teaching blocks in the foreground were the first to be refurbished. That on the right hand side has the new foyer canopy and entrance. The large, entirely re-clad teaching block is at the rear and between is the hall which is connected to the rest of the school with new covered walkways.

Opposite: The main teaching block viewed across adjacent playing fields. The built-in natural ventilation louvres and irregular window pattern are absorbed into the colour composition which becomes lighter towards the sky. The sixth form block shows as a prominent orange bay.

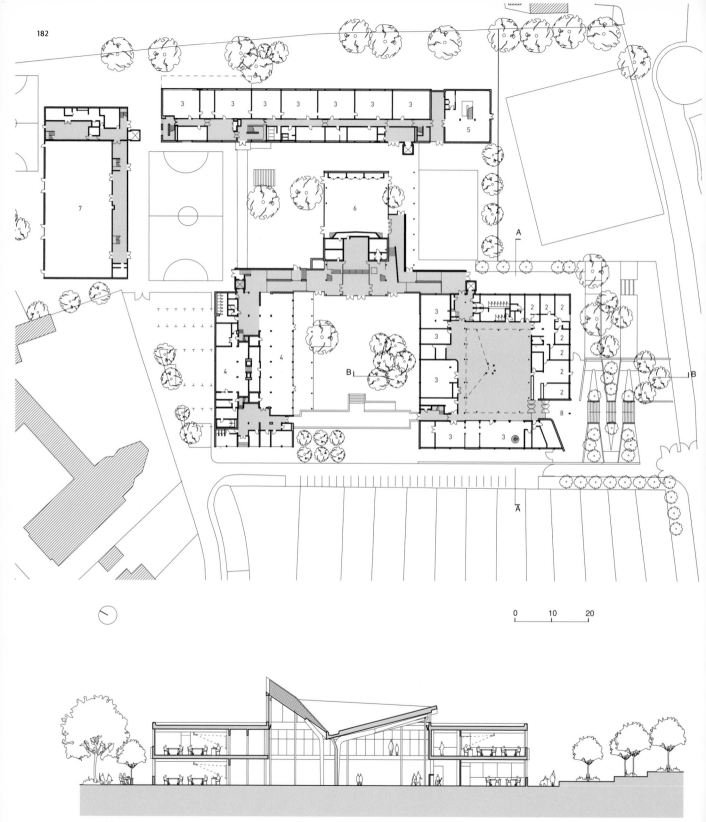

Opposite top: Ground plan.

1 reception
2 office/administration
3 teaching space
4 dining/kitchen
5 library
6 school hall
7 sports hall
8 entrance

Top: Interior of entrance foyer. The space is used for a variety of school functions and by local people.

Opposite bottom and bottom: Sections through the entrance foyer showing the tree-like structure of the roof.

BB

0   5   10

On arriving in London in 1962, too late to have taken the '11 Plus' examination that determined whether a child's future would be academic or vocational, I started at the local secondary modern school (vocational). Given a second chance at '13 Plus' I then went to the local grammar school (academic) and then the Labour government of 1964–1970 transformed secondary education, abolishing selection at the age of 11. Both my schools merged into a single comprehensive school and this series of flukes meant that I experienced all three major state systems for secondary schooling. The original ambition of the 1944 Education Act was that vocational skills taught in secondary modern schools would have the same esteem as academic skills taught in grammar schools. Sadly that is not how society saw it, and the advent of comprehensive schools has made little difference to a fundamental inequality, the low status of vocational education. The teachers involved in some of our recent school projects have fresh and inspiring visions that are addressing this deep rooted problem. For the Jo Richardson Community School Design Exemplar project, for example, a restaurant for visitors run by catering students was provided near the entrance and that had implications for the planning of the kitchen, technology and entrance areas.

In the 1980s and 90s there was a backlash against child centred education and the comprehensive system, on the grounds of figures for examination and test results indicating poor delivery of basic academic skills, and a perception that children's immaturity was being indulged. No doubt many educationalists strayed far from the rigour of Steiner and Piaget and lacked the talent of Montessori or Neill. No doubt the examination performance and minimum standards that traditional methods secured — at the expense of the development of innate abilities — were better than what was achieved by a system inadequately resourced or insufficiently committed to take up the challenge of real child-centred education. Whatever the full explanation, consequent politicisation of children's education has resulted in swerves in government policy and the growing micro-management of education through measures such as the National Curriculum, literacy and numeracy initiatives and a large increase in performance measurement bureaucracy. It seems that recent governments have thought education to be too important to be left to teachers, just as French Prime Minister Georges Clemenceau, in 1917, thought that war was too important to be left to generals.

In the meantime private education, while retaining many aspects of traditional classroom teaching has itself become far more sensitive to the differences between children and because of much higher teacher to pupil ratios, greater resources and often more home support, is able to focus guidance to individuals in a way that state school teachers struggle to do. Happily the teaching profession in the UK state schools has not abandoned the steady shift in education towards realising each child's potential despite enormous problems of discipline and order, despite being bullied and humiliated by ministers and civil servants and attacked by some commentators prejudiced against modern educational thought.[9] Our many teacher friends demonstrate how far teaching in the best British schools has come from 'chalk and talk' and how the focus in schooling has shifted from teaching to learning. The government today rightly promotes 'personalised learning' and the 'every child matters agenda', but David Miliband, when Schools Minister in 2004, felt compelled to say that "personalised learning is not a return to child centred theories."[10] Child centred education is dead; long live child centred education!

For us as architects a shift from teaching to learning means a shift from teaching environments to learning environments. As with health environments and certain work environments in such a shift the focus changes from designing for the convenience of the suppliers of the service – teachers, doctors, airline staff – to designing for the experience of those the service is for – students, patients, passengers. That does not mean in any way diminishing the convenience of the providers; fortunately this is not a zero sum game. On the contrary a close study of everyone's needs enables designers to improve the environment for the teachers as well as for the students, parents, the community and visitors.

A multi-billion pound programme, Building Schools for the Future (BSF) is currently underway to rebuild or refurbish every one of England's 3,500 secondary schools before 2020, tax revenues permitting. Also involving primary schools and a number of new city academies, this is a programme at an even larger scale than post-war school building. At that time many local authorities, with their large in-house architects and engineers departments, developed planning and construction principles to accord with teaching methods, that they applied consistently across a large number of projects.[11] School building systems on a national scale were also devised and a great mass of shared knowledge about designing schools was built up and enshrined in central government guidance called "Schools Building Bulletins".

The great legacy of collective knowledge enshrined in these Bulletins and periodically updated still guides the functional design of schools and their parts. Unlike the post-war schools programme the current one is being delivered through a system whereby a joint venture company, 70 per cent owned by a competitively selected private consortium and 30 per cent by public bodies, takes on the responsibility of developing the school buildings, associated play space and the ICT provision of a Local Education Authority and of maintaining it in a useable state for a fixed period. The integration of all the disciplines and voices is potentially very beneficial, as is the intent of ensuring that longer term operation and maintenance is taken into account in design. However, the design and construction procurement process chosen by government at the start of this programme threatens these benefits by weakening direct links between the designer and client in the vital preparatory stages. The competitive process and commercial confidentiality poses a challenge to knowledge sharing, which the design and educational community must now themselves promote.

Olney Campus, Annexe to Ousedale School, Buckinghamshire, 2004–2007

This school, an annexe of a large school six miles away, was built as part of Milton Keynes Borough Council's programme of reconfiguring secondary education by making separate provision for 11 to 14 year old children. On its seven acre site, once a sloping wheat field on the edge of the village, the building consists of two parallel blocks at right angles to the contours so that the ground slopes up between them making a terraced social space. Of the two blocks one is a three-storey rectilinear teaching wing, the other is a less regular two-storey wing that accommodates the facilities shared with the community: sports, assembly, music and drama. The entrance to the school is in a glazed link between the wings and the first view upon entry is of the terrace and, beyond, the original hill. Further up the hill the first floor of the wings, including the dining area, has level access to external play and social spaces.

Teaching spaces are orientated north or south to reduce the penetration of low easterly and westerly sun and internally have large glazed panels creating a sense of openness and bringing light into the corridors. Airshafts either side of the corridors provide natural air ventilation to the classrooms. In part to meet the tight budget the external walls are all clad in fair-faced concrete blockwork; but to subvert the utilitarian connotations of the material the blocks are laid on end and have a ribbed pattern. They are interrupted by large windows and areas of timber mullioned curtain walling with occasional coloured glass panels. The roof, a unifying element, folds in planes of varying pitches over the three distinct elements of the building.

Top: Central court looking up the hill towards the large windows of the dining room. The tall windows divided with an opening vent light the adjacent library and connect it with the court.

Bottom: Cross-section.

Opposite top: Central landscaped court — the heart of the School.

Opposite bottom: Entrance approach.

0   5

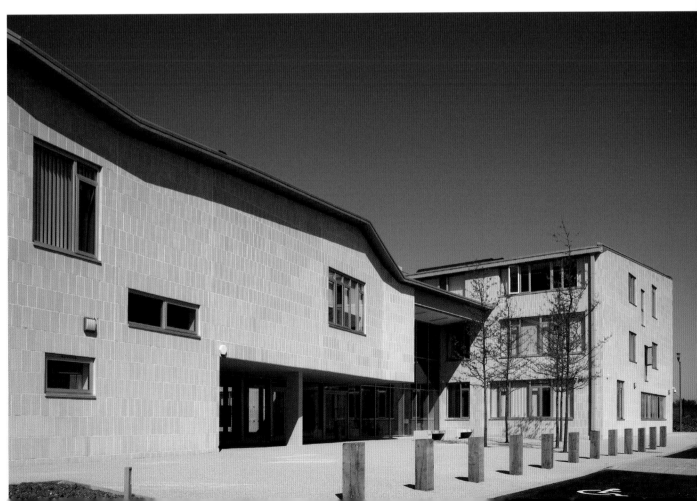

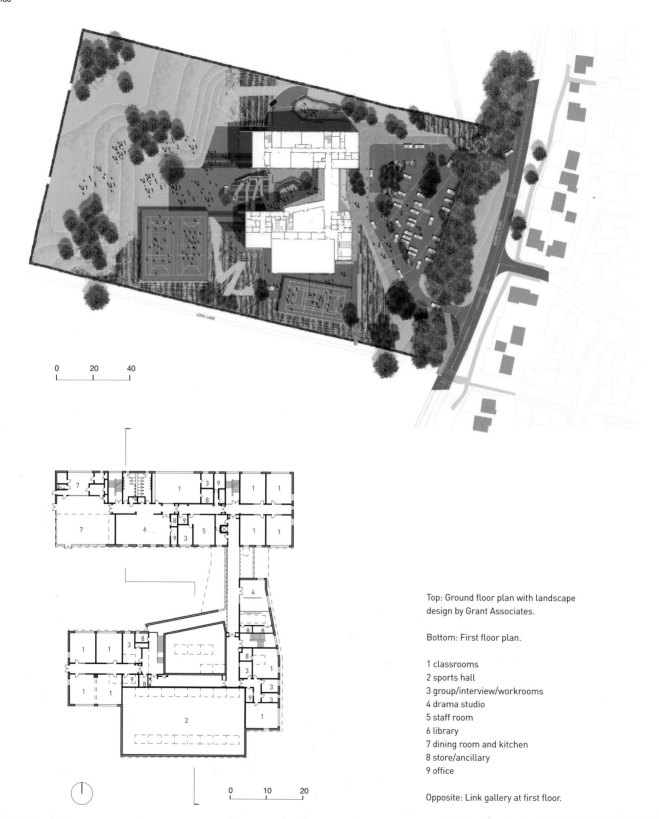

Top: Ground floor plan with landscape design by Grant Associates.

Bottom: First floor plan.

1 classrooms
2 sports hall
3 group/interview/workrooms
4 drama studio
5 staff room
6 library
7 dining room and kitchen
8 store/ancillary
9 office

Opposite: Link gallery at first floor.

Top: Entrance at dusk.

Bottom: Study model of the scheme.

Opposite: Looking back from the central court towards the link and entrance.

Front page of "The School We'd Like" article in *Education Guardian*, 5 June 2001.

The brief for a school

The school designer's task today is very much more complicated than it was during the post-war period. Traditional classroom teaching must be accommodated alongside or in the same space as revolutionary methods whereby students follow their personal learning programme, which might entail being in a large lecture-like session of 60 to 70 people followed by solitary study and work, or group work; there are different ideas about how a school as a whole is best organised, and these are different again for primary and secondary schools; controversy surrounds the extent to which pupils with special educational needs should be integrated into the mainstream; information and communication technology can enable entirely new ways of learning and teaching that may make previous provision redundant; and the degree of engagement with and openness to the local community varies hugely. All that could be accommodated by tailoring each school to its particular set of pedagogies and operational policies, but it is likely that a new headmaster, new governors or new local authority leadership may wish to implement a different set in the not too distant future. And in any case technology and society keeps evolving apace. In the 1960s how teachers taught was pretty clear; now there are numerous ways of learning. But some things, from managing behaviour to creating a sense of pride and belonging, do not change, and often it is these things that make the difference between an environment that supports learning and one that inhibits it. Our design approach is therefore to plan school buildings to be as adaptable to different pedagogies and operational arrangements as possible while focusing on the experience of students, teachers and visitors.

If you ask students what matters to them they would not name any of the areas listed in the paragraph above. In 2001 *The Guardian* ran a competition called "The School We'd Like" which attracted 15,000 entries. With many imaginative ideas about submarines, roof lights, colourful spaces and a school without walls, the following pragmatic suggestions about the environment featured most prominently:

Laptops so we could continue our work outside and at home.
Drinking water in every classroom, and fountains of soft drinks in the playground.
Clean toilets that lock, with paper and soap, and flushes not chains.
Large lockers to store our things.
A swimming pool.

In numerous surveys of school childrens' concerns, the condition of toilets, safety from bullying, security of personal possessions, good social space and good play facilities repeatedly rank high. Evidence from a number of studies has shown that well designed school environments improve educational outcomes. Naturally a good fit between the teaching methods and the layout is essential but it is just as important to have good daylighting, fresh air, easily supervised circulation spaces well worked out in conjunction with patterns of class changeover, and a good balance of outdoor and indoor social spaces. There are other design characteristics not specific to pedagogies and operational policies: the image the school building presents to its locality; the facilities for staff; the movement of goods and people; dealing with cars and cycles; the engineering solutions; and safety and security.

Overarching all these is the capacity of the design to inspire students, staff and visitors. That is what some of the children in *The Guardian* competition were getting at when they also suggested schools like giant submarines with waterproof maps of the underwater world, voice activated pencils, and rocket launch pads to take them to the planets to study the solar system. At one of our presentations a supportive head teacher said that without an inspiring and distinctive design he would not be able to convince his pupils that the promised transformation in their education would actually happen and would find it difficult to win their co-operation, or attract them to come to school in the first place.

The building can also literally be a teaching tool. In our designs of the Millennium Centre in Dagenham, 1997, and the Discovery Centre in Great Notley, 2001, sustainable construction techniques are displayed by exposing parts of the construction. At the Ashburton Learning Village the large photovoltaic array, and the rainwater harvesting tank are connected to meters in the social space so that students can measure and understand how much energy is being generated and water conserved. At The Charter School the giant steel tree that supports the rain-collecting inverted cone shaped roof has transparent rainwater pipes to bring the weather inside. In the design of the Bremer School, which has a technology specialism, the steel entrance canopy and the concrete frame structure are devised to display the building's engineering principles. Abstract patterns based on trees and printed circuits are recessed into areas of exposed cast concrete so that in arts classes students might 'complete' the building by infilling the recesses.

Ashburton Learning Village, Croydon, London, 2003–2006

The school and the local public library, a quarter of a mile away, have been combined to create a new type of local resource to the mutual benefit of both. The head teacher's report is that the previous frequent vandalisation of the library has stopped, reader numbers are up and students not previously seen there are visiting. The school hall is in demand as a rehearsal and performance venue for local musicians via the Croydon Music Service and the sports hall and other areas have regular non-school use through the borough's Continuing Education and Training Service.

The building forms a backdrop to a new neighbourhood piazza on Shirley Road, its deep and wide canopy expressing the 'under one roof' nature of the project. The entrance past the library with its coloured louvred window leads to the three-storey high school street with a sinuous gallery at each upper level, and dappled light from high up coming through a 200 m² array of photovoltaic cells. On one side of the street are the school's hall, drama studio and sports hall. On the other side are classroom wings with outdoor social spaces in between. The classrooms are arranged either side of a trapezoidal space that widens towards the end such as to be useable for break out sessions or an IT resource area. Some of the classrooms can also open into this space to allow flexibility in teaching methods. In this 'school without corridors' all the classrooms also have visual connections with the circulation areas via large glazed vision panels.

The design, construction and facilities management was procured through the government's Private Finance Initiative. To deal with the decreased control of detail we rely on large simple moves such as the structure of the main hall with its big curved laminated timber portal frame and profiled steel structural roof deck. At the same time the long term view favours inclusion of durable elements like the slate flooring throughout the ground floor.

Top: The school 'street' at ground level view, with a slate floor and curved galleries, The orange elements identify the staff bases at the entrance to the wings.

Bottom: Cross-section.

Opposite: School street from first floor — the 200 m² photovoltaic cell array along the high level windows is visible top left.

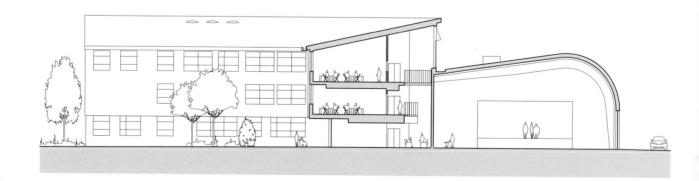

| 0 | 5 | 10 |

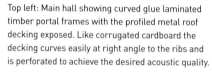

Top left: Main hall showing curved glue laminated timber portal frames with the profiled metal roof decking exposed. Like corrugated cardboard the decking curves easily at right angle to the ribs and is perforated to achieve the desired acoustic quality.

Top right: External social space between wings.

Bottom: Public entrance with the louvres to the library beyond.

Opposite: Ground floor plan.

1 pupil entrance
2 public entrance
3 library
4 dining area/kitchen
5 teaching spaces
6 sports hall
7 school hall
8 dance area
9 changing rooms
10 office/administration
11 mobile library garage

The parts of a school

In 2003 the Department for Education and Skills, in preparation for the Building Schools for the Future programme, selected a number of architects to produce 'Exemplar Designs' for secondary and primary schools in a number of different contexts. Our design for a community school on a restricted city site embodies approaches to most of the issues highlighted in the passages above. The design recognised that teaching and learning were changing and that such change was likely to be a constant aspect of the brief. The design therefore had to be adaptable to accommodate both conventional and innovative pedagogies. But this did not mean that the form and structure of the whole school must somehow be indeterminate. We saw the school as having two principal spatial realms: one comprising spaces for formal teaching/learning, and the other comprising all the other spaces of the school: the arrival and circulation spaces as well as the social, performance, learning resource and ceremonial spaces. The first we named the "learning rig" to reflect its adaptability by users. The second consists of two parts: the 'civic ground', being the entry, arrival and special spaces open to the local community, and the 'light links', which contain vertical circulation giving access to the learning rig. The learning rig would be a series of platforms suspended at first floor level and above and access to these could easily be limited to the school community only. The civic ground occupies the whole ground floor of the building and contains the entrance lobby, the school hall, the dining areas, access to the library/learning resources centre, the sports hall and all the in between circulation and lingering spaces. The urban streetscape flows into the civic ground with the minimum restrictions required for security and with the design of the external and internal spaces well integrated. The major special spaces of the civic ground, namely the main hall, the dining spaces, the sports hall and the library core, are analogous to distinguished public buildings of a town; while the formal teaching spaces in the learning rig are analogous to its houses. Although devised for a multi-storey secondary school building on a restricted site, the spatial differentiation of our DfES Exemplar can apply to any school building. On a typical two- or three-storey secondary school, instead of the civic ground there may be a school street or square containing the same elements. The learning rig idea translates into 'fingers' or 'blocks' of accommodation in the typologies we have developed to guide our designs.

Left: DfES Exemplar Design, 2003. Computer image of the interior of an open plan learning space created by joining up traditional classrooms.

Centre and right: Early design sketches of the circulation and classrooms of the Treehouse School, Haringey, London, 2003.

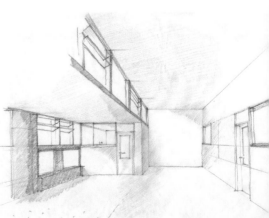

Learning spaces

The change of teaching practice does not simply mean moving away from classrooms to another type of spatial arrangement, it means the co-existence of several kinds of space. The classroom remains the unit of measurement in terms of area and funding, and so we have devised ways of dissolving the 'box' of the classroom and merging it with adjacent 'boxes' and circulation to make larger teaching/learning areas, which can permit both open plan layouts and smaller group work rooms or bays and areas for individual study. The design of the building's structure and environmental systems are key to permitting such adaptability. The environmental services design, daylight and natural light, thermal comfort, fresh air and good acoustics are fundamental to creating the physiological conditions to support the concentration and communication which is essential to learning, and indeed the staff's capacity to teach.

On top of these core principles of design need to be overlaid the particular qualities needed for primary, secondary or special needs environments. We helped build the brief for a school for children in the autistic spectrum by spending time in classrooms and engaging closely with the teachers. As a result the design of the Treehouse School is focused on making a core of very calm and orderly spaces, especially in the primary education areas on the ground floor, where stimuli unwelcome to the children can be kept out. However, the aim of the school is to enable the children to function in the real world as they grow up. Other parts of the school are therefore more like mainstream classrooms, including specialist teaching areas.

A school without corridors

Progressive primary schools of the 1960s and 70s began to adopt layouts whereby instead of opening off a corridor classrooms were arranged in clusters around an activity space. Our design for the temporary home of Prior Weston School re-using some nearby de-commissioned buildings organised the school around an open plan library and ICT resource space made by roofing over a yard to form the 'heart' of the school.

The central street of the Ashburton Learning Village, with its two upper level galleries, leads to the school's three wings, the sports, main and dining halls and the library. In the wings the classroom spaces are arranged either side of a trapezoidal central space that gets wider moving away from the entrance such that at the ends of the wings there is a day-lit space big enough for a break out session or to create an ICT resource area. If the classrooms are opened up with their sliding screens then a large open plan area can also be created. A roof light and openings in the second and first storeys means that daylight floods all the way down to the ground. The head teacher at Ashburton describes it as a school without corridors.

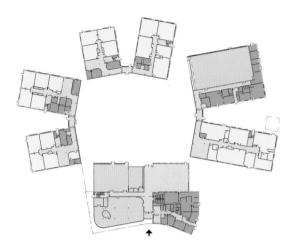

Withywood Academy

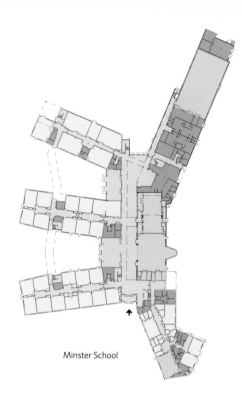

Minster School

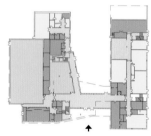

Olney Campus

Ashburton Learning Village

Bremer School

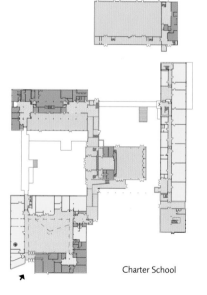

Charter School

Key

Administration and services

Teaching

Special spaces — main hall, libraries and sports halls

Circulation including social and dining spaces

Where corridors are unavoidable, as at Minster School and Olney Campus, we try to ensure that they are designed so classrooms on one side of a corridor can be combined later in different ways; that they have areas of natural light and that the pattern of circulation round the building and its external spaces naturally promotes smooth flows as well as pools of activity.

The school in its community

Plans of six schools to the same scale. 1:2000. The 1,500 place Minster School, 2007, the 1,200 place Ashburton Learning Village, 2006, illustrate the 'street and wings' typology whereby the major spaces of the schools are placed along one side of a street, and from the other side are entered wings of classrooms/ learning spaces. The 900 place Bremer School, 2008, is a variation of this typology with the main hall and sports hall placed at the end of the street and specialist learning spaces along one side. The 1,200 place Withywood Academy, 2008, illustrates a 'cloister' typology in which the major spaces as well as classroom clusters form individual buildings making 'shopfronts' along an open-sided walkway encircling a central landscaped court. The 600 place Olney Campus, 2007, has a hybrid arrangement: a 'fat' wing with the main hall and sports hall as well as some classrooms, and a 'thin' wing with classroooms, library and dining hall joined by a transparent entrance link. The typology of Charter School, originally built in the late 1950s and remodelled in 2003, has a seried of interlinked two-storey courtyards with the main spaces and a separate large five-storey teaching block.

More and more schools today are 'community schools'. Not just schools also used by the community, these are a genuinely shared resource, with dual use of the sports facilities, performance spaces, the main hall, the library, and perhaps other social spaces. The school may also have a police office, and a primary health care point. There may be adult education classes using other parts of the school, to promote 'lifelong learning'. A feature of the community school is that community use is not restricted to out of hours, and this presents a particular design challenge. From the school's point of view it is not desirable to have strangers wandering around and from the local community's point of view the presence and dynamics of a large number of teenagers can be intimidating. In our Design Exemplar for the Jo Richardson Community School we devised entry for the community and for the students along two separate axes at right angles to each other, a principle retained in the finished building, designed by Architecture plb.

The design aspects of the interface between a school and the local community are interesting but there is potentially a much more significant re-imagining of boundaries between a secondary school and the community in general. A number of strands are coming together to make this likely. While it has become widely recognised that children before puberty should not be seen as miniature adults, the age at which they begin to transform into adults has been getting younger and younger. At the same time, compared with 25 years ago, young people have far more and increasing autonomy. It follows that the school environment must call for spaces that are more 'normal', more like the world outside: a place where the 'school citizen' increasingly exercises the freedoms and the responsibilities of an adult citizen. But where is the boundary of such a place? Real working environments, offices, shops, restaurants, factories, studios, could surely also be learning environments, where school students go for vocational education, for example, using real tools and meeting real customers; Dewey's and Gandhi's 'learning by doing' reinvented for the twenty-first century. In the meantime the concept of lifelong learning has become more widely recognised not least to serve a labour market where continuous professional development is seen as essential and jobs and careers for life far from the norm. After hours, schools have huge reservoirs of space well suited to lifelong learning/adult education. The school is set to pour out into the community as the community pours into the school. It is too early to say exactly what these shifting boundaries may mean for the design of schools but multiple uses of space, adaptability and the integration of information and communication technology can only gain in importance.

Residential and Daycare Facilities, Essex, 1987–1991

MacIntyre, a charity dedicated to providing care, support and education to children and adults with learning difficulties, had acquired a village farmhouse with a frontage onto the main street and a large L-shaped site to the rear, with an ambition to create self-contained housing and daycare facilities for 15 people with learning difficulties. Replacing the more traditional hospital ward accommodation for young adults at a local hospital, the project was based on MacIntyre's successful approach of using horticulture as therapy. The charity wanted a sensitive design that helped overcome the stigma attached to such facilities so that mutually beneficial contact may be made with the village community.

A group of three houses, each with five resident bedrooms, dining and living rooms, staff accommodation, wcs, stores, etc., could have created an intrusive jump in scale in this small village where even the high street has a domestic character. The existing farmhouse has been retained and converted to make living spaces and extended with a long tail of bedroom accommodation barely visible from the high street. Two new houses of the same 'tadpole' design are placed at right angles round a courtyard at the rear of the site. Each house has alternative social spaces, including a conservatory to give residents maximum choice in sociability and privacy. The third side of the courtyard is closed by the day centre with reception and office, therapy rooms and staff rest areas.

The structure of the buildings is simple load bearing blockwork clad in buff bricks and large areas of black stained ship-lap timber boarding as traditionally used on local barns. The roofs are of silvery profiled aluminium with generous overhangs created by curving the sheets at ridge and eaves. The monopitch roofs make for a noble scale on the entrance courtyard elevations and a cottage scale towards the surrounding farmland.

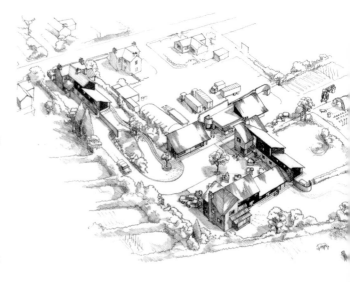

Top: An aerial sketch of the site — a farm courtyard surrounded on three sides by arable land.

Bottom left: Courtyard view. External walls are primarily constructed with buff coloured brick with black stained feather-edged timber boarding on blockwork.

Bottom right: The cottage scale on the private side of the houses in 2007.

Opposite bottom: The steep monopitch roofs have a simple timber rafter construction with profiled aluminium sheeting and deep bracketed eaves.

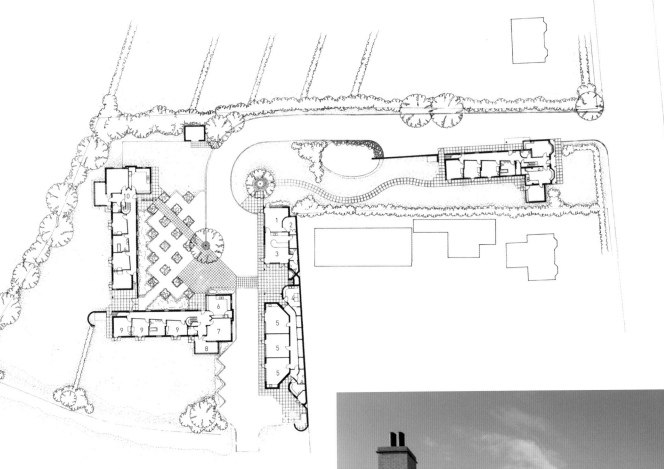

Top: The ground floor plan showing the 'tadpole' layout of the three houses, with a head containing the social spaces and a tail with most of the bedrooms.

1 reception
2 office
3 kitchen/tea room
4 laundry
5 therapy rooms
6 kitchen dining room
7 living room
8 conservatory
9 bedrooms
10 entrance

The revolution that occurred in the way that primary school children were taught in many ways anticipated the way any 'learner' is coming to be regarded today. Secondary schooling is already being tuned more to the individual person and now higher education establishments, as they compete to attract good candidates, are also waking up to the importance of seeing the world from the student's point of view. As we suggested in the submission for the DfES Exemplar Design "The twenty-first century learning environment must be sensual rather than austere, flexible rather than rigid."

1 Jackson, Phillip, *Life In Classrooms*, Orlando: Holt Rinehart and Winston, 1974, originally published 1968.

2 Snyder, Benson R, *The Hidden Curriculum*, New York: Alfred A Knopf, 1970.

3 Paul Goodman's 1962 book *Compulsory Miseducation*, Harmondsworth: Penguin Books, 1971 and Ivan Illich's 1971 book *De-schooling Society*, Penguin Books, 1973, were both radical and influential attacks on institutional schooling.

4 Living in India in the late 1980s, seeing children as young as three taking exams, the purpose of most schooling appeared to me to be to convert the child into a middle aged adult in the shortest possible time.

6 John Dewey's declaration of 1897, *My Pedagogic Creed*, contains these passages:

I believe that the only way to make the child conscious of his social heritage is to enable him to perform those fundamental types of activity which make civilisation what it is.

I believe, therefore, in the so-called expressive or constructive activities as the center of correlation.

I believe that this gives the standard for the place of cooking, sewing, manual training, etc., in the school.

I believe that they are not special studies which are to be introduced over and above a lot of others in the way of relaxation or relief, or as additional accomplishments. I believe rather that they represent, as types, fundamental forms of social activity; and that it is possible and desirable that the child's introduction into the more formal subjects of the curriculum be through the medium of these activities.

Dewey, John, 1897, "My Pedagogic Creed", *The School Journal*, vol. LIV, no. 3, January 1897.

7 Tagore's educational work is best known through the university he set up in Santiniketan but he also had strong views on conventional schooling: "In this critical period a child's life is subjected to the education factory lifeless, colourless, dissociated from any contact with the universe, within bare white walls staring like eyeballs of the dead. We are born with that god given gift of taking delight in the world, but such delightful activity is fettered and imprisoned, muted by a force called discipline which kills the sensitivity of the child's mind which is always on the alert, restless and eager to receive first-hand knowledge from Mother Nature. We sit inert, like dead specimens of some museum, while lessons are pelted at us from high, like hailstones on flowers." Tagore, Rabindranath, "Talks in China" quoted in Devi Prasad, *Education for Living Creatively and Peacefully*, Hyderabad: Spark-India, 2005.

8 "Education, for most people, means trying to lead the child to resemble the typical adult of his society... but for me and no one else, education means making creators... You have to make inventors, innovators not conformists."

Conversations with Jean Piaget, JC Bringuier, Chicago: Chicago University Press, 1980.

AS Neill founded (1921) and ran Summerhill School in Leiston, Suffolk. Controversially children were not required to attend class. The school is still going strong. "No one is wise enough or good enough to mould the character of any child. What is wrong with our sick, neurotic world is that we have been moulded, and an adult generation that has seen two great wars and seems about to launch a third should not be trusted to mould the character of a rat." Neill quote on mug sold by the schools as merchandising.

9 "Egalitarians... are committed to the mind-bending, results-twisting, socially suicidal philosophy that no-one must fail and instead all must have prizes. This is what lay behind the comprehensive schools, bent upon the equality of the lowest common denominator. It's what lies behind the obsession that everyone must gain a university degree of equal value. It's what lies behind the blackmailing of the universities to turn away the best-qualified pupils because they come from good schools. It's what lies behind 'child-centred' education, which is based on the premise that nothing should be done to hurt a child's feelings. Thus pupils have been told a series of lies — that answers are correct when they are not, that they can read when they can not, and that their work has reached a required standard when it has not." Phillips, Melanie, "Prince Charles Was Right", *Daily Mail*, 22 November 2004.

10 Rt Hon David Miliband, Minister of State for Education *"Choice and Voice in Personalised Learning"* 18 May 2004, DfES Innovation Unit/Demos/OECD Conference.

11 Saint, Andrew, *Towards a Social Architecture: The Role of School Building in Post-War England*, London: Yale University Press, 1987.

Prior Weston School, London,
2003–2004

Awaiting the construction of its new permanent campus Prior Weston School, with its well established child centre ethos, parent involvement and high achievement levels was merged with a nearby school with a falling role and traditional teaching methods. Our design for transforming the shabby 1960s buildings adopted a two-fold approach: to create a shared open plan IT and library space as a large foyer at the heart of the school by enclosing a hard play area between the three existing blocks, and to place at the front of the site a new cluster of three open-sided classroom spaces with a central shared group space. These two new insertions were constructed using a timber framed cassette system fabricated off-site making it possible for the project to be completed in the six week period of the summer holiday for £400,000. Instead of concrete foundations timber pallets carry the structural loads. These speeded up erection and avoided having to deal with tricky ground conditions.

The buildings together create a new entrance courtyard centred on a Eucalyptus tree. The head teacher describes how the new environment helped her to break down the inhibitions of the parents of the traditional school and to engage them in the new culture. One expression of this culture is her own open door policy operated from blue polycarbonate cabin in the foyer adjacent to the school administrator. Older children from the school worked with an artist to create a large artwork stencilled onto to the fibre cement cladding panels on the street.

Top: The roof-lit central building accommodates the open cabins housing the administration team, head teacher's office and reception, as well as open library and teaching spaces.

Bottom: View from Bunhill Row. The street presence of the school was strengthened with a colourful design created by artist Sian Tucker, along with a group of children from the school.

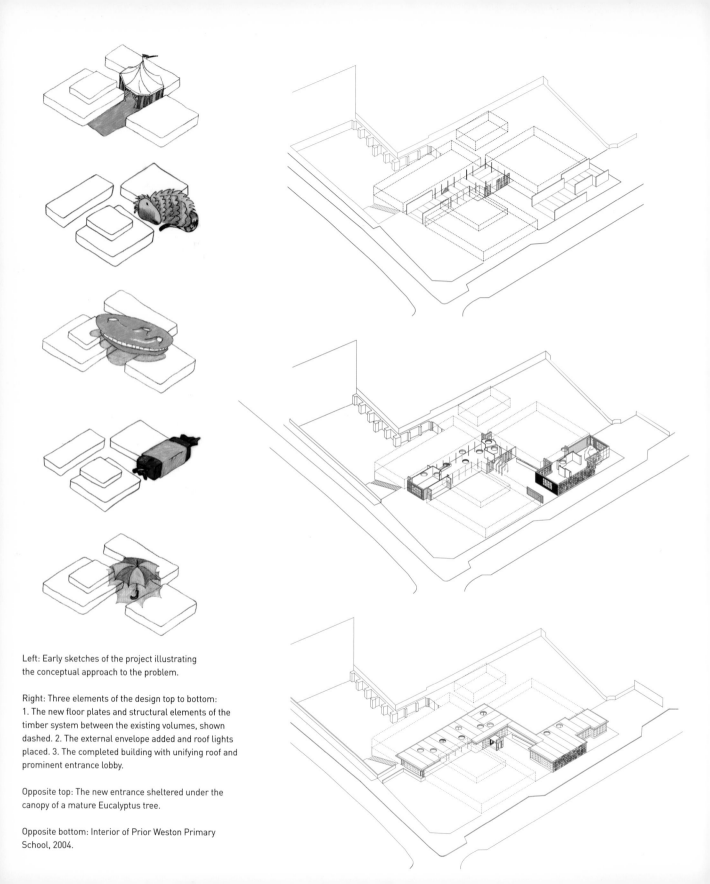

Left: Early sketches of the project illustrating the conceptual approach to the problem.

Right: Three elements of the design top to bottom:
1. The new floor plates and structural elements of the timber system between the existing volumes, shown dashed. 2. The external envelope added and roof lights placed. 3. The completed building with unifying roof and prominent entrance lobby.

Opposite top: The new entrance sheltered under the canopy of a mature Eucalyptus tree.

Opposite bottom: Interior of Prior Weston Primary School, 2004.

LIMITS

This chapter positions climate change and sustainability in the context of familiar limits, such as finance, that we as designers must work with. It explores how environmental considerations have informed our approach and how the urgency of the climate change threat will require a change of culture in design.

The resource envelope

The broad scientific consensus that has emerged about potentially catastrophic climate change, and about its causation in human activity, is triggering a keener and wider consciousness of the limit of the earth's capacity to support ever increasing human consumption. This consciousness must lead to a new view of the whole relationship between buildings and the limits that their construction and operation confront; rather than being seen simply as obstacles to overcome and then be forgotten, limits will become an integral part of design value.

In all made things the quality of design is recognised through using or experiencing them and not through knowing what obstacles were overcome, or resources expended, to achieve the finished result. And yet working within the constraints of available resources or, as often, ingeniously overcoming them to produce a desired result, is the very stuff of design. Design can display an almost magical ability to expand this 'resource envelope' by creating far greater value than its initially apparent potential. But little of this will be evident at the point of use of the building or other artefact. Sometimes with buildings of a recent date such issues may feature in discussion of their design value. There has been continuing controversy over the £400 million cost of the Scottish Parliament building, 2004, ten times the original budget, leading to the questioning of its eligibility for design prizes. That the almost universally loved Sydney Opera House, 1978, cost vastly more than the budget at the competition stage is mentioned rarely nowadays; it is recognised as the universal symbol of the city and has paid for itself many times over as an attractor. The costs of the Henry V Chapel at Windsor, the Taj Mahal or the Pantheon, are a matter of interest only to some very specialised historians, if known at all.[1]

The operating costs of buildings, heating, cooling, cleaning and maintaining, are, of course, also affected by design. Though a significant issue for owners and managers, costs rarely enter evaluations of architectural design. But this must now change with the recognition of a new kind of cost, the degrading through human activity of the earth's capacity to sustain life as we know and desire it. That a building has been designed and built, and is capable of being operated, with close to zero use of carbon will in the next decades be a major factor in how it is valued. The extent of the global harm caused by apparently harmless products, like plastic bags, though known for a long time, is still being quantified and will need to be accounted and legislated for. The challenge for us is how to see all these limits in the round, holistically, and to make them a natural part of designing.

Great Notley Discovery
Centre, 2001.

For our practice, to do this is to continue to follow a seam that has been present in the work from the start, a mixture of environmental consciousness and an attraction to economy of means both as a poetic and a financial concept. Now these need to be pursued with greater determination, knowledge and clarity. As practice partner Ian Goodfellow puts it: "Within a few years we will look back and barely recognise some of our architectural preoccupations, our synapses will be so reconfigured and keenly focused on addressing climate change."

Sustainability

Sustainability is intrinsically an holistic approach, but this quality has caused confusion as a brief examination of the idea will show. Although the science of ecology has a history going back to the nineteenth century, the significant milestones in the raising of a general awareness of the limits of the earth's resources and our enormous dependency on them are quite recent: the publication of the report of the Club of Rome, *The Limits to Growth*, 1972, followed by the 1973 oil crisis, for example. Throughout the 1970s consciousness grew about the adverse impact of human activity on the balance of natural systems. RIBA President Alex Gordon's "Long Life Loose Fit Low Energy" initiative of 1972– 1974 was a prescient response many of whose principles remain relevant. In schools of architecture research began early in the decade on autonomous buildings that would make no net demand on external servicing or energy sources. The UK Building Regulations introduced thermal insulation of dwellings in 1976 and measures to conserve fuel and power for the first time in 1985.

In 1987 the World Commission on Environment and Development published *The Brundtland Report: Our Common Future*. This document is the source for the term "sustainable development" defined as development that "meets the needs of the present without compromising the ability of future generations to meet their own needs".

Sustainability may be amongst the least precise of concepts that practitioners, policy makers and the public have ever had to grapple with. There are literally 100s of definitions whose imprecision was neatly summarised at a workshop held at Shell: "Sustainable development — one of the slipperiest

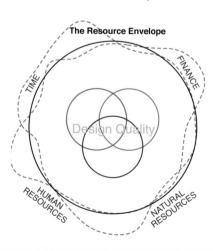

The Resource Envelope

TIME   FINANCE

Design Quality

HUMAN RESOURCES   NATURAL RESOURCES

Left: The sedum and moss covered roofs on Brixton Hill Surgery, London, 1993.

Right: Resource Envelope diagram conceptualising the relationship between design quality and limits in the Construction Industry Council's *Design Quality Indicator*. Although all buildings have to be built within a limited envelope of financial, natural and human resources, intelligent and innovative designs can change the envelope's size and shape.

pieces of soap you are ever likely to find in the shower." The Brundtland definition, for example, is dependent on the meaning of three un-measurable, and potentially conflicting, values: "the needs of the present", the "needs of future generations" and the "ability of future generations to meet them". The ideal of equity and redress of poverty were strong elements of "Our Common Future", whereas in many corporations sustainability was recruited as a measure of business viability. That the word sustainability means different things to different people must itself be a major factor in sustaining the concept and its proliferation. Though the elasticity of the term may raise eyebrows, it is well established in discourses about the built environment and development. The ability of people to use it in practical ways recalls the famous quip "It's all very well in practice, but will it ever work in theory?"

Filling the moral vacuum left in the secular realm after the collapse of socialism it seems that sustainability has offered a rational and ethical guide to action that allows avoidance of political polarisation. It extends the ideal of equity to an inter-generational dimension so cementing the principle that actions must take into account long term impact. And now that the ideology of the supremacy of the unfettered market is widely discredited, having failed to look after the interests of the poor and the long terms interests of all, sustainability offers a one word guide to the regulation of the market.

While the main reason for the establishment of sustainability as a good thing was a consciousness of environmental limits, it was always clear that development could not focus on the environment alone and had to be related to economic and social factors. For example, if in attempting to protect the environment we reduce development too drastically, it may cause economic decline with adverse impact on social structures and resulting overall poorer quality of life for a community. Such logic gave rise to the concept of the "triple bottom line" where economic, environmental and social factors are weighed together in assessing the sustainability of developments. Not surprisingly, yet another definition on the Internet describes sustainability as the "study of the interconnectedness of things". The UK government defined a sustainable community through as many as eight components.[2]

The more sustainability is presented as the general interconnectedness of everything the more complex becomes the means of measuring success with potentially more confusion about the goals of development. The growing realisation of the unprecedented threat posed by climate change promises a new perspective to adopt, for climate change presents an altogether harsher challenge: drastically reduce greenhouse gas emissions or end life on earth, as we know it.

Climate change

The wide scientific consensus by 1990 about the phenomenon and potential consequences of global warming added a new urgency to the environmental debate.[3] While the few surviving climate change sceptics today do not deny that global warming is occurring, they cannot accept that it is almost certainly man made and caused by greenhouse gas (GHG) emissions. The scientists who found the correspondence between global temperatures and atmospheric carbon dioxide levels over 800,000 years of data do not claim that cause and effect is absolutely proven, but for most policy makers and practical people, like architects, the precautionary principle overrides any residual doubt. Mitigating climate change is a wise precaution because if the consensus predictions, let alone the more extreme ones, are correct the consequences of inaction are catastrophic. The extinction of species has already accelerated. It is likely, though not proven, that some heat and flood related human deaths have climate change as root cause. Flooding and desertification leading within the next few decades to millions of displaced people, "climate change refugees", might only be the beginning of the real impact of climate change.

Climate change is inescapably a global problem. If the whole world were to live at the levels of material consumption enjoyed in the West it would require the capacity of three earth ecosystems. We only have one planet. Once upon a time this could be seen as rather an abstract concept that required an active belief in the equality of all to be of any real consequence. But the consequences of climate change unlike those of poverty do not distinguish between rich and poor, north and south. Now, along with rapidly rising consumption in the rest of the world, carbon emissions are rising equally fast, there being a very close correspondence between Gross National Product and GHG emissions.[4] This global problem requires a global solution such as Contraction and Convergence, which would lead to agreed national emissions limits far more comprehensively than the Kyoto Protocol.[5]

Folded back into the complex view of sustainable development, climate change helps establish priorities and actions. The 'triple bottom line' thinking outlined above can lead to an argument for holding back on environmental measures because of their immediate and local economic implications. But what if slightly less abundance is the price to be paid for survival? What if an apparent reduction in material affluence leads to a higher quality of life? Whereas higher GDP has led to higher GHG emissions it has proven not to lead to greater happiness.[6] That is not an argument for reducing GDP but for seeing it in less absolute terms; a key indicator but not the paramount one. What if we see the climate change threat as a cultural wake-up call as much as a technical challenge?

Buildings and the use of buildings are responsible for around half of total greenhouse gas emissions. If we take into account the impact that the planning of settlements has on transport of

Sketch of the Millennium Centre set in the landscape of Eastbrookend Country Park and the Chase Nature Reserve, 1997.

people and goods, architecture and town planning can be seen as amongst the most significant fronts in the efforts to reduce emissions and dependency on fossil fuels. Buildings are also the most conspicuous manifestation of affluence and their size and glitter today a marker of success. For us as architects there is a technical challenge for design to reduce emissions; but also a cultural challenge to shift the markers of success towards design with a keen, intelligent, and undaunted consciousness of limits, rather than the pursuit of visual hyperbole.

The environment at Penoyre & Prasad

By the beginning of the 1980s the fledgling discipline of environmentally conscious design, focusing mainly on passive measures such as solar gain, had taken root in a few architectural practices, including Edward Cullinan Architects where Greg Penoyre and I were working, and in engineering practices like Büro Happold and Max Fordham. In 1988, at the founding of Penoyre & Prasad, we had not heard of the Gaia hypothesis, first published by James Lovelock a decade earlier, but we must have imbibed its broad outline by osmosis somewhere along the way; for we discovered we had independently concluded that the earth should be conceived of as a single living organism of which humans are a part. Many people joining the practice since have reinforced the principle that to think of humans as separate from and in a position to dominate nature is a fallacy to be resisted.

From the early years designing low energy buildings with natural cooling was an important concern for us. In 1990 we took part in a limited competition to convert an animal experimentation laboratory into the new Greenpeace HQ and proposed a combined heat and power plant (CHP), natural ventilation and solar control, as well as high levels of insulation. In the design of Brixton Hill Surgery, 1991, we employed a sedum and moss roof to reduce solar gain in a single-storey garden extension planned around a courtyard cooled by a fountain. The design and specification of Woodlands Nursing Home and The Rushton Street Medical Centre, both 1993, aimed for a comprehensive approach to energy efficiency, combining passive measures, concerning the form and fabric, with active measures, concerning the engineering systems. Engineers had started using Computational Fluid Dynamics (CFD) to model thermal performance, which could take into account the crucial ingredient of occupant behaviour. And we were able to design in techniques for ensuring good air quality without throwing out heat with the stale air.

In 1995 we won a limited competition to design The Millennium Centre for the London Borough of Barking & Dagenham; to be a showcase of the then emerging concept of sustainable design, and an education resource for a nature reserve and new country park created by the greening of a large landfill site. In this project, together with Max Fordham, the environmental services engineers, and Büro Happold, the structural engineers, we re-thought every aspect of construction from the point of view of sustainability. The design team adopted a common sense meaning of sustainability as the ability "to go

on doing it", the 'it' being particular servicing or material selection strategies. At a time when the ideal of autonomy for individual buildings was still prevalent this approach clearly pointed, for example, to rejecting an independent sewerage system in favour of connecting to the mains. As an exemplar, the building should not be incorporating techniques that would be difficult to replicate, such as treating sewage on site and putting wastewater through reed beds. However, rainwater harvesting and re-use passed the test of sustainability because the client could go on doing it. In the design of the Millennium Centre we considered the energy used in the manufacture of building materials and components, 'embodied energy', as well as operational energy. However, materials with high embodied energy, such as aluminium, were not ruled out if they could be recycled easily. Recycling extended to the whole building and also the site. Instead of concrete piled foundations, the structure is supported on 22 galvanised steel screw anchors wound into the ground through the landfill to an average depth of 11 metres. This method virtually eliminated the use of energy hungry concrete, and the extensive health and safety measures, labour and energy that would have been required in excavation of this partially contaminated site. We repeated this concept of 'touching the ground lightly' for our temporary school for autistic children in Bloomsbury. When the school moved the building was taken down, and the screw anchors withdrawn, leaving no trace behind.

Principles of sustainability run through the designs of the Millennium Centre and the subsequent Discovery Centre at Great Notley Country Park in Essex, 2001, but environmental consciousness is not worn on the sleeve. Their architecture, in terms of human experience and registration with the landscape, has its own presence. Sustainable design can inspire new forms but form does not have to be dictated by sustainability.

The lessons of these projects, with a client intent on setting an example, have now become part of everyday practice, limited only by other clients' ambitions and budgets. In the DfES Exemplar School Project, 2004, the environmental services engineers Atelier Ten devised with us a modular heat recovery system, which would be embedded within the facade of the building and offered very low energy use. The glazing on the facade employed light bending technology to increase natural light levels deep into the backs of the rooms, so enabling more space efficient layouts. A number of our schools projects use natural ventilation chimneys and light wells to illuminate and ventilate classrooms without energy hungry artificial cooling.

Bottom left: A screw anchor foundation being driven in.

Bottom right: Cross-section, Discovery Centre for Sports and Leisure, Great Notley Country Park, 2001. Arrows indicate heating and natural ventilation strategies.

Opposite: The Treehouse School temporary accommodation at Coram Fields, London, 2001, fitted tightly in amongst mature London planes and was removed together with its screw anchor foundations in 2005, leaving no trace.

0   5

The Millennium Centre, Eastbrookend Country Park, London, 1995–1997

Eastbrookend Country Park and Chase Nature Reserve occupy 80 hectares of heathland previously scarred by mineral extraction and landfill. The Millennium Centre acts as a gatehouse to the park, has facilities for the park rangers, a classroom with science benches, together with permanent and temporary displays to explain the ecology, the history and the flora and fauna of the area. The borough council's aspiration was that the visitors, particularly school children, could be educated through the building in how to manage, maintain and respect the environment. The construction being integral to this message, the design embodies a rigorous attitude to sustainable development. Siting and orientation were informed by maximising the effectiveness of photovoltaic panels on the roof, by prevailing winds and the presence of a sheltering copse. The foundations are almost concrete free, using steel screw anchors that avoid disturbing the five to ten metres of landfill. The ground floor is constructed like a pavement, with sand and precast slabs over foamed glass insulation. The structure maximises the use of reconstituted and small section softwood (timber as a crop), and sparingly employs recyclable steel and aluminium. The fabric is heavily insulated with blown pulped newsprint and external shutters further preventing heat loss. The natural ventilation system uses stack effect as well as cross ventilation. Rainwater is recycled and a wind turbine generates enough electricity for the computers.

A desire to mount photovoltaic panels facing due south at 45 degrees generated the prominent profile of the building and makes a tall timber-clad wall with small openings facing north to the entrance approach. The south, by contrast, is more extensively glazed and delicate.

Top: Competition entry sketch of the entrance.

Bottom: Close up of timber cladding showing details of re-entrant corner, the sharp edge of the curved aluminium roof stops short of the vertical cladding.

Opposite top: The south elevation from the park. A viewing gallery cantilevers from the east facade of the building.

Opposite bottom: The north facade is more closed with smaller windows.

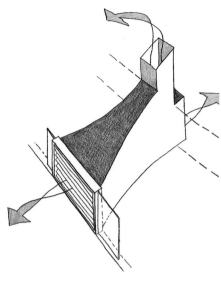

Top left: Ducts aiding the natural ventilation of the building are expressed in the circulation corridor.

Top right: Diagram of an individual duct.

Bottom: A wind turbine acts as a sign for the Centre while making a contribution to the energy supply together with photovoltaic panels.

Top: Ground and first floor plans. Visitor display areas and an education space are located on the ground floor and orientated to the south. A kitchen, wcs and stores form a strip of rooms along the north edge. Above these are the park ranger's facilities, from which they can survey the surrounding landscape.

1 exhibition/teaching/activity space
2 reception
3 store
4 office
5 display
6 entrance
7 ha-ha

Bottom: Section through the building. Laminated timber joists spanning between steel posts form the main spaces. Most of the envelope of the building is of composite timber construction clad with aluminium on the roof and fireproofed timber boarding on the walls. The natural ventilation strategy is indicated with arrows following alternative air paths through the building.

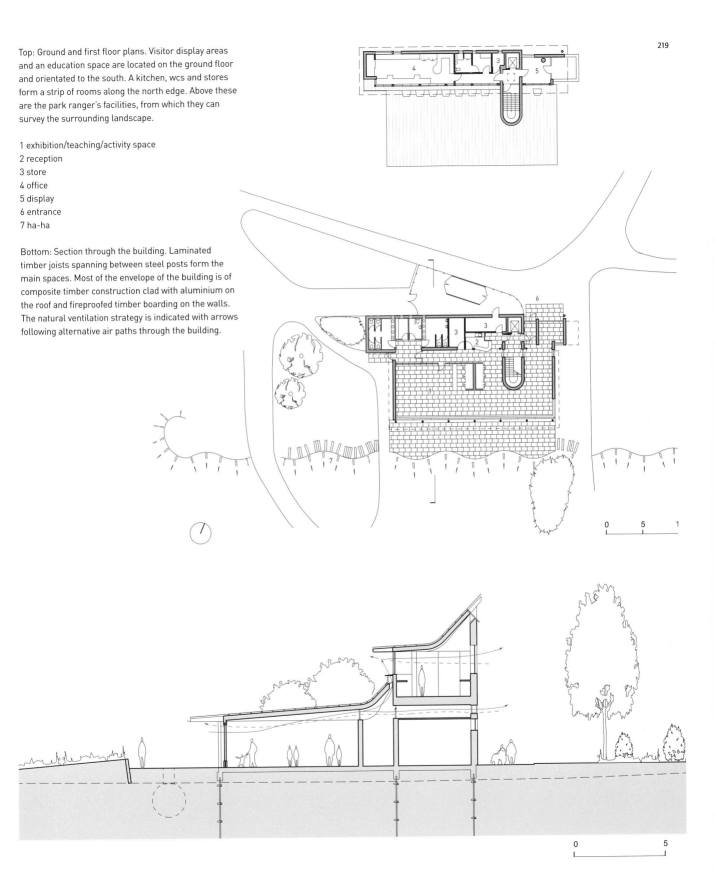

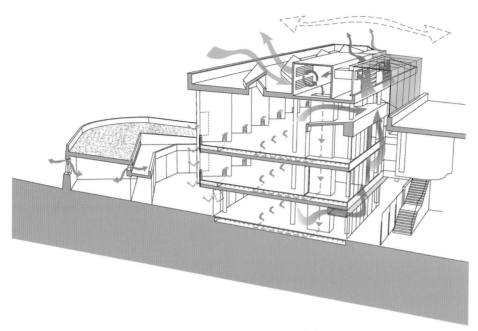

Diagram of the environmental strategy for the University of Portsmouth Library, 2007, indicating ventilation air flows.

The mixed mode ventilation design of the Portsmouth University Library, 2007, uses an atrium to create up-draught to draw in fresh air, and the thermal mass of the concrete structure to cool it in the summer. In the winter a pump recovers the heat from stale air to warm incoming fresh air. The orientation of the building, and the geometry of its southerly facade are optimised to reduce solar gain. We have concentrated on the fit between building and environments and letting this play a subtle part in the expression of the architecture. One of the most promising energy reducing technologies is the ground source heat pump, which uses the constant temperature of the ground at a certain depth to both heat the building in the winter and cool it in the summer. Unfortunately, because of cost constraints this was omitted from the design.

Green Wrythe Lane Integrated Health Centre in south London illustrates a common design problem: dealing with conflicting demands of natural ventilation and noise exclusion. This has been done through incorporating acoustically absorbent ventilating louvres as part of the window design. Together with a number of other measures, the building has achieved an 'Excellent' rating in the NHS's Environmental Evaluation Tool (NEAT). Such tools are not only essential for evaluation but also help raise market awareness of sustainability. The developer at our Parrock Street mixed-use project in Gravesend agreed to spend a modest extra amount to ensure that two of the homes were rated 'Excellent' under the Ecohomes evaluation scheme. Their rapid sale illustrates the growing demand for environmentally sustainable homes, which, of course, also have lower energy bills.

It is now viable to build zero carbon homes and low carbon non-domestic buildings. But some 75 per cent of the built stock of 2050 already exists and is very energy hungry. The scope for increasing the energy efficiency of this stock may be limited but has to be exploited to the full. Our renewal of The Charter School, Dulwich, 2003, incorporated a number of measures to greatly reduce the energy use of this 1957 design with its low insulation levels and summertime overheating. The measures were designed to be visible to students so that the school building itself became part of learning about sustainability. Similarly at the new Ashburton School and Library in Croydon, the 200 square metre photovoltaic array and rainwater harvesting system are connected to visual displays that the students can monitor.

Transcending limits

Environmental capacity together with finance, time and other resources should be seen as inter-related limits to which design must imaginatively respond. But they also have their own distinct characteristics and environmental capacity is the priority that helps give perspective to the whole. For an owner or operator of a building its running costs and any financing of its capital costs are important design influenced factors. Typically a small fraction of the total costs of ownership, they are weighed against the functionality they offer and the other value they add to the business. These value equations are complex and it is often difficult to place economic value on intangible benefits of good design such as employee wellbeing or brand enhancement. Nevertheless, economic factors are quite tangible. In contrast, the environmental and social impacts of buildings are less immediately obvious. They are not borne by individuals and organisations and many of them take a long time to become apparent. But government regulations are making such impacts more evident. A European Union Directive has made it mandatory to display an Energy Performance Certificate in every public building. This makes the environmental credential of the building a manifest part of its economic and cultural value.

There will have to be a binding global agreement to limit carbon emissions if the world is to have any chance of mitigating climate change. Such an agreement will in effect determine a per capita maximum emission limit, thought to be around two tonnes of carbon dioxide equivalent per year; one fifth of the present UK average. Such an agreement may be accompanied by various trading schemes, domestic and international, that will have the effect of turning carbon into currency, so making the limits of emissions as visible in valuing design as limits of money.

It would be logical to think that regardless of any impact on the planet, a number of measures to improved sustainability were directly in the client's interest because of long term savings in running the building. Studies show that investment in green technology shows good returns on capital. But in both the private and the public sector the linkage between capital and revenue costs of buildings is very weak because the two generally fall under separate budgets or separate ownership. The UK government's Private Finance Initiative should, in principle, convert the long term cost of running a building (management, maintenance, energy and repairs) and the 'first cost' (the cost of construction) into a single number, such as the Net Present Value or the annual Unitary Charge. In practice it has failed to do so, partly because of the poor intellectual development and integration of facilities management as a discipline but mainly because the uncertainty of future energy cost levels has led to energy costs being taken out of the equation and not included in the annualised payment.[7] So in most of our PFI and PPP projects, the client pays for the energy used separately from the payment for the building, creating no incentive for the private sector partner to reduce energy use. In the commercial office or residential rental markets greater divisions of responsibility for capital and revenue costs prevail and act as a disincentive to investment in sustainable design.

However many definitions of sustainability there may be, the long view is at the heart of the idea. The long view means seeing a building's short term costs in the context of the whole life value it will deliver. This in turn means that we as architects, with co-professionals, need to engage with clients' objectives and resources at a much earlier stage than is currently the norm, better to match them with each other. Construction budgets are often set on historical precedents with lower performance requirements than today's. This usually leads in mid-design to so-called value engineering, often a euphemism for plain cost cutting. An example of true value engineering, in contrast, is the real granite counter in our Belmarsh Prison Visitor Centre toilets, which together with the strong colour scheme lends an unexpectedly posh character to facilities that are traditionally severely utilitarian and frequently vandalised. During the design prudent control of the budget allowed a small amount of extra money to be allocated for the counter. Consciousness of the difference between looking cheap and insulting to visitors as opposed to being cheap, led us to devise a distinctive colour scheme and specify the granite. It has helped reduce vandalism and added long term value that more than pays for the stone. Demonstrating long term value at far bigger but also at such smaller scales will be the key to making the cultural transition away from a lowest cost mentality.

We are not today hampered by technology so much as by attitudes. William McDonough, a pioneer of sustainable architecture, says: "We talk of throwing things away; but where is 'away'?" One third of all waste produced in the UK is construction waste, and around one third of all material arriving at a building site turns into construction waste. And with that, all the energy that went into manufacturing the materials is wasted. How can we help to design out such waste?

Technological advances, particularly in energy generation, will in the long term play a large part in arresting and even reversing climate change. Carbon free energy, driven by the nuclear fusion taking place in the sun, is tantalisingly all around us. Not just heat and light but also wind, waves and the energy stored in plants. If we could capture one six-thousandth of the sun's energy falling on earth it would be enough for the world's current power requirements. In the meantime there is an array of highly promising established technologies to be working with. Our approach should be to work in harmony with natural forces as much as possible to ensure that basic design moves like location, orientation and building form minimise mechanical heating, cooling and ventilation; and then to provide this reduced heat and power with plant that uses carbon minimal technologies; and

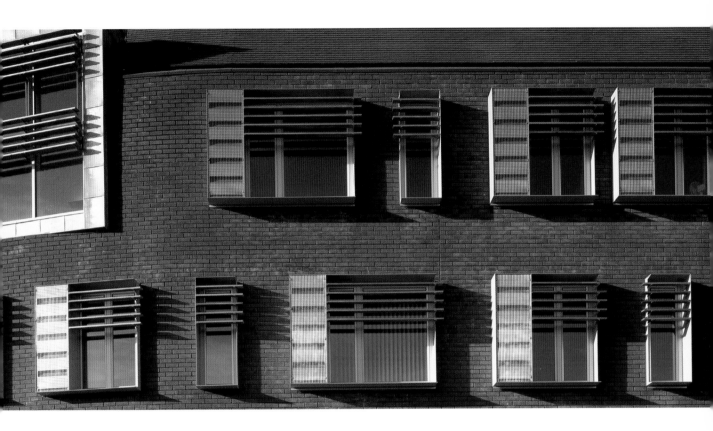

Sound attenuating louvres allowing natural ventilation on a noisy site, Green Wrythe Lane Primary Care Centre, Carshalton, 2006.

finally to use carbon neutral energy sources to run the plant, including on site energy generation where appropriate. We will almost certainly be designing for a changed climate and could learn from hotter and wetter parts of the world how the manner of use of buildings can reduce energy use.

In the thirteenth century, the Pueblo people of what is now the southwest of the United States built the settlement of Betatakin in stone within a vast cave in the cliff face of a mesa. The arch of the cave shades its 135 rooms in the summer and lets in the sun in the winter. The mesa acts as a rain store ensuring supply through drought years. These ancestors of the present day Hopi had a profound understanding of the natural world, its possibilities and limits. That a civilisation of evident artistic accomplishment but without our science, technology and material prowess could thrive in such inhospitable terrain is an inspiration for us to harness the natural world sustainably and turn limits into assets.

1 As the well-known British journalist Paul Finch puts it: "No one says "Hey, lets go and see that new film, I hear it came in 10 per cent under budget"."
2 The Sustainable Communities Plan has the following eight indicators:
Governance: Well-run communities with effective and inclusive participation, representation and leadership.
Transport and Connectivity: Well-connected communities with good transport services and communications linking people to jobs, health and other services.
Services: Public, private and community and voluntary services that are accessible to all.
Environmental: Providing places for people to live in an environmentally friendly way.
Equity: Fair for everyone in our diverse world and for both today's and tomorrow's communities.
Economy: A thriving and vibrant local economy.
Housing and the Built Environment: High quality buildings.
Social and Culture: Active, inclusive and safe with a strong local culture and other shared community activities.
Source: The Academy of Sustainable Communities, 2006.
3 In 1988, the United Nations' Intergovernmental Panel on Climate Change (IPCC) was set up to prepare for the Earth Summit held in Rio de Janeiro in 1992. In 1990 the scientific working group of the IPCC, drawing on 170 scientists from 25 countries, published a report stating that human activity increasing greenhouse gas emissions "will enhance the greenhouse effect, resulting on average in an additional warming of the Earth's surface". It calculated that an immediate 60 per cent reduction in CO_2 emissions would stop the build-up of carbon dioxide. Also, in the same year, 747 participants from 116 countries took part in the Second World Climate Conference. The conference statement reported that "a clear scientific consensus has emerged on estimates of the range of global warming which can be expected during the twenty first century. If the increase of greenhouse gas concentrations is not limited, the predicted climate change would place stresses on natural and social systems unprecedented in the past 10,000 years." In the meanwhile, an appeal signed by 49 Nobel Prize winners and 700 members of the NAS stated, "There is broad agreement within the scientific community that amplification of the Earth's natural greenhouse effect by the buildup of various gases introduced by human activity has the potential to produce dramatic changes in climate.... Only by taking action now can we insure that future generations will not be put at risk."
Source: Global Warming; The History of an International Scientific Consensus, www.environmentaldefense.org, 2003.

4 Global Commons Institute, 2004, www.gci.org.uk.
5 The Kyoto Protocol, ratified in 2006 binds its developed nation signatories to reduce emissions by set percentages within a certain time. For the UK government its basic effect should be to reduce emission by 60 per cent by 2050. "Contraction and Convergence" is a framework proposed by the independent Global Commons Institute based on setting an equitable per capita annual maximum carbon emission allowance across the globe and concluding an international treaty to bind countries to achieving it. For the UK it is estimated to mean a 80 per cent reduction in emission by 2050. "Cap and trade" is based on setting national and corporate carbon allowances and allowing international trade in these whereby allowances can be exchanged for money or goods. Some trade in carbon allowances already exists, following Kyoto. Domestic tradable carbon quotas, as so far unsuccessfully pursued in the UK parliament by Colin Challon MP, are based on setting personal carbon allowances and then allowing trade in them.
6 Layard, Richard, *Happiness: Has Social Science a Clue?* Lionel Robbins memorial lecture, London School of Economics, March 2003.
7 All 3,500 schools in England are to be rebuilt or refurbished in the next 12 years, a rate of almost a school a day. The programme appears to provide just the large scale of demand for devices like photovoltaic panels that should make them affordable. The delivery mechanism is generally a public private partnership, but there appear to be no mechanism the government is willing to use to exploit such a potential.

Betatakin, fourteenth
century Pueblo village
within a large cave,
Navajo National
Monument, Arizona.

Selected Projects

Selected projects 1988–2007. Bold typeface indicates the inclusion of a project summary in the book.

Publications
AJ–The Architects' Journal
AT–Architecture Today
BSJ–Building Services Journal
AR–The Architectural Review

BD–Building Design
HD–Hospital Development
RIBAJ–RIBA Journal
FDM–Facility Design and Management

- **GP surgery for seven doctors, Manor Place, Walworth, London, for doctors Higgs, Haigh, MacKay and Reyburn, £600,000 1986–1991**
  AJ, 29 Aug 1996, p. 42
  HD, vol 25, no 10, Nov 1994, pp. 31–33
  Deutsche Bauzeitung, vol 126, no 5, May 1992, pp. 32–35
  GP Business, 6 Mar 1992, p. 110
  AJ, vol 195, no 7, 19 Feb 1992, pp. 28–39, 41–43
  AJ, vol 191, no 1, 3 Jan 1990, pp. 32–67
  AJ, vol 191, no 2, 10 Jan 1990, p. 37

  Structural Engineer–Trigram Partnership
  Services Engineer–Fulcrum Engineering Partnership
  Cost Consultant–Ken McCarthy
  Contractor–EC Sames Ltd

- Conversion of Oast House, Whatlington, East Sussex, for private clients, £130,000, 1987–1989

- **New Maltings renovation and additions to house with a new pool, Nayland, Suffolk, for private clients, £250,000, 1987–1989**
  East Anglian Daily Times Supplement, 12 Sep 1996, p. 20
  Individual Homes, Jul/Aug 1992, pp. 14–20
  BD, 4 Oct 1991, p. 7
  Country Life, 28 Feb 1991, pp. 44–49
  AR, vol 188, Dec 1990, pp. 62–65

  RIBA Regional Award 1991

  Structural Engineer–Jampel, Davison & Bell
  Cost Consultant–Stern and Woodford
  Contractor–Cadman Builders Ltd

- **New residential and day provision for people with learning disabilities, Essex, for North Thames Regional Health Authority & MacIntyre, £950,000, 1987–1991**
  RIBA Regional Award 1992

  Structural Engineer–Harris & Sutherland
  Services Engineer–Woodcocks Building Services Engineers
  Cost Consultant–Low & Low
  Contractor–FJ Construction

- Loft conversion, Bassett Road, Kensington, London, for private clients, £70,000, 1988–1989

- Competition design for a mixed-use development at the fire station site, Surrey Quays, Rotherhithe, London, for Space Interspace Ltd, 1988

- Refurbishment of house at Campden Hill Road, Kensington, London, for private clients, £100,000, 1989–1991

- Design for a new Chapel and internal alterations St Jude's Church, East London, for the Parish of Clapton Park and Diocese of Southwark, 1989–1992

- Competition design for Greenpeace Headquarters, Islington, London, for Greenpeace, 1989

- Design for a new shop and therapy rooms for people with learning disabilities, Westoning, Bedfordshire, for Macintyre, £80,000, planning 1989

- Design for a psychotherapy day hospital, day centre and homes for the elderly mentally ill, St Olave's Hospital Site, Rotherhithe, London, for Bellwinch Homes Ltd and South East Thames Regional Health Authority, £4.6m, planning 1989

- GP surgery for four doctors, Coldharbour Lane, Camberwell, London, for doctors Puri and Charles, £250,000, 1989–1991
  BD, 19 Nov 1993, pp. 12, 14, 16
  AT, no 27, Apr 1992, pp. 22–49

- Design for new office and studio development, Wapping, London, for Pierhead Properties Ltd, £3m, planning 1990

- Conversion of a warehouse to offices, Camden, London, for the Anti-Apartheid Movement, £250,000, 1990–1991, demolished

- *Civic Monument* stage set design for a travelling performance by Marty St James and Anne Wilson, for the Artangel Trust, £10,000, 1990
  AJ, vol 192, no 10, 5 Sep 1990, p. 89

- Competition design for a mixed development in Limehouse, London, for the London Docklands Development Corporation, £7.5m, 1990
  BD, no 994, 13 July 1990, pp. 12, 14–15

- Conversion of a house to sheltered housing for people with learning disabilities, Sevenoaks, Kent, for Moat Housing Society and MacIntyre Housing Association, £300,000, 1990–1992

- Conversion of a 1950s community building to doctors' surgery, Iveagh House, Brixton, London, for doctors Konzon and Kheraj, £130,000, 1990–1992. subsequent extension £350,000, 1996–1998
  BD Interiors, Feb/Mar 1999, pp. 31–32
  BD, 2 July 1993, p. 6

- Restoration and alterations to a Grade II listed Georgian house, Mill Hill, London, for private clients, £200,000, 1991–1993
  BD, 2 July 1993, p. 6

- Competition design for a cultural centre, Central Samarkand, 1991

- Competition design for housing at Coin Street, South Bank, London, for Coin Street Community Builders, £1.1m, 1991
  AJ, vol 194, no 10, 4 Sep 1991, p. 27

- Consultancy in connection with the art installation *Steam* at the Chisenhale Gallery, London, for Rose Finn-Kelcey, 1991

- House extension in a conservation area, Camden, London, for private clients, £75,000, 1991–1992

- Two houses at Vicarage Park, Plumstead, London, Southwark Diocesan Housing Association with New World Housing Association, £145,000, 1991–1993

- GP surgery for seven doctors, Brixton Hill, London, for doctors Bennett, Williams, Wilkie and Evans, £500,000, 1991–1993
  BD, 10 Jan 1992, p. 15
  Building Supplement, vol 260, no 7881, 24 Feb 1995

- Intensive care and coronary care unit, Jeddah, Saudi Arabia, for the International Hospitals Group, £2m, 1992–1994

- 12 new houses, Ellison Road, Streatham, London, for Asra Housing Association, £700,000, 1992–1994

- 29 new houses, Grove Street, Deptford, London, for ASRA Housing Association London and Quadrant Housing Trust, 1992–1995

- Four flats for people with learning disabilities, Tooting, London, for MacIntyre Housing Association and Servite Homes, £500,000, 1992–1995

- **GP surgery and health centre, Rushton Street, Hackney, London, for East London and the City Health Authority, £1.4m, 1992–1996 subsequent alterations 2000–2001 and 2005–2007**

Design Week, vol 12, no 18, 9 May 1997, p. 19	Civic Trust Award Commendation 2000	Structural Engineer—Whitby & Bird Engineers
AJ, vol 205, no 16, 24 Apr 1997, pp. 29–37	Civic Trust Award Commendation 1998	Services Engineer—Max Fordham & Partners
HD, vol 28, no 4, Apr 1997, pp. 21–24	RIBA Award 1999	Cost Consultant—Peter W Gittins & Partners
The Independent Supplement, 18 Jan 1994, p. 21		Contractor—John Barker Construction Limited

- Design for a new house in a conservation area, Mill Hill, London, for private clients, £250,000, planning 1993–1994

- Competition design for a visitor's centre at Langdon Cliffs, Dover, for the National Trust, £600,000, 1993

- **40 bed nursing home for the elderly mentally infirm, Woodlands Nursing Home, Lambeth, London, for West Lambeth Community Care (NHS) Trust, £1.6m, 1993–1995**

HD, Mar 2000	RIBA Architecture Award 1997	Structural Engineer—Büro Happold
Caring Times, Oct 1998, p. 15	UCB Care Home Award 1997	Services Engineer—Büro Happold
Nursing Home Business, vol 2, no 7, Sep 1998, p. 21		Cost Consultant—Cyril Sweet & Partners
RIBA , 97/1, 1997		Landscape Architect—Livingstone Eyre Associates
Sunday Telegraph, 21 July 1996		Contractor—Fitzpatrick
AJ, vol 203, no 22, 6 June 1996, pp. 26–27		
BD, 24 May 1996, p. 17		
HD, vol 27, no 1, Jan 1996, pp. 21–24		
RIBAJ, vol 102, no 11, Nov 1995, pp. 58–65		
BD 26, Nov 1993, p. 40		

Flats and work space on fire station site, Rotherhithe, competition, 1988.

Coldharbour Lane Surgery, 1991.

Restoration and alteration design for listed Georgian house, Mill Hill, 1993.

Brixton Hill Surgery, 1993.

- Masterplan for housing and council works depot rationalisation, Low Hall Depot and Langthorne Hospital Site, 1993

- Proposals for the refurbishment of an art gallery, Hampstead, London, for Catto Gallery, planning 1993

- Design for new house at St Georges Hill, Weybridge, Surrey, for private clients, £350,000, planning 1993–1994

- 17 housing units in Barnsbury, Islington, London, for Barnsbury Housing Association, £1.2m, 1993–1996

- Four new houses for people with learning disabilities, Crosby Close, St Albans, Hertfordshire, for MacIntyre Housing Association, £850,000, 1993–1996
  AT, no 79, June 1997, pp. 20–22, 25

- New visitors' reception centre for Belmarsh Prison, Greenwich, London, for a charitable trust, £600,000, competition win 1993–1995
  AJ Focus, Apr 1997, pp. 9–10
  AJ, vol 203, no 12, 28 Mar 1996, pp. 29–39
  RIBAJ, vol 103, no 2, Feb 1996, pp. 6–7, 9
  AJ, 23 Nov 1995, p. 11
  BD, 11 Feb 1994

- Bethnal Green urban design framework study, East London, for Bethnal Green City Challenge Company, 1994

- **Newhaven Downs House, 50 bed nursing home and day centres for frail elderly and elderly mentally infirm, Newhaven, East Sussex, for South Downs Health (NHS) Trust, £3.4m competition win 1994–1997**
  AJ Focus, vol 14, no 9, Sep 2000, p. 46
  The Independent Review, 22 Feb 1999, p. 9
  Building, vol 263, 23 Oct 1998, pp. 36–41
  Nursing Home Business, vol 2, no 7, Sep 1998, p. 21
  Construction South, vol 4, no 9, 1996, pp. 14–15
  AJ, vol 201, no 5, 2 Feb 1995, pp. 34–35
  FDM, Dec/Jan 1994–1995, p. 18
  BD, 15 Apr 1994, p. 1

  UCB Care Home Award Finalist 1997
  Lewes District Council Design Award 1997

  Structural Engineer—Büro Happold
  Services Engineer—Büro Happold
  Cost Consultant—John Rowe Associates
  Contractor—Mansell Construction Services

- Competition design for Cardiff Bay Opera House, £45m, 1994

- GP surgery for five doctors, Westminster, London, for doctors Tlusty and Rich, £500,000, 1994–1997

- Design for the refurbishment of The Christian Community Church, Temple Lodge, Hammersmith, for The Christian Community, £500,000, 1995–planning 1999

- **The Rollercoaster Centre for Young People, Bridgwater, Somerset, for Sydenham SRB Trust Ltd, £440,000, 1995–1997**
  RIBAJ, vol 105, no 10, Oct 1998, pp. 44–49

  Civic Trust Awards Commendation 1999

  Structural Engineer—Duncan & Millais Engineers
  Services Engineer—HGa
  Cost Consultant—Slade Parry Partnership
  Contractor—CS Williams

- **New visitor's education centre for Eastbrookend Country Park and the Chase Nature Reserve, Dagenham, East London, for the London Borough of Barking & Dagenham, £650,000, 1995–1997**
  British Architectural Profile, Issue 1, 2001, p. 43
  AT, no 87, Apr 1998, pp. 38–47
  Building, vol 263, 30 Jan 1998, pp. 38–42
  AJ, 30 Nov 1995, p. 7

  Civic Trust Awards Commendation 2000
  RIBA Award 2000,
  Aluminium Imagination Award 1999
  AIA Excellence in Design Award 1999
  Design Sense Short-list Award 1999
  Green Apple Award 2004

  Structural Engineer—Büro Happold
  Services Engineer—Max Fordham LLP
  Cost Consultant—Peter Gittins & Associates
  Contractor—RG Carter London Ltd.

Belmarsh Prison Visitors Centre, 1995.

House for people with learning disabilities,
St Albans, 1996.

Newhaven Downs Polyclinic,
1998.

- **The Pulross Centre—Brixton Intermediate Care Centre, South London, for West Lambeth Community Care (NHS) Trust, £2.4m, competition win 1995–2000**

  Techniques et Architecture, June 2002

  HD, May 2001,

  AJ, 22 Mar 2001, pp. 32–41

  BD, 1 Dec 2000, p. 2

  Civic Trust Awards Commendation 2004

  Building Better Health Care Awards

  High Commendation 2002

  NHS Estates Design Excellence Awards

  Finalist 2001

  Structural Engineer—Dewhurst MacFarlane & Partners

  Services Engineer—Max Fordham LLP

  Cost Consultant—Dobson White Boulcott Ltd.

  Landscape Architect—Livingston Eyre Associates

  Contractor—Neilcott Special Works Ltd.

- Community health building, Neptune Health Park, Tipton, West Midlands, for Sandwell Health Care NHS Trust , £2.1m, 1995–1998

  HD, vol 31, Issue 11, Nov 2000, p. 20

  NHS Executive Quarterly, vol 8, no 2, 1998–1999, pp. 21–25

- Design for 42 houses and flats and doctor's surgery in Camden, for St Pancras Housing Association and Camden & Islington FHSA, £3.5m, planning 1995

- Competition design for performing arts centre, North London, for Latymer School, £3m, 1996

- Masterplan for 50 bed nursing home, day centres and outpatients department, Chester-le-Street, Durham, for North Durham Community Health Care NHS Trust, 1995–1996

- Administration offices, Bombay, India, for British Airways, £500,000, 1995–1996

- Fit out of GP surgery, Camden, London, for Camden & Islington FHSA, £75,000, 1995–1996

- Design competition for the Maysbrook Health Centre, East London, for Barking and Havering Family health service authority, £1.3m, competition win 1996

- Newhaven Downs Polyclinic, Newhaven, East Sussex, for South Downs Health (NHS) Trust, £670,000, 1996–1998

- Masterplan of the Wolverhampton Learning Quarter, Wolverhampton, £22m, 1996

- **Alterations to Snape Maltings Concert Hall, Snape, Suffolk, for The Aldeburgh Foundation, £3m, competition win 1996–1999**

  AT, April 2001, pp. 18–30

  Building, vol 264, 27 Aug 1999, pp. 38–50

  RIBAJ, vol 106, no 8, Aug 1999

  Soundings Autumn, 1999, p. 111

  RIBA Award 2001

  Civic Trust Awards Commendation 2001

  Structural Engineer—Price & Myers

  Services Engineer—Max Fordham LLP

  Cost Consultant—Hyams & Partners

  Acoustics Engineer—Arup Acoustics

  Contractor—Sindall Norwich Ltd

- **New additions and alterations to Grade II listed Wolverhampton Civic & Wulfrun Halls, Wolverhampton, for Wolverhampton Metropolitan Borough Council, £3.5m, competition win 1996–2001**

  AJ, Jan 2003, pp. 31–37;

  AJ, vol 205, no 16, 24 Apr 1997, pp 10–11

  Civic Trust Award 2004

  Structural Engineer—Büro Happold

  Services Engineer—Max Fordham LLP

  Cost Consultant—Wolverhampton City Council

  Contractor—Mansell Construction Services

- Conversion of existing houses to maisonettes and flats, West London, for Notting Hill Housing Trust, £350,000, 1997–1999

- The Quick and the Dead, Art and Anatomy touring exhibition for the South Bank Centre, £15,000, 1997–1998

- Competition design for housing at Newington Green, North London, for The Peabody Trust, 1997

- Design for the Multi-cultural Arts Centre, Cardiff, for CADMAD, £3.3m, 1997–1998

  Touchstone, Issue 6, Oct 1999, p. 21

  AJ, vol 207, no 20, 21 May 1998, p. 19

The Quick and the Dead exhibition design, 1998.

CASPAR housing competition, Leeds, 1998.

Wolverhampton Learning Curve masterplan, 1998.

- **Alterations and refurbishment of Grade II* listed Sheffield City Hall, for Sheffield City Council, £12m, 1997–2005**

  AT, Feb 2006, pp. 62–68

  AJ, vol 208, no 15, 22 Oct 1998, pp. 29–47

  Civic Trust Awards Commendation 2006

  RIBA Yorkshire White Rose Awards

  Commendation 2006

  Project Manager–Barraclough English & Wright

  Structural Engineer–Ove Arup & Partners

  Services Engineer–Ove Arup & Partners

  Cost Consultant–Barraclough English & Wright

  Contractor–HBG Construction North East Ltd

- Competition design for CASPAR housing (City Apartments for Single People at Affordable Rents), Charlotte Street, Birmingham, for The Joseph Rowntree Organisation, 1998

- Chailey Westfield Rehabilitation Centre, East Sussex, for South Downs Health (NHS) Trust, £925,000, 1998–2000

- The Discovery Centre for Sports and Leisure, Great Notley Country Park, Essex, for Countryside Properties Ltd, £1.2m, 1998–2001

  AJ, 1 June 2001, pp. 19–29

  AJ, vol 211, no 18, 11 May 1999

- Refurbishment and reconfiguration of Tower Hamlets College, Poplar, London, for Tower Hamlets College, £3m, 1998–1999

- Tibetan Buddhist Temple, L'Engayresque, Herault, France, for Rigpa, £7m, 1998–planning 2000

- Design for Paces School and Training Centre for children with cerebral palsy, High Green, Sheffield, for Paces High Green Centre, £3m, competition win 1998–2000

- New commercial offices, 125–135 Freston Road, Kensington, London, for Stade Properties Ltd, £3.3m, 1998–2000

  Royal Borough of Kensington News, June 2002

- Teviot Community Access Centre, Tower Hamlets, London, for the London Borough of Tower Hamlets, £1m, 1998–2000

- Four maisonettes, Cambridge Gardens, West London, for Notting Hill Housing Trust, £280,000, 1998–2000

- Four houses and five flats, 78–86 Whitehorse Road, Stepney, East London, for LABO Housing Association, £900,000, 1998–2001

- Competition design for CASPAR housing, North Street, Leeds, for The Joseph Rowntree Organisation, 1998

- Housing with provision for people with special needs, Priory Works, Muswell Hill, London, for Notting Hill Housing Trust and Willmott Dixon Housing, £1.5m, 1999–2001

- Conversion of two Grade II listed buildings to 11 flats, Gloucester Gardens, West London, for Notting Hill Housing Trust, 1999–2001

- Design for the Walnut Tree Walk School, Lambeth, London, for Lambeth Education Directorate and Governors, £2.6m, competition win 1999–planning 2001

  Building, vol 265, 1 Sept 2000

  AJ, vol 210, no 15, 21 Oct 1999, p. 13

- House extension, Wandsworth, south London, for private clients, £50,000, 1999–2001, with Nick Alexander

  RIBAJ, March 2001

- **Remodelling of 1950s LCC school to create The Charter School, Dulwich, London, for the Governors and The London Borough of Southwark, £18m, 1999–2003**

  Teachers, Dec 2001

  Surface, May 2001

  BD, 12 April 2001, pp. 10–11

  FX, Jan 2001,

  RIBAJ, Jan 2001, pp. 40–46

  RIBA Regional Award 2003

  Civic Trust Awards Commendation 2004

  Aluminium Imagination Award 2003

  FX International Design Awards Finalist 2001

  Daily Telegraph, 20 Dec 2000, p. 17

  Project Manager–Osprey Mott MacDonald Ltd

  Structural Engineer–The Babtie Group

  Services Engineer–Southwark Building Design

  Cost Consultant–Franklin & Andrews

  Landscape Architect–Watkins Dally

  Contractor–Mansell Construction Services

- Design study for new primary school and centre of excellence for visually impaired children, Lambeth, London, for Lambeth Education Directorate and Governors, 1999–2000

Walnut Tree Walk School, 1999.

Commercial offices, Freston Road, 2000.

Community Access Centre, 2000.

- Design for new house for six pupils with Learning Difficulties, Womaston School, Walton, Powys, Wales, for Macintyre Housing Association, £200,000, 1999–2000

- **Urban regeneration and spatial master plan for Central Gravesend, Kent, for Gravesham Borough Council, 1999–adopted 2000**
  Ecotech, 4 Nov 2001
  AJ, 2 Nov 2000, p. 26

- Competition design for housing association headquarters and residential accommodation, Hartshill Road, Stoke-on-Trent, for Staffordshire Housing Association, £3m, 2000

- Design study for housing and mixed development, Paragon Road, Hackney, London, for The Peabody Trust, planning 2000

- Housing at Elsdale Street, Hackney, London, for The Peabody Trust, £4.5m, 2000–2003 (phase 1) 2006 (phase 2)

- Reconfiguration of Wolverhampton Childrens library for Wolverhampton City Council, £140,000, 2000–2001

- Design for 137–139 Freston Road, Kensington, London, for Stade Properties Ltd, 2000

- Design study for an adult centre at East India Dock Road, London, for Tower Hamlets College, £500,000, 2000

- Design for a mixed use development of offices and business units at 167–185 Freston Road, Kensington, London, for West London Self Storage, £13.4m, 2000–planning 2003

- Design study for new college and residential accommodation at the Poplar site, London, for Tower Hamlets College, 2000–2002

- TreeHouse centre for autism education, Muswell Hill, London, for The TreeHouse Trust, £8m, 2000–ongoing

- Temporary accommodation for school for children with autism, Coram Fields, London, for The TreeHouse Trust, £300,000, 2000–2001–dismantled 2004

- **130 dwellings (Step one of Gravesend Masterplan), Lord Street, Gravesend, Kent, for Gravesham Borough Council, Barratt Eastern Counties and Hyde Housing Association, £13.5m, 2001–ongoing**

  Employer's Agent–Dobson White Boulcott Ltd.
  Project Manager–Acorn Project Management Ltd
  Structural Engineer–RLT Engineering
  Services Engineer–Atelier Ten/Whitecode Design
  Landscape Architect–Colvin & Moggridge
  Contractor–Barratt Eastern Counties

- Design of new sheltered housing and alterations to Mercers Trinity Hospital, Greenwich, London, for The Mercers Company, £6m, 2001–2002

- Urban design study for the Eden Grove neighbourhood, Eden Grove, Barnsbury, London, for Barnsbury Housing Association, 2001–2002

- Conversion and extension of a former school to 11 flats, Eden Grove, Barnsbury, London, for Barnsbury Housing Association, 2001–ongoing

- Design of the Charles Darwin forum, Downe, Kent, for The Charles Darwin Trust, £9m, Competition win 2001–planning 2003

- The SCORE Complex, Community Sports and Health Care Facility, Leyton, East London, for SCORE Trust with English Partnerships, £9.9m, 2001–2005

- Shared ownership accommodation, Milborne St, London, for The Peabody Trust, £2.4m, 2001–ongoing

- Community treatment and care centre with Todd Architects, Castlereagh, Belfast, Northern Ireland, for South and East Belfast Health and Social Services Trust, £6m, 2001–ongoing

Housing Association HQ, Staffordshire, 2000.

House extension,
Wandsworth, 2001.

Sheltered housing, Trinity Hospital,
Greenwich, 2001.

- **The Arches Treatment and Care Centre with Todd Architects, Holywood Arches, Belfast, Northern Ireland, for South and East Belfast Health and Social Services Trust, £8.6m, 2001–2005**

  HD, Feb 2007, pp. 9–12
  Urban Building, Sep/Oct 2006, pp. 58–60
  Building, Sep 2006, pp. 42–45
  AJ, Jun 2006, p. 48
  Building, 7 Apr 2006, p. 8

  RIBA Award 2006
  Building Better Healthcare—Best Primary or Community Care Design Award 2006
  Building Better Healthcare Award 2006

  Project Manager—Health Estates Northern Ireland
  Structural Engineer—Price and Myers
  Services Engineer—Max Fordham LLP
  Cost Consultant—White Young Green
  Landscape Architect—Gillespies LLP
  Contractor—Farrans Construction Ltd

- **The Bradbury treatment and care centre, Lisburn Road, Belfast, Northern Ireland, for South and East Belfast Health and Social Services Trust, £6m, 2001–2006**

  Building Better Healthcare Awards —Commendation 2006
  Building Better Healthcare—Best Use of Art in Hospitals Award 2006

  Project Manager—Health Estates Northern Ireland
  Structural Engineer—Price and Myers
  Services Engineer—Max Fordham LLP
  Cost Consultant—White Young Green
  Landscape Architect—Gillespies LLP
  Contractor—Farrans Construction Ltd

- Masterplan and development strategy for Dulwich Community Hospital site, Dulwich, South London, for Dulwich Community Hospital Project Board, Southwark, 2001–2002

- Alterations and refurbishment to existing buildings, Arbour Square, Tower Hamlets, London, for Tower Hamlets College, £850,000, 2002–2003

- Dulwich Community Hospital, Dulwich, south London, for Building Better Health for Lambeth, Southwark & Lewisham NHS LIFT, £37m, 2002

- Design study for the redevelopment of Acton Town Hall, West London, for Ealing Council, 2002

- Design for the Roehampton Community Hospital, London, for South West London NHS Trust, 2002

- Proposals for housing at 143 York Way, Camden, London, for Notting Hill Housing Trust, 2002

- Competition design for Kentish Town integrated care centre, for Camden and Islington Health Authority, £7m, 2002

- **Conversion of an existing building to The Rich Mix Multi-cultural Arts and Resource Centre, Bethnal Green, London, for the The Rich Mix Cultural Foundation, £11m, earliest proposals 1997, 2002–2005**

  Blueprint, July 2006, p. 24
  BD, May 2006, pp. 12–15

  Aluminium in Renovation Award 2007

  Project Manager—Bovis Lend Lease
  Structural Engineer—Ove Arup & Partners
  Services Engineer—Ove Arup & Partners
  Cost Consultant—Peter Gittins & Associates

- **The Richard Desmond Children's Eye Centre, Islington, London, for Moorfields Eye Hospital NHS Foundation Trust/ Balfour Beatty Procure21 Ltd, £14.5m, 2002–2006**

  HD, May 2007, pp. 18–20
  Lighting, May 2007, pp. 4, 5, 8
  AJ, 26 April 2007, pp. 23–25
  FX, April 2007, pp. 40–43
  Optician, 6 April 2007, pp. 14–15

  Project Manager—Hunter & Partners
  Structural Engineers—Price & Myers
  Services Engineers—Arup
  Cost Consultant—Turner and Townsend Cost Management
  Contractor—Balfour Beatty Construction Ltd.

- Competition entry "Designs on Democracy", Yorkshire, for Bradford Metropolitan District Council sponsored by RIBA and Demos, 2002

- Poplar Riverside Masterplan, Ailsa Street, Poplar, London, for Leaside Regeneration Ltd, London Borough of Tower Hamlets and London Development Agency, £97m, 2003

- Housing and Rosa Morison Day Centre for people with learning difficulties, Barnet, London, for Notting Hill Housing Trust, £3.6m, 2003–2007

  UK Construction, April 2006, p. 73

Roughsleepers housing, Hackney, 2003.

Mixed-use development, Freyton Road, 2003.

Charles Darwin Forum, Kent, 2003.

- PFI bid design for Clacton schools, Clacton-on-Sea, Essex, for Jarvis Construction, £20m, 2003

- Exemplar school design for Jo Richardson Community School, Barking Reach, London, for London Borough of Barking & Dagenham, £25m, 2003

- **Ashburton Learning Village, Croydon, London, for Norwest Holst Construction Ltd, for London Borough of Croydon, £18m, 2003–2006**
  AT, Oct 2006, pp. 50–57

  BD, plus, May 2006, pp. 18–20

  Structural Engineer—Curtins Consulting Engineers

  Services Engineer—Jones King Partnership/Sub-Rosser & Russell

  Landscape Architect—fira

  Contractor—Jarvis Construction and Norwest Holst Ltd/Sub-Gale Construction Co Ltd

- Competition design for a new music department, for Bedford School, 2003

- Competition design for offices and light industrial units, North Kensington, London, for Chelsfield, £20m, 2003

- Refurbishment and alterations to the Grade II* listed Wolverhampton Central Library, for Wolverhampton Metropolitan Borough Council, £6.5m, 1998–2003

- **Sheltered housing for the elderly, Collier's Gardens, Bristol, for Brunelcare, £5.3m, 2003–2006**
  AJ supplement, 7 July 2006, pp. 30–31

  Inside Housing, Feb 2006, p. 10

  Housing Design Award 2006

  National Homebuilder Design Award 2006

  Structural Engineer—Structures 1

  Services Engineer—Büro Happold

  Cost Consultant—Andrew Wilson Partnership

  Landscape Architect—Colvin & Moggridge

  Contractor—John Sisk & Son Ltd

- Competition design for alterations to Grade II listed Geoffrey Chaucer School, Walworth, London, for Southwark Council, £20m, 2003

- **Heart of Hounslow Health Centre, Hounslow, London, for Building Better Health for Ealing, Hammersmith & Fulham and Hounslow NHS LIFT, £15.3m, 2003–2007**
  Structural Engineer—Price & Myers

  Services Engineer—Whitby Bird

  Cost Consultant/Employers representative—Davis Langdon LLP

  Landscape Architect—Whitelaw Turkington

  Contractor—Willmott Dixon Construction Ltd

- **Secondary School Design Exemplar, Building Schools for the Future, for DfES/Schools Capital Design Guide, £17m, 2003**
  Building Schools Journal, July/Aug 2006, pp. 14–15

  Structural Engineer—Alan Conisbee & Associates

  Services Engineer—Atelier Ten

  Cost Consultant—Dobson White Boulcott Ltd.

  Landscape Architect—Grant Associates

- **Extension to Prior Weston School, Islington, London, for London Borough of Islington, £470,000, 2003–2004**
  Building Innovations, Issue 3, 2005, p. 45

  AT, Mar 2005, pp. 48–53

  RIBA Award 2005

  Civic Trust Awards Commendation 2006

  Structural Engineer—Alan Conisbee & Associates

  Services Engineer—Rivendell Electrical Ltd

  Cost Consultant—Dobson White Boulcott Ltd.

  Contractor—Framework CDM

- Design study for St Aidans Primary School, North London, for Haringey Council Education Services, 2003–2004

- Carlisle Health and Wellbeing Centre with Todd Architects, Lincoln Avenue, Belfast, Northern Ireland, for North and East Belfast Trust, £6.35m, 2003–2007

- New Health and Wellbeing Centre with Todd Architects, Andersonstown Road, Belfast, for North and West Belfast Trust, £11m, 2003

- Competition design for Civic Headquarters, Bethnal Green, London, for London Borough of Tower Hamlets, £30m, 2003

Jo Richardson Community School, Barking,
Exemplar Design, 2003.

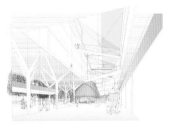

Clinic HQ competition, Bethnal Green, 2003.

SCORE Community and Sports Complex, Leyton, 2005.

- 79 new apartments, Hounslow, London, for Capital and Provident Regeneration Ltd with Metropolitan Housing Trust Ltd., £7m, 2003

- Cloister Road GP surgery, Ealing West, London, for Building Better Health for Ealing, Hammersmith & Fulham and Hounslow LIFT, £780,000, 2003–2006

- Central Streatham Health Centre, Lambeth, London, for Building Better Health for Lambeth, Southwark & Lewisham LIFT, £8m, 2003–2007

- Grand Union Primary Care Centre, for Building Better Health for Ealing, Hammersmith & Fulham and Hounslow LIFT, £5.2m, 2003–ongoing

- Green Wrythe Lane Primary Care Centre, Carshalton, Surrey, for Building Better Health, for South West London LIFT, £4.3m, 2003–2006
  BD, March 2007, pp. 14–18
  AJ, 2 Feb 2007, pp. 38–40
  HD, Feb 2007, pp. 16–19
  Building, 17 Nov 2006, p. 70

- Design for 104 live-work units, Wick Lane, Tower Hamlets, East London, for Silverpeak Ltd, £15m, 2004–ongoing

- Crowndale Medical Centre, West Norwood, London, for Building Better Health for Lambeth, Southwark & Lewisham LIFT, £3m, 2004–ongoing

- **The University Library, Portsmouth, Hampshire, for The University of Portsmouth, £7.6m, competition win 2004–2007**
  AT, April 2007, pp. 28–41
  Building Services Journal, May 2007, pp. 32–36

  Project Manager–Davis Langdon LLP
  Structural Engineer–Gifford & Partners
  Services Engineer–Gifford & Partners
  Cost Consultant–Denley King Partnership
  Landscape Architect–JCLA
  Contractor–Fitzpatrick Contractors Ltd

- Design study for the new Haringey Heartland Secondary School, London, for Haringey Council Education Services, 2004–2005

- Archive centre and artist accommodation at the Red House, Aldeburgh, Suffolk, for the Britten-Pears Foundation, £500,000, 2004

- Preston area regeneration masterplan, Surrey with Urban Practitioners, for Reigate and Banstead Borough Council, 2004–2005

- **Secondary School Campus, Olney, Buckinghamshire, for Milton Keynes Council, £8.5m, 2004–2007**

  Structural Engineer–Adams Kara Taylor
  Services Engineer–Atelier Ten
  Cost Consultant–Dobson White Boulcott Ltd.
  Landscape Architect–Grant Associates
  Contractor–ISG Jackson Ltd

- New Minister School, secondary school, Southall, Nottinghamshire, for The Minster School, £24m, competition win 2004–2007

- The Merchants' Academy, City Academy, Withywood, Bristol, for DfES and Society of Merchant Venturers, £15m, 2004–2008

- Building Schools for the Future for a secondary school, for Bristol BSF with Excell Learn, Bristol, for Laing O'Rourke Group Ltd, £18.2m, 2005

- Competition design for the Golden Lane School Campus, Whitecross Street, London, for London Borough of Islington, £12m, 2005

- Crawley Public Library, register office and social services accommodation, Crawley, West Sussex, for West Sussex County Council, £12.75m, 2005–2008

- Frederick Bremer School, secondary school, Waltham Forest, London, with Bouyges UK Ltd and London Borough of Waltham Forest, £22m, 2005–2008

- Competition design for New Cross Gate NDC Centre and associated housing, South London, for London Borough of Lewisham New Deal for Communities, £20m, 2006

Brixton Building Schools for the Future, bid design, 2005.

Central Streatham Health and Joint Service Centre, 2007.

The Minster School, Southwell, 2007.

- Secondary school for Islington BSF on Highbury Grove School, North London, for Willmott Dixon Construction Ltd and John Laing plc, £18m, 2006–2007

- Refurbishment of the Alan Garner Adult Education Centre, Wolverhampton, for Wolverhampton City Council, £800,000, 2006–2007

- New primary school, nursery and youth centre, Crouch Hill, North London, for London Borough of Islington, £11.5m, competition win, 2006–ongoing

- Masterplan for a community centre and housing on a former gasworks site in North Deal, Kent for SEEDA, 2006–ongoing

- Masterplan of an integrated and sustainable community, Goodmayes Hospital site, Essex, for East Thames Housing Group, 2006

- Extension and refurbishment of The Wren Academy secondary school, Finchley, London, for DfES Academies Division, £15m, 2006

- Upton Park masterplan for a new retail hub with 500 residential units, Green Street, Upton Park, for East Thames Group, £26m, 2007

- The Gardens, 26 large family homes for the Orthodox Jewish Community, Stamford Hill, East London, for Agudas Israel Housing Association, £6m, 2007

- Design study for two new primary schools, South London, for the London Borough of Lambeth, 2007

- Woodside High School inclusive learning campus, Haringey, London, for Haringey Council Education Services, £24m, 2007

- New primary school and children's centre, John Perryn School, Ealing, West London, for Willmott Dixon Construction Ltd, £7.5m, 2007

- Extension and refurbishment of St Marks Academy, Merton, South London, for DfES Academies Division, £6m, 2007

- 70 new flats and maisonettes, Isle of Dogs, London, for East Thames Group, £12m, 2007

- Kindergarten, primary and secondary school, King David's Campus, Liverpool, for Liverpool City Council and Norwest Holst, with Nightingale Architects, £20m, 2007–ongoing

- 60 extra care flats and 40 sheltered flats for market sale, London Borough of Havering, for East Thames Group, £14m, 2007

The Merchant's Academy, Bristol, 2008.

Crawley Library, 2008.

Office Members

Neil Allfrey
Lyn Ang
Sumit Arora
Sarah Ashley
Nathalie Bagnoud
Melanie Bax
Leigh Baxter
Twahaa Begum
Akshat Bhatt
Robert Bird
Tracey Bishop
Lily Blair
Mario Boche
Joanna Bridges
Andrea Bycroft
Gabrielle Calver
Lucy Cartlidge
John Ceclich
Rajan Chaudhary
Adam Cole
David Cole
Stephen Coleman
Michael Cooke
Louise Corbin
Dominic Cox
Tessa Cox
Liz Crawford
Joelle Darby
Max de Rosee
Simon Dennison
Mark Devitt
Simon Dove
Justine Duggan
Tanja Eichenauer
Holly Fisher

Bernard Fitzsimons
Henry Fletcher
Jacqueline Gabbitas
Donna Gage
Kristian Garrecht
Thomas Gilbey
Richard Gooden
Ian Goodfellow
Peter Grove
Diane Harrington
Harriet Harriss
Lester Hawksby
Wayne Head
Ben Hebblethwaite
Christian Held
Logan Hepworth
Mark Hindley
Alan Holloway
Anthony Holmes
Rebecca Holmes
Angela Hopcraft
Gillian Horn
Gareth Hoskins
Jane Howson
Bridget Isibor
Dann Jessen
Inderpaul Johar
Dan Jones
Simon Jones
Masashi Kajita
Fleur Kay
Hadas Keren
Emily Keyte
Shiraz Kidwai
Simon Knox

Annelie Kops
Sabine Kuehnast
Ashish Kumar
Tonja Lauener
Lily Le Brun
Markus Lemanski
Peter Liddell
Edward Liu
Chris Lomas
Johanna Maatta
Euan Macdonald
Sally Mackay
Kathryn Manning
Pippa Mansell
Rafael Marks
Ana Matic
Katherine McNeill
Viola Metzger
Phyllida Mills
Fran Mitchell
Tze-Ting Mok
Peter Morris
Abdullah Motaleb
Jean Murphy
Amarjit Myers
Megumi Nagai
Sophie Noble
Simone O'Hanlon
Giles Oliver
Adedayo Omikunle
Ian Oppenheim
Caroline Osewe
Richard Owers
Pavandeep Panesar
Elizabeth Parker

Manushi Patel
Rachel Pattinson
Greg Penoyre
Emma Phipps
Kevin Pollard
Aanand Prasad
Rahul Prasad
Sunand Prasad
Caroline Pullen
Catherine Purves
Jordi Rafols
Noam Raz
Sally Rendel
Clare Richards
Teresa Richford
Julia Robinson
Mark Rowe
Crispin Ryde
Gesa Schenk
Stephanie Schultze-Westrum
Emma Seidel
Leonard Sequeira
Andrew Siddall
Joseph Simpson
Madalein Simpson
Inderpaul Singh Johar
Camilla Smith
Barry Smyth
Louise Souter
Gareth Stokes
Sarah Susman
Kerry Swift
Yoko Takahashi
Helen Taylor
Duncan Thomas

Claire Tilling
Mark Tinker
Richard Trew
Peru Tsen
Steven van der Heijden
Chakradhar Vittala
Jamie Wakeford
Stephen Ware
Alex Warnock-Smith
Isabelle Watson
Denise Webber
Julia Wedel
Nicole Weiner
Hannah Wells
Bob Wills
Suzi Winstanley
Kirsty Yaldron
Ying-Soo Yau

Credits

Purpose: p.16 bl Ref: Rob Krier 'Urban Space' br courtesy Venturi, Scott Brown and Associates, Inc. p.17 tl©Sandra Lousada/NAI, Rotterdam bl©Louis Hellman p.24©James Morris p.26 bl UFA courtesy of the Kobal Collection br©Henry Grant Collection/Museum of London p.28 bl©Dennis Gilbert/VIEW tr©Morley Von Sternberg p.29©Dennis Gilbert/VIEW p.30 bl©Morley Von Sternberg top©Morley Von Sternberg p.35 top Image by Hayes Davidson p.36 centre©David Grandorge **Construction:** p.40 br©Sue Barr/VIEW p.42 tr©Morley Von Sternberg p.43©Marcus Peel p.44 tl©Dennis Gilbert/VIEW bottom©Dennis Gilbert/VIEW p.46 courtesy of Architect's Journal, published 24 April 1997. p.47 bl courtesy of Edward Cullinan Architects p.48 bl©Michael D. Gunther/www.art-and-archaeology.com p.48 bottom centre courtesy of Stevensons of Norwich Ltd. p.50©Dennis Gilbert/VIEW p.52 bl©Helene Binet br©Richard Bryant/arcaid.co.uk p.54 bottom Portsmouth Museums and Records Service: Ref DC/PM/1/8 p.55©Tim Crocker 07 p.57©Tim Crocker 07 p.59©Tim Crocker 07 p.61 br©Dennis Gilbert/VIEW bl©Morley von Sternberg p.63©Tim Crocker 07 **Context:** p.64©Dennis Gilbert/VIEW p.66 tr©Morley Von Sternberg p.67©Morley Von Sternberg p.68 top©Morley Von Sternberg p.70 tl©Dennis Gilbert/VIEW p.71 bl©Dennis Gilbert/VIEW p71 br©Sally Rendel/Rietveld Gerrit/DACS 2007 p.72 br©Hans Werlemann p.72 bm©Architectural Press Archive/RIBA Library Photographs Collection p.73 br©Tim Crocker 07 bl©Dennis Gilbert/VIEW p.76 bottom©Andrew Southall p.77©Tim Crocker 07/Design for Homes p.78 br©Tim Crocker 07/Design for Homes bl©Andrew Southall p.79©Tim Crocker 07/Design for Homes p.80 br©Matthew Pull p.82 courtesy of St Bartholomew's Hospital Archives p.83©Houston Green Photography p.85©Morley Von Sternberg p.86©Morley Von Sternberg p.87©Morley Von Sternberg p.88 bl©Chris Gascoigne/VIEW p.89©Morley Von Sternberg **Art:** p.90©Morley Von Sternberg p.92 tl©Zaha Hadid p.93 bl Architectural Press Archive/RIBA Library Photographs Collection. p.93 br©Shuhei Endo Architect Institute p.95 tr©Edwin Morgan p.97 bl©Sokari Douglas Camp/Licensed by DACS 2007 p.98 bottom (second, third and fourth images)©Alison Turnbull courtesy of the artist and Matt's Gallery, London p.100 Photography by Lyndon Douglas/www.lyndondouglas.com p.101©Cassius Taylor Smith/Wordsearch p.102 top Photography by Lyndon Douglas/www.lyndondouglas.com br©Cassius Taylor Smith/Wordsearch bl Photography by Lyndon Douglas/www.lyndondouglas.com p.104 Photography by Lyndon Douglas/www.lyndondouglas.com **Time:** p.106©Dennis Gilbert/VIEW p.109©Peter Cook/VIEW p.110 tr©Peter Cook/VIEW bl courtesy of the Britten-Pears Library p.111 top©Peter Cook/VIEW p.112 tl©Peter Cook/VIEW p.113©Peter Cook/VIEW p.114 bl©Sheffield City Archive br John Havinden/RIBA Library Photographs Collection p.116 bottom centre©Adrian Pingstone, 2005 br©West 8/photo: Jeroen Musch p.118 tr Reproduced with the permission of Wolverhampton Archives and Local Studies p.119©Dennis Gilbert/VIEW p.120©Dennis Gilbert/VIEW p.121 tl©Dennis Gilbert/VIEW p.124 tl©The National Gallery, London. p.125 top©Guido Guidi, Fototeca Carlo Scarpa p.126 bl Edward Stuart Bale/RIBA Library Photographs Collection tr E. Vincent Harris/RIBA drawings collection p.127©Dennis Gilbert/VIEW p.128 tr©Dennis Gilbert/VIEW p.129©Dennis Gilbert/VIEW **Care:** p.130©Marcus Peel br Gustav Welin/Aalto Foundation p.133 top Tecton/RIBA drawings collection p.134 bl courtesy of John Haworth br©FLC/ADAGP, Paris and DACS, London 2007 p.137©Dennis Gilbert/VIEW p.138 tl©Dennis Gilbert/VIEW tr Rijksmuseum, Amsterdam p.139 bl©Dennis Gilbert/VIEW p.140 Dell and Wainwright/RIBA Library Photographs Collection p.144©Sue Barr/VIEW p.146 bl Paulmegaheyphotography.com p.147 top©Dennis Gilbert/VIEW p.148©Dennis Gilbert/VIEW p.151 Paulmegaheyphotography.com p.156 tr©Dennis Gilbert/VIEW p.157 Dennis Gilbert/VIEW p.159©Dennis Gilbert/VIEW p.160©Dennis Gilbert/VIEW p.161 tr©Dennis Gilbert/VIEW p.162 bl photographer unknown br©David Grandorge p.164©Dennis Gilbert/VIEW p.166©Dennis Gilbert/VIEW p.167©Dennis Gilbert/VIEW p.168 tl©Dennis Gilbert/VIEW bl©Dennis Gilbert/VIEW p.169 bl©Livingston Eyre Associates p.171©Mandy Reynolds/Fotoforum p.172 br©Grant Smith/VIEW tr©Geremy Butler p.173 top©Geremy Butler **Learning:** p.174©Tim Crocker 07 p.176 br©English Heritage/NMR p.178 courtesy of David Trood p.179 bl©Josh Taylor/Bedales School p.180 bl©David Grandorge tr©Dennis Gilbert/VIEW p.181©Kilian O'Sullivan/VIEW p.183©Dennis Gilbert/VIEW p.186 tr©Tim Crocker 07 p.187©Tim Crocker 07 p.188 courtesy of Grant Associates p.189©Tim Crocker 07 p.190 top Tim Crocker 07 p.191©Tim Crocker 07 p.192 tl©Guardian News & Media Ltd. 2001 p.194 tr©Tim Crocker 07 p.195©Tim Crocker 07 p.196 tl©Morley Von Sternberg tr©Tim Crocker 07 bl©Tim Crocker 07 p.202 bl©Dennis Gilbert/VIEW br©Morley Von Sternberg p.203 br©Dennis Gilbert/VIEW p.205 Raf Makda/VIEW p.207©Raf Makda/VIEW **Limits:** p.215©Morley von Sternberg p.217©Dennis Gilbert/VIEW p.218©Dennis Gilbert/VIEW p.223©James Brittain **Timeline:** p.228 bc and bl©James Morris bl©Sue Barr/VIEW p.230 bc©Sue Barr/VIEW p.231 br©Dennis Gilbert/VIEW p.232 bl©Raf Makda/VIEW

Acknowledgements

Sally Rendel led the production of this book for Penoyre & Prasad. Logan Hepworth, Emily Keyte, Tze Ting Mok, Elizabeth Parker, Caroline Pullen and Bob Wills produced the specially prepared plans and cross sections. Catherine Purves, Becky Holmes, Fran Mitchell, Bridget Isibor, Emma Seidel and Isabelle Watson helped with the picture research and administration. Greg Penoyre, Gillian Horn, and Ian Goodfellow helped guide the image selection and layout and, with Giles Oliver and many others in the office, constructively commented upon the essays, which were written by Sunand Prasad. Thanks to all at Black Dog Publishing, especially Duncan McCorquodale, Matthew Pull and Shumi Bose.

© 2007 Black Dog Publishing Limited and the authors. All rights reserved.

Black Dog Publishing Limited
Unit 4.4 Tea Building
56 Shoreditch High Street
London
E1 6JJ

Tel: +44 (0)20 7613 1922
Fax: +44 (0)20 7613 1944
Email: info@blackdogonline.com

www.blackdogonline.com

All opinions expressed within this publication are those of the
authors and not necessarily of the publisher.

British Library Cataloguing-in-Publication Data.

A CIP record for this book is available from the British Library.

ISBN: 978 1 904772 67 5

All rights reserved. No part of this publication may be reproduced, stored in a
retrieval system, or transmitted, in any form or by any means, electronic, mechanical,
photocopying, recording, or otherwise, without prior permission of the publisher.

Every effort has been made to trace the copyright holders, but if any have been
inadvertently overlooked the publishers will be pleased to make the necessary
arrangements at the first opportunity.

Black Dog Publishing is an environmentally responsible company. *Transformations*
is printed on Fedrigoni SYMBOL Freelife Satin, an environmentally-friendly ECF
woodfree paper with a high content of selected pre-consumer recycled material
from well managed forests.

architecture art design
fashion history photography
theory and things

www.blackdogonline.com